Is Killing Wrong?

STUDIES IN PURE SOCIOLOGY

Donald Black, Editor

IS KILLING WRONG?

A STUDY IN PURE SOCIOLOGY

MARK COONEY

University of Virginia Press • Charlottesville and London

University of Virginia Press

Printed in the United States of America on acid-free paper

First published 2009
First paperback edition published 2012
ISBN 978-0-8139-3304-7 (paper)

9 8 7 6 5 4 3 2 1

The Library of Congress has cataloged the hardcover edition as follows:

Library of Congress Cataloging-in-Publication Data
Cooney, Mark, 1955–
Is killing wrong? : a study in pure sociology / Mark Cooney.
p. cm. — (Studies in pure sociology)
Includes bibliographical references and index.
ISBN 978-0-8139-2826-5 (cloth : alk. paper)
1. Murder. 2. Homicide. 3. Criminal psychology. 4. Criminal justice, Administration of. I. Title.
HV6515.C65 2009
364.152'3—dc22 2009001837

FOR NICK AND ZARA,
AND FOR MARY

CONTENTS

	Preface	ix
1	The Morality of Homicide	1
2	Pure Sociology	18
3	The Vertical Dimension	36
4	The Organizational Dimension	63
5	The Radial Dimension	91
6	The Normative Dimension	109
7	The Cultural Dimension	132
8	The Relational Dimension	156
	Conclusion	185
	Notes	203
	References	217
	Index	241

PREFACE

Right and wrong fascinate us. Their conflict provides a large part of our entertainment and education. Morality is the stuff of ancient myths, television documentaries, Hollywood movies, parental guidance, detective stories, courtroom dramas, learned debates, religious homilies, Shakespearean tragedies, and quotidian gossip. Part of the attraction lies in the very ambiguity of the central notions themselves. We know, for example, that what comes to be defined and treated as right and wrong are not entirely stable across societies or time periods: one tribe thinks nothing of infanticide, another abhors it; drinking alcohol is outlawed across the nation today, but tolerated a decade earlier. Yet we know relatively little about why morality varies. To say it varies because of "culture" is to say almost nothing at all.

Sociologists have long been interested in issues of morality. Today, their work is usually categorized under the rubric "deviance and social control." But while theories of deviance abound, theories of social control are few and limited in scope. Sociologists have given far more thought to explaining variation in deviant behavior than to variation in sanctions for deviant behavior, to explaining why people do wrong than to explaining why others penalize conduct as more or less wrong. Fortunately, there is one major exception.

Over the past one-third of a century, sociologist Donald Black has developed a startlingly new theory of morality. He argues that morality varies not from culture to culture as much as from case to case. Moral variation is primarily found at the level of conflicts, and can be observed in the variable sanctions or penalties that law and popular justice mete out to wrongdoers. One person is harshly punished, a second does the same thing and gets off lightly, a third is rewarded and praised. What explains such variation, Black argues, is the social structure or geometry of cases—their location and direction in social space. Is the complaint directed upward (against status superiors) or downward (against status inferiors)? Are the parties close (e.g., intimates) or distant (e.g., strangers)? How do the social characteristics of third parties, such as witnesses, allies, judges, and jurors, augment or modify the case's core shape? Alter the case geometry, as known by the social identity of the parties, and the outcome will change as well.

Black's conception of social geometry is an intrinsic part of a new theoretical system he has invented, known as pure sociology. Pure sociology explains social life without references to standard features of virtually every other social theory. It ignores the human mind. It ignores the ends or goals toward which people and groups are said to strive. It even ignores people as such: its subject matter is not the behavior of individuals but the behavior of social life.

Pure sociology, then, is more than a little weird. It is also more than a little improbable. It predicts, for example, that morality varies geometrically in the same way across all societies and at all times. It predicts that the same principles explain the severity of sanctions among nomadic hunter-gatherers and modern urban dwellers, among our ancestors ten thousand years ago and our descendants ten thousand years hence (if there are any).

Some evidence exists to support Black's extravagant claims. But they have not been subjected to a systematic confrontation with the evidence on their own terms. That is the purpose of this book. I take a single form of deviant behavior and examine whether the sanctions visited upon those who commit it line up in the way Black's theory predicts. The particular form of deviance I choose is homicide. Homicide and its penalties have been studied by anthropologists, historians, sociologists, criminologists, lawyers, and others, resulting in a body of research literature unprecedented in quantity and quality. Homicide has the additional advantage of being the offense least likely to conform to Black's theory—its widely acknowledged gravity means it is the most likely to be handled in an even-handed manner. Homicide therefore provides the best and the sternest test of Black's theory. If the theory is correct, the morality of homicide depends on its social geometry. But does it? Is killing, in fact, wrong?

This book has had an unusually lengthy gestation period. I first became interested in the penalties for homicide in the early 1980s when I undertook a cross-cultural study of the topic for my SJD dissertation at Harvard Law School. After completing the research phase of the project, I took a teaching position in the Department of Law at the University of Zimbabwe. Perhaps it was the distance, physical and social, from home, but my time in Zimbabwe, while personally rewarding, led to an intellectual reorientation, a disillusionment with the ephemeral and normative nature of traditional legal scholarship and a kindling of interest in the scientific character of sociology. On leaving Zimbabwe, I decided to enroll at the University of Virginia for a PhD in sociology. There, I finished my SJD dissertation and began PhD research—a series of interviews with men and women incarcerated for murder or manslaughter that focused on the formal and informal sanctions they and their family had suffered as a result of the homicide. After completing the dissertation and several papers, my attention then shifted, somewhat perversely, to homicide itself. I published a book and several articles on lethal violence. That work behind me, I found myself attracted once again to the original topic—the legal and popular response to homicide. With fresh eyes, I began to explore additional sources of information, reading widely in, for instance, the historical and human rights literatures in an effort to acquire the broadest possible familiarity with the subject. The present book is the culmination of my research.

Over the years I have received much help from many people. My greatest intellectual debt is to Donald Black, whose "Sociology of Law" course inspired my interest in sociology in general and pure sociology in particular. He supervised my two dissertations and has continued to provide a great deal of stimulation and support for this and other projects. Conversations with M. P. Baumgartner have always been enlightening and enjoyable. James Tucker has been a source of friendship and wisdom for many years. More recently, the two Scotts, Phillips and Jacques, have been good friends and great sounding boards. Others to whom I am grateful for penetrating comments on this and earlier work include Roberta Senecahl de la Roche, Barry Schwartz, Heath Hoffmann, and Callie Burt. The University of Georgia has provided a supportive environment for my endeavors, and I wish to mention, in particular, the three individuals who have headed the Department of Sociology since my arrival for various kinds of assistance they have provided me over the years: Gary Fine, Woody Beck, and William Finlay.

I thank the Virginia Department of Corrections for granting me access to the state's prisons, and especially Larry Gunther and John Jarvis, who facilitated my work there. I am deeply indebted to the prisoners themselves for telling me their stories, each unique, each humanly tragic. And I am grateful too to their family members, who shed considerable additional light on the cases and their aftermaths in the community.

Finally, I owe more than I can communicate to my family: my parents, siblings, children, and, above all, my life partner, Mary. This much I know for certain: without their encouragement and backing, this vessel would never have left port, let alone arrived at its destination. Thank you, each and all.

Is Killing Wrong?

1 THE MORALITY OF HOMICIDE

"Thou shalt not kill." No moral principle is more basic, widely understood, or universally accepted. Everybody knows from a young age that human life is sacred, and to take it willfully is the most wicked thing a human being can do. The principle is articulated in homes, schools, churches, and courtrooms, repeated by spiritual and temporal leaders, and reinforced by the dramas of good and evil, factual as well as fictional, that entertain and enthrall us. Not every culture phrases the prohibition as we do, and not every culture may make it their number one taboo, but the proscription of killing appears to be universal across human groups (see, e.g., Linton 1952; Hoebel 1954: 286; D. Brown 1991). Without it, how would societies survive? True, there are exceptions, such as killing in self-defense and during wartime. But precisely because self-defense and war are special cases, they do not undermine the general principle. Killing within a society (the focus of the present book) is wrong, pure and simple, and any deviations have to be sternly justified (see, e.g., Devine 1978; McMahan 2002: chap. 3). And because it is wrong, homicide must be punished consistently and evenly.[1] The rich are not to be favored over the poor, the more educated over the less educated, the native born over the newly arrived. Those who take human life are to be sanctioned, one and all, even-handedly.

This high-minded principle has only one enemy: reality.

MORAL REALITY

Look not at what people say or think, but at what they do—adopt a sociological rather than a philosophical perspective—and the most striking feature of human killing is the sheer variability of responses it evokes. While one homicide triggers the utmost severity, a second elicits no sanctions at all. Whatever the moral principles or legal rules state, the penalties and punishments actually inflicted upon those who kill differ widely in severity and type across time and place. Indeed, so variable is the handling of homicide that, far from being evil, certain killings are treated as the epitome of virtue, their perpetrators enjoying not just public approval but social acclaim (see Kooistra 1989). One such person was James Grant, accused of murdering Rives Pollard, a newspaper editor, in Richmond, Virginia, in 1868.

PRAISING THE KILLER

> The Saturday, November 21, number of Pollard's paper, the *Southern Journal,* contained a scandalous report of the flight of a young woman, her secret engagement, and her possible marriage. The story did not name the woman but provided enough detail that readers could identify her as Mary Grant, daughter of one of the richest men in Richmond, William H. Grant. The article brought into question Mary's virtue and the ability of the men of her family to protect her. Many read it as a slur on the Grant family's honor, and wondered how the family would seek satisfaction.
>
> Three days later, Pollard was shot and fatally wounded as he alighted from a carriage outside his office. Police officers quickly determined that he had been killed by buckshot fired from the upper windows of the building opposite. Searching the building, the police broke open a third-floor door and found a man armed with four guns, including a double-barreled shotgun loaded with buckshot. One of the barrels had recently been fired. The window facing the street on which Pollard had been killed was propped open with a hairbrush and the sill was blackened. The man was James Grant, William Grant's eldest son, Mary's brother. The police took him into custody. As he was led out onto the street, cries of "Three cheers for Grant" could be heard from the assembled crowd.
>
> Within three hours of the shooting, a coroner's jury had convened, examined the body, and heard police and civilian testimony. The verdict was announced in less than an hour: Pollard had died from gunshot fired "by some person unknown to the jury."

> Nevertheless, some three months later, Grant was indicted for Pollard's murder. The trial was delayed because the court could not find sufficient jurors who were not convinced of Grant's innocence: out of a jury pool of over 380 people, only two were deemed fit to serve. The others were dismissed for remarks such as "I would sooner hang the jury than the prisoner."
>
> After the court turned to other towns to form a jury pool, the trial began. Grant pleaded not guilty. The prosecutor presented additional evidence of guilt: that two of the guns found on Grant on the morning of the shooting had been recently purchased by Grant himself, that Grant had obtained the key to the room the night before, that no guns were kept there, and that the room's tenant had met Grant there at 7 AM on the morning of the shooting and drunk a glass of wine with him.
>
> The judge reminded the jury several times of its duty to apply the law of the land. After deliberating for only forty minutes, the jury came in with its verdict: not guilty. The spectators packed into the courtroom gallery erupted in jubilant approval. The defendant left the courtroom in triumph, surrounded by a throng of well-wishers. (see Hamm 2003)

Grant was lauded by his friends and neighbors because he had defended his family's good name, or honor. Because such notions of honor are no longer found among modern elites, it is tempting to dismiss the case as a quaint reminder of a bygone era. That would be a mistake, for both a narrow and a broad reason. Narrowly, lethal conflicts over personal and family honor remain a reality in places as diverse as the Middle East and the poor urban communities of modern America. In cultures in which honor looms large, those who kill in its name continue to garner admiration and respect (see, e.g., Shakur 1993; Peratis 2004).

More broadly, defense of honor is only one of two broad scenarios in which those who take human life are lionized. The Jívaro of the Ecuadorian Amazon are not the only people among whom a man gains great prestige "by helping the people of his locality in eliminating their enemies" (Harner 1972: 112). The enemy slain in these heroic killings may assume different forms. In rural Laos, for instance, individuals who assassinate village leaders who have abused their positions of power are "often admired, occasionally even revered" (Westermeyer 1973: 123).[2] A Celtic cross in County Donegal, Ireland, memorializes three men who ambushed and killed Lord Leitrim, a highly unpopular Anglo-Irish landlord, and two employees as they were traveling to evict yet another tenant from his estate in 1878 (Thomson 1974: 196). The killers' deed is even commemorated in that most democratic of poetic forms, a drinking toast:

> Here's to the hand that made the ball
> That shot Lord Leitrim in Donegal.[3]

Permanent glory also attaches to the Montana vigilantes who killed fifty-seven people between 1864 and 1870, including, and most notably, a corrupt sheriff, Henry Plummer:

> To this day, the men who banded together and killed the sheriff are revered as great heroes in Montana. The shoulder patches worn by members of the Montana Highway Patrol bear the numbers 3-7-77, the mysterious warning the vigilantes posted on doors or tent flaps when they wanted to drive someone into exile. A high school in Helena, the state capital, calls its football field Vigilante Stadium and its yearbook *The Vigilante.* Bozeman has a Vigilante theater company. Several of the vigilante leaders went on to successful careers as legislators, lawmen, governors, and judges. One was a founder of Creighton University, another served as U.S. senator when Montana achieved statehood. Their exploits have been written about by authors of every stripe, from hacks to Mark Twain, and even caught the attention of Charles Dickens. (F. Allen 2004: xvi)

Even today, the killing of certain enemies will elevate the killer's standing among the law-abiding. People who eliminate notorious thugs, thieves, or troublemakers in crime-ridden neighborhoods, for instance, may reap admiration and applause for their service to the community (see, e.g., Kubrin and Weitzer 2003: 171–77). Killers can still be heroes.

THE CONTINUUM OF POPULAR JUSTICE

Showering praise on the killer is clearly not the only, or even the most common, way ordinary people respond to homicide, today or in earlier societies. Popular justice takes many forms (Black 1993).[4] At different times and places, those who take human life are ignored, forgiven, boycotted, banished, denounced, hunted, attacked, kidnapped, enslaved, tortured, assassinated, lynched, and mutilated. They flee, negotiate, recruit allies, seek protection, summon mediators, beg forgiveness, make amends, pay restitution, have their property destroyed, and launch counterreprisals. Conveniently, these many forms can be reduced to a small number of categories, ranked according to their severity. Let us consider each category briefly.

The severity of popular justice

Praise	Toleration	Shunning	Compensation	Self-help
LESS SEVERE				MORE SEVERE

If praise represents social approval, *toleration* consists of taking no moral action in response to a homicide (Black 1990: 58). Toleration is purest when the homicide is simply ignored—the killing is surrounded by a circle of silence. In less pure forms, mild sanctions are imposed—the victim's family criticizes the killer, or gossips about him behind his back, or defines him as mentally ill (most killers are male). Toleration should not be mistaken for approval. People may dislike, even hate, the killer, but do little or nothing to him. In no known society is every homicide tolerated, although the Gebusi of New Guinea come close. In the period 1940–82, almost nine out of every ten Gebusi homicides were of individuals or their kin suspected of injuring others through acts of sorcery and whom the community believed deserved to die, a judgment usually accepted by the victim's kin, albeit reluctantly, with the result that killers typically went about their daily business free from punishment, stigma, or the obligation to make payment (Knauft 1985: 116–23; compare Knauft 2002). The Gebusi are unusual in tolerating such a large proportion of their killings, but in most societies at least some killings have no moral repercussions: the homicide itself dies.

Shunning—the curtailment or elimination of interaction following a conflict (Black 1990: 49)—is the first category of truly negative sanctions or penalties. People who kill are often given the "cold shoulder." Friends no longer drop in, acquaintances do not pause to say hello, people turn away in the street. Even their family and friends may be ostracized. Shunning of this type is the most severe popular sanctions that killers today typically experience (though not the most severe sanction they ever experience). But shunning comes in more coercive guises as well. The Cheyenne Indians, for instance, banish certain killers from the tribe altogether for a period of years (Llewellyn and Hoebel 1941). Shunning, then, is a matter of degree, and can vary significantly in amount and severity across cases.

Compensation is the payment of wealth, such as livestock, crops, slaves, or money, following a conflict (Black 1987). Killers and their families making restitution to the victim's family for their loss is a common practice in many preindustrial societies. Yet these payments can rarely be taken for granted, typically requiring delicate negotiations between the two sides that may, as with the nomads of Tibet, extend over many days or even weeks, perhaps with the aid of a mediator (see, e.g., Ekvall 1964: 1142–47). Once the parties agree to pay and accept compensation, the risk of being attacked that typically hangs over the killer's side lessens, but does not always dispel. The Mae Enga of New Guinea are by no means the only group among whom victims' families "reserve the right to avenge the homicide in kind, even after accepting the killer's pigs" (Meggitt 1977: 123). To encourage the payment of compensation, some cultures have scales that stipulate the sum to be paid for a homicide. In practice, these sums only serve as starting points in the negotiations between the two sides. The amount actually sought and paid will vary from case to case: some lives cost more than others.[5]

Self-help—the most severe of the popular sanctions—is the use of aggression in retaliation for the homicide (Black 1990: 44). Most often it is the family, friends, or neighbors of the victim who pay back the killing with a killing of their own (vengeance). Sometimes, though, it is the community at large that engages in self-help, as when a town denounces or, more extremely, lynches a killer. Either way, the person attacked is not always the killer himself: under conditions of "collective liability," any member (or perhaps any male member) of his family, neighborhood, or tribe is a potential target (see, e.g., Stauder 1972: 165–66). Lethal self-help, like all forms of popular justice, varies in severity. In less severe cases, just one person is killed; in the most severe cases, an entire group is tortured, slaughtered, mutilated, and eaten. Between these extremes lies feuding—the "precise, extended, and open exchange of killings, usually one death at a time" (Black 2004a: 153). Feuding in the wake of homicide occurs in many regions of the world, including the arid deserts of North Africa and the Middle East (see, e.g., Peters 1967), the Balkan highlands (see, e.g., Hasluck 1954), the rain forest of South America (see, e.g., Chagnon 1977), the lush tropical lands of the Philippines (see, e.g., Kiefer 1972), and the Hindu Kush mountains of northern Pakistan (see, e.g., Aase 2002). But in none of these places is feuding automatic: only certain kinds of killings trigger a cycle of retaliatory violence. Again, individual cases vary.

FROM POPULAR JUSTICE TO LAW

In the earliest human societies, all justice was popular, and homicides were handled through some combination of praise, toleration, shunning, compensation, and self-help. Over the centuries, control over the handling of homicide has shifted from society to the state. Today, legal officials normally step in following a homicide, seeking to arrest, try, convict, and sentence killers. In the process, capital punishment has replaced feuding and lynching, and prison sentences have supplanted compensation payments. How did this transformation come about? And how complete is it?

Law is a product of the state. From its birthplace in Mesopotamia some five thousand years or so ago, the state has spread in various forms across the globe. With it, law has expanded and popular justice has shrunk, gradually but inexorably. The first states resulted from the emergence of a central authority capable of enforcing at least some of its rulings. These aborning states did not enjoy anything close to a monopoly of violence, especially in remote areas, their leaders having to be content with modest goals such as "deferring violence, encouraging arbitration, limiting reprisal" (R. Fletcher 2003: 116). Early legal systems therefore often tolerated, or were forced to tolerate, severe popular sanctions such as feuding (Wallace-Hadrill 1959). Often, the state's first step in establishing permanent legal authority over homicide was to continue the system of compensation payments prescribed by prelegal codes, but to stiffen it with the threat of sanctions for those who would not settle peacefully.

Only gradually did punishment displace compensation. It typically did so centrifugally, from the capital outward, coming first to major population and economic centers, later to smaller settlements, and latest of all, to isolated outlying regions. In Britain, the Crown had established jurisdiction over English homicide cases as early as the thirteenth century. The king's judges traveled throughout the country, hearing cases and investigating suspicious deaths in provincial centers. Although a large number of killers were able to flee, the state was able to identify and outlaw many of them, and few—perhaps only those of higher social standing—appear to have been able to escape prosecution by paying compensation (Given 1977; Hanawalt 1979; Powell 1989: 100–103). In the outlying regions of Wales, Ireland, and Scotland, however, many homicide cases continued for several more centuries to be settled by a transfer of wealth, usually with official blessing (R. Davies 1969; Nicholls 1972: 53–57; Wormald 1980). Until the end of the sixteenth century, for example, homicides among the Scottish elite, or those who had elite patronage, were often handled by a panel of arbitrators who got the parties to agree in writing to a compensation payment and to sign (along with their maternal and paternal kin) a letter of forgiveness. To finalize things, a judge might be asked to certify the agreement and issue a formal legal pardon to the killer (Wormald 1980; K. Brown 1986: chap. 2). The British Isles were not unique. The kingdom of Sweden prescribed death for many homicides, but as late as the sixteenth century the courts usually allowed the killer to save his life by paying compensation to the victim's family and a fine to the king, particularly when the killing occurred outside Stockholm, the capital (Ylikangas 2001: 15–28; Karonen 2001: 99–104).

Gradually, though, homicide cases came to be dominated by the state rather than the victim's family (see, e.g., Dean 2001: 5–9, 104–7). The state, in turn, came to be dominated by professionals. In England, for example, the prosecution could long employ a lawyer, but did not do so with any regularity until the 1730s. That same decade saw the relaxation of the rule that a defendant could not be represented by counsel, although, initially, the lawyer was largely confined to cross-examining the prosecution witnesses (Beattie 1986: 352–62). As the eighteenth century progressed, medical evidence, for the prosecution and defense, increasingly came to be given by scientifically trained doctors, and full autopsies were held more often (Gaskill 2000: 272–78). The year 1829 brought the demise of the venerable but haphazard system of preindustrial policing, with its local constables, night watchmen, and thief-takers, and the creation of the first modern professional police force, the London Metropolitan Police, a development that was soon widely copied by European and North American cities (see, e.g., Walker 1998: 51–54). Shortly afterward, police departments developed special units to investigate major crimes such as homicide. The Metropolitan Police, for example, created its first specialist detectives in 1842 (see Innes 2003: 12). The latter half of the century saw increasing reliance on scientific methods and personnel in Britain, continental Europe, and America. Coroners or medical examiners began to conduct autopsies more routinely and more thoroughly. Experts came to provide evidence on fingerprints, toxicology, ballistics, and other matters, further professionalizing homicide investigations and trials (Lane 1997: 200–213; Farmer 2007: 48–52). By the end of the nineteenth century, the modern system of prosecuting homicide was largely in place.

The advent of professionalized law has restricted, but not eliminated, popular justice (see Cooney 1994a). Popular sanctions continue to be leveled against those who take the lives of others. Many killers in modern society are shunned to one degree or another by their or the victim's family members, friends, and neighbors; some find themselves threatened with violence, and a smaller number are actually beaten or killed (see, e.g., Shakur 1993). In parts of the world where state control is more nominal than real, popular justice is all the more prominent. Peoples residing in mountains, jungles, deserts, and other remote areas may effectively govern themselves, handling homicides after their own fashion, without state intrusion. The legal systems of many industrializing countries are often quite porous, enabling most killers to avoid arrest so that any real sanctions they experience are popular. Even where the state is more highly organized and legal officials handle more cases, as in modern America, substantial legal and popular penalties may still be found in tandem. Law and popular justice, then, are not mutually exclusive; a mixture of legal and popular sanctions is usual in state societies.[6]

THE VARIABILITY OF LAW

The advent of law has changed the types of sanction imposed on killers. Yet it has not changed a fundamental feature of those sanctions: variability. The modern legal system is a large bureaucratic machine, processing killers according to a standard set of procedures, but the results it generates are still far from uniform. One killer is sent to the death chamber, a second to prison for several years, and a third is set free. As with popular justice, the possible outcomes can be arranged in order of how strongly they repel social actors, or their severity.[7]

The severity of law

Praise Toleration Arrest Prosecution Conviction Probation Therapy Imprisonment Death

LESS SEVERE MORE SEVERE

Praise, the most lenient result, is the most rare as well. Since legal systems typically prohibit killing on pain of severe penalties, rewarding killers blurs the message government sends to the people. Still, there are instances where killers receive official praise. In premodern Japan, for example, government officials could authorize the close relatives of a homicide victim to avenge the killing and were known to shower plaudits and gifts on those who did so successfully (Mills 1976: 528, 539). Sheriffs in medieval China who killed dangerous criminals were eligible for promotion, and the more bandits they killed, the greater their chance of career advancement (McKnight 1992: 269–75). Today, Brazilian police officers who kill multiple suspected criminals may be similarly singled out for promotions and pay increases (see, e.g., Cavallaro 1997). Citizens, too, may benefit from slaying others: nineteenth-century America is not the only society in which the government offered monetary rewards for the capture of notorious outlaws "dead or alive" (see, e.g., Taub 1988).

In the vast majority of cases, however, the range of legal variability stretches from toleration (no official action taken) to the death penalty. Both extremes appear often in early legal systems, as homicide offenders often attracted either very severe or very lenient penalties. In thirteenth-century England, for instance, a homicide conviction carried a mandatory death sentence, but one-half of all killers identified by the authorities were able to flee the clutches of the law, and another quarter managed to secure an acquittal. All told, twelve out of every thirteen accused killers avoided being convicted and executed (Given 1977: 93). Many third world societies today exhibit similar patterns, being unwilling or unable to punish most perpetrators. In Brazil less than 8 percent of homicides, one official has estimated, are successfully prosecuted (see Jahangir 2004: paragraph 55). A dearth of reliable data makes it impossible to say how typical of less-developed nations the Brazilian numbers are. What is more certain is that homicides in the world's wealthier nations tend to result in more convictions.

In modern America, about which most is known, homicide cases enter the legal system when the police are notified of, or discover, the killing.[8] Dead bodies are difficult to conceal, and most homicides probably come to the notice of today's professional police forces. But not all. An unknown number of American homicide victims are never found, their corpses burned, drowned, buried, or otherwise disposed of surreptitiously. These killings leave no official trace.

Once the police discover a possible or likely homicide victim, they send the body for autopsy to the coroner or medical examiner.[9] If the autopsy suggests or confirms foul play, the legal process is set in motion. The case then goes through a series of decision-making stages, at each of which it may drop out for one reason or another.

- Arrest, the first stage, occurs in about two-thirds of the cases in which police judge the homicide to be criminal (Federal Bureau of Investigation 2005). The remaining homicides are effectively tolerated.
- After police have charged the offender, the case is sent to a grand jury for indictment and/or a preliminary hearing (depending on the jurisdiction) to establish probable cause that the defendant is guilty. Of those charged with murder, only about 3 percent have their cases dropped at these two stages (Baumer, Messner, and Felson 2000: 286).
- The case then goes to court where acquittal eliminates about 20 percent of the remaining offenders. (Of those remaining, approxi-

mately half plead guilty and half are found guilty at trial [Baumer, Messner, and Felson 2000: 86]).

- Of those convicted, a small number (less than 1 percent) are declared insane and sent indefinitely to a psychiatric hospital for treatment (Callahan et al. 1991). The vast majority receive prison sentences. The numbers vary from jurisdiction to jurisdiction, but typically about 90 percent receive prison sentences, 5–10 percent receive probation, and 1–5 percent receive the death penalty (in jurisdictions that permit it). In California, for example, 89 percent of those convicted of homicide in 1999 were sentenced to prison, adult or juvenile; 5 percent received unnamed other sentences; and 6 percent were sentenced to death (California Department of Justice 2000: 37, 41).[10]

In sum, at least one-third of Americans who kill are never arrested; at the other extreme, a very small number receive a death sentence. Most end up somewhere in between, convicted and sent to prison, though for widely dissimilar durations.

EXPLAINING MORAL REALITY

Law and popular justice, then, will often be mobilized following a homicide. The severity of popular and legal sanctions may therefore converge or diverge.[11] Popular justice and law may both be lenient (as in James Grant's case). Or popular justice may be severe and law lenient (e.g., when a crowd lynches a man acquitted of murder). Or popular justice may be lenient and law severe (e.g., where a killer is executed by the state but attracts few or no communal sanctions). Or both may be severe (e.g., an attempted lynching followed by an execution).

The critical question is, what explains this wide variation? Why do homicides attract such drastically different sanctions, legal and popular? Let us begin with what the experts say.

MORAL AND LEGAL THEORY

Moral teaching and legal theory hold that the key to explaining case-by-case variation is the deviant's conduct and mental state. The culpability of conduct depends on the degree of harm caused (for example, injury versus death) and the degree of aggressiveness with which the defendant acted (self-defense mitigates seriousness). A killing provoked by the victim is less blameworthy than a killing not so provoked. Culpability also depends on whether the defendant acted intentionally or merely carelessly, and whether the defendant acted freely or under some kind of pressure or compulsion. A law professor put the point well:

> The underlying question in evaluating a homicide is actually very simple. To what extent was the killer acting from within rather than under the pressure of external circumstances? To what extent was he or she self-actuating or autonomous in choosing to take the life of another human being? The more self-actuating the killer's actions, the more he or she is to blame and the more severe the punishment deserved. . . .
>
> The most culpable form of homicide is the one that reflects planning, thinking, and calculated action. The least culpable form is the one that occurs with minimal input of the killer's personality: the killing occurs spontaneously, under the heat of passion, under the pressure of circumstances, triggered by external factors. (G. Fletcher 1995: 22)

Legally and morally, then, factors such as premeditation, accident, and self-defense are crucial to judging homicide.

The factors specified by legal and moral theory matter, but they are far from being the only ones to matter. Some premeditated killings are wholly or partially tolerated, even when not committed in self-defense. James Grant is hardly the only killer who acted with apparent premeditation, and without any threat to his own life, to escape legal punishment. Similar results can be seen today. As just one example, consider a case from a Houston study:

> A young man, 21 years old, was planning to leave his wife and to move in with a male partner. The man's mother objected strongly to his plan. One day, the young man and his new partner accidentally bumped into the mother at a shopping mall. The man and his mother again argued about his decision. As the man exited a store, his mother took out a .22 caliber pistol and shot him in the back of the head. Despite the intentional nature of the killing, the victim being unarmed, and the absence of any attack on

the mother by her son or his partner, she was sentenced to just five years imprisonment (see Lundsgaarde 1977: 87–88). To put this result in context: The mother's sentence was more lenient than that received by many people convicted of possessing small amounts of illegal drugs.

Striking though this real-life example is, some preindustrial societies go further and dismiss issues of intentionality and self-defense altogether. The nomadic Bedouin people of North Africa and the Middle East, to cite one example, traditionally did not distinguish between accidental, deliberate, or defensive killing. They cared little about the killer's state of mind; what mattered was that the victim's family had lost a member. A killing must be repaid in kind: "There should be one grave opposite the other," a popular Bedouin motto states. Hence, they sought revenge whether the killing was intentional or not (Ginat 1997: 15). Today, the Bedouin have become more sedentary, farming plots of land and working for wages. Even so, they remain unimpressed by killers' excuses or justifications (Ginat 1997).

SOCIOLOGICAL THEORY

If legal and moral theory provides limited assistance in predicting the fate of those who kill, perhaps sociological theory can fill the void. After all, sociologists have long been fascinated by law and social control. Disappointingly, though, most of their theories turn out to be of little help.

Cultural theory, for example, explains legal outcomes with the values of the setting in which it is judged (see, e.g., Hoebel 1954). According to this view, the explanation of the tolerant overall treatment of homicide in, for example, the Houston study lies in the tolerant values toward violence of the Houston population: The residents of the city, accustomed to a high rate of homicide and living in a state renowned for its frontier past, understand and even admire those prepared to use violence; if others die in the process, well, they probably deserve to. This line of explanation runs into the problem, however, that the outcomes of Houston homicide cases of the time were far from uniform. While there was a good deal of leniency, there was also some severity. Certain defendants received long sentences, and some were even sentenced to death (Lundsgaarde 1977). The culture was a constant, but the case outcomes varied. Culture alone cannot explain the handling of the cases.

Nor do the classic sociological theories of Karl Marx, Émile Durkheim, or Max Weber fare much better. All three men had important insights into the social context of law, but each of them was more concerned with legal variation across societies than individual cases.

For Marx, law reflects and reinforces social class divisions; it is a means by which the ruling class rules (see, e.g., Cain and Hunt 1979; H. Collins 1982). But neither Marx, nor Engels, nor any of the conflict theories inspired by them predicts how police officers, grand juries, prosecutors, judges, and juries will decide particular cases (e.g., Turk 1969; Quinney 1970). What happens, for instance, if the homicide takes place, as most do, within the working class? Will the legal officials—who tend to come from and represent the higher classes—take a lenient view, perhaps regarding it as an outlet for destructive energies that might otherwise be channeled in a more revolutionary direction, or will they treat it severely in order to establish a peaceful social order that allows capitalism to flourish most effectively? Marxism provides no clear answer.

For Durkheim (1893), law reflects and reinforces social solidarity, the sense of unity that binds members of a society together. Durkheim proposed that as a society's division of labor becomes more differentiated, its dominant style of law changes. Penal sanctions imposed by the community give way to compensatory sanctions flowing from one party to the other. Although this was the first testable theory of law, it did not extend to sanction variability within a society—why, for example, one case attracts punishment and another compensation.[12]

For Weber (1925), law reflects and reinforces rationalization, the relentless trend toward more organization, order, rules, and predictability that pervades modern life. Law has evolved into a seamless system of rules logically applied by a staff of trained professionals. Weber held that this increase in formal legal rationality brings greater equality of case outcomes. But his thesis does not explain why formally identical cases may still have very different results. Weber addressed case outcomes in general, not the winning or losing of particular legal cases.

Modern sociological theory is no more helpful. It addresses the issues from a branch of criminology known as deviance and social control, which analyzes, for example, when the state is and is not likely to define behavior as criminal (see, e.g., Becker 1963). But while theories of deviance abound, theories of social control are scarce, especially at the level of individual cases.[13] Criminology has a wealth of competing explanations for why individuals engage in violence, drug use, and other forms of behavior commonly defined as deviant (see, e.g., Cullen and Agnew 2006). Yet it is bereft of rival case-level theories of social control—sets of interlinking propositions from which, say, a defendant's sentencing in a Houston courtroom can be deduced. Nor does any other field or theoretical tradition fill the gap. Rational choice theory, for example, explains behavior with the calculated choices made by self-interested individuals (see, e.g., Coleman 1990). However, it is not clear why it is in the interests of a judge to impose a lenient sentence on a mother who publicly executes her son in broad daylight when presumably he sentenced other killers more severely. More damagingly, it is not even clear that the judge's interests can be measured with any precision anyway, based as they are on subjective preferences locked away in the mind, to which there is no known key.

Perhaps the failure of these theories is due to the nature of morality. Perhaps moral variation is simply random, a matter of good or bad luck. Perhaps the attribution of good and bad obeys no logic. Perhaps human morality is meaningless.

Before drawing that stark conclusion, however, one final theory must be considered: pure sociology (Black 1976, 1995). Pure sociology is a new way of thinking about the individual and society (Black 1995, 2000b; see also Baumgartner 2002). It is not a theory of human behavior, but a theory of social behavior. It treats social life as a realm of reality independent of biology or psychology that obeys laws of its own. The job of the pure sociologist is to uncover these laws, to explain the fundamental principles of social existence. Pure sociology was first applied in the study of legal conflict, though it can be adapted to address any and all aspects of social life. If valid, it should explain the handling of homicide cases—it should predict who is arrested and indicted for homicide, who is convicted and who is acquitted, who gets the death penalty and who gets life imprisonment, as well as who bears the brunt of popular ire and who is treated as a folk hero. It is our best hope for a theory of social morality. But what exactly is pure sociology? And does it work? These are the questions this book addresses.

Killing is a fact of human life. From the earliest times to the present, people and groups have resorted to lethal violence from time to time in dealing with their opponents and enemies. True, some cultures are extremely peaceful, their members invariably handling conflicts in nonaggressive ways, shunning lethal violence (see, e.g., Howell and Willis 1989). But homicides occur within the great majority of known societies, albeit in widely varying numbers. Moreover, these societies are of all types, at every stage of socioeconomic development. Perhaps the least violent are the simple hunter-gatherers, small bands of people who forage for survival and who use their mobility to move away from conflict and avoid violence. But even simple hunter-gatherers, such as the Bushmen of the Kalahari, are known to kill on occasion (e.g., Lee 1979: 382–400).

Homicide, then, is a near universal. So too is the prohibition on homicide. What is far from universal, however, is the response to homicide, its social morality (see, e.g., Waters 2007). In real life, there are good killings and bad killings (Wilson 1996). So it was in earlier societies, and so it is today, even as jurisdiction over homicide has passed from society to the state. Nowadays, popular sanctions may be reduced to a supporting role in most places, but they share at least one central feature with legal sanctions: variability. This perpetrator is not even arrested, but that one is prosecuted, convicted, and sentenced to spend the rest of his days in a cage. Some killers are lauded and lionized, while others are excoriated and executed.

Knowing that severity varies is one thing: knowing why is quite another. The critical question is, what explains the variability in sanctions imposed on those who take human life? Law and morality fail to provide a satisfactory answer. So does conventional sociology. However, a bold new body of ideas finally promises to do so: pure sociology, the subject of the next chapter.

2 PURE SOCIOLOGY

It is possible to overstate the role of law in the modern world, but it is equally possible to understate it. Law is found in every realm of contemporary life. It penetrates, to one degree or another, virtually every corner of our social universe—our places of work and leisure, our homes and schools, our shopping malls, highways, airports, and even our wildernesses. It reaches across the entire society, claiming jurisdiction over every person, group, and corporation. No town or city remains unpoliced. Jails and prisons pepper the landscape, and courthouses command prominent city sites. On the civil side too, litigation proceeds apace, one source of a relentless barrage of legal activity. Every day, police arrest suspects, lawyers file suit, prosecutors press charges, grand juries hand down indictments, judges issue rulings, and juries decide the fate of defendants.

At first glance, law presents a bewildering array of actions, far too varied and voluminous for the layperson to understand. Better leave law to the experts, then. And for much of its history, law was the exclusive domain of lawyers. But in the nineteenth century, outsiders such as Karl Marx and Émile Durkheim began to take a hard look at law, arguing that it is influenced by, and influences, its social environment (Cain and Hunt 1979; Durkheim 1893). These thinkers drew attention to law's social context, even if they did not manage to formulate a testable theory of the case. Later, a new generation of scholars began to systematically apply the newly discovered techniques of social science to the study of legal conflicts, including ethnographic observation, statistical analysis, and the testing of hypotheses. In doing so, they uncovered patterns of legal behavior that were at best only dimly perceived previously, such as the reluctance of many businessmen to sue for breach of contract (Macaulay 1963), the tendency of judges to be stricter than jurors on defendants (Kalven and Zeisel 1966), and the greater success enjoyed by repeat players over one-shot litigants in lawsuits (Galanter 1974). Important as their work was, the social scientists lacked a framework that would explain their findings. They lacked a theory.

Theory is the highest form of scientific activity, and theorists are the most acclaimed scientific thinkers. A theory explains a large body of findings and predicts many others. Going beyond the known facts, a theory constellates patterns of empirical reality into a system of ideas that can be tested and refined by others. Developing new theories requires great intelligence, but intelligence is everywhere in science. More searchingly, original theory requires insight, imagination, innovation: the ability to see the world anew. Hence its rarity.

Eventually, law found its theory. The year 1976 saw the publication of a remarkable book, *The Behavior of Law.* In a little over one hundred pages, the author, Donald Black, laid out a general sociological theory of legal conflict. The theory consists of a set of propositions that purport to explain the outcome of all legal cases, criminal and civil, in all legal systems at all times. Which victims call the police? Who gets arrested? When will grand juries indict? Under what conditions will merchants sue one another? Who wins in courts? What explains the size of damage awards? Which cases get the ultimate penalty? *The Behavior of Law* addresses these and a host of related questions. And it does so in a radically new way.

THE BEHAVIOR OF LAW

Law, for Black, is governmental social control (and social control is the definition of and response to deviant behavior). Law in this sense is a quantitative variable, known by the severity of sanctions a case attracts (as measured by how far the case progresses in the legal system). In criminal cases, an arrest is more law than no arrest, an indictment more law than a "no bill," a conviction more law than an acquittal, and a long sentence more law than a short sentence. Similarly, in civil cases, contacting a lawyer is more law than not contacting, filing suit more law than not filing, a decision in favor of the plaintiff more law than a decision in favor of the defendant, and a large damage award more law than a small damage award.

Law also varies in style. There are four styles: penal, compensatory, therapeutic, and conciliatory. The penal style treats deviance as a crime that requires punishment; the compensatory style frames wrongdoing in terms of debt and restitution; the therapeutic style sees deviance as an illness that can be overcome with help; while the conciliatory style emphasizes the repair of ruptured relationships. Each style varies quantitatively so that one can speak of the quantity of penal law (measured, for example, by severity of sentence) or the quantity of compensatory law (measured, for example, by the size of damage awards).

THE GEOMETRY OF LAW

What explains variation in the quantity and style of law? For centuries, aspiring lawyers have been told that the key to understanding law is to study its rules and principles. But having mastered the contents of statutes, judgments, and scholastic commentaries, neophyte lawyers are often disappointed to find that their hard-won knowledge conforms only approximately to the way cases are handled in the real world. Once they encounter actual cases, recent graduates of American law schools—perhaps the best formally educated young lawyers in history—almost invariably find they have been taught much that is irrelevant and have not been taught much that is relevant. When, for example, will the police arrest a suspect and when will they let him walk? The written law is an uncertain guide: empirical research shows that not only do the police frequently fail to make an arrest when the law permits it but they also sometimes arrest when the law forbids it (Black 1980: 180–86). When will the district attorney seek the death penalty? Alas, the answer will not be found in the statutes and precedents. When will a jury convict and when will it acquit a defendant? Again, the formal law does not provide much assistance: two technically identical cases may produce diametrically opposite results from the same jury (see, e.g., Ugwuegbu 1979).

When the rules run out, lawyers invoke the human element in law, or "discretion" (Baumgartner 1992a). Discretion means that legal officials must sometimes make personal decisions that are, by their nature, unpredictable. One prosecutor reviews a homicide and concludes that it should be charged as a murder; another, equally well trained and experienced, sees it as no more than a manslaughter case. But this approach only gives the problem a name. To say that legal outcomes are based on discretion does not explain anything; it merely camouflages the lack of an explanation.

The Behavior of Law proffers an explanation. Exhibiting a new form of sociological thinking, later known as pure sociology, it proposes that, holding constant the conduct of the parties, *case outcomes vary with their location and direction in social space, or their social geometry.* Thus, to explain the handling of a case—the amount and style of law it attracts—look to see whether it is upward or downward, or traverses large or small expanses of social space.

Social space accommodates all the major variables that sociologists have discovered over the years to be important in explaining social life, including social class, the division of labor, social networks, and marginality. Most of these explanatory variables are derived from the theoretical systems devised by the great sociological thinkers of the past. By incorporating their powerful variables into a single framework, pure sociology creates an even more powerful system or paradigm based on five dimensions of social space. The *vertical* dimension refers to wealth and its distribution, a favorite source of explanation for Karl Marx and Frederick Engels (1848) and their followers; the *organizational* dimension refers to the collective aspects of existence, a niche explored by thinkers such as Max Weber (1922) and Guy Swanson (1971); the moral or *normative* dimension refers to social control (anything that defines and responds to something as deviant)—and was favored terrain for sociologists such as William Graham Sumner (1906) and Erving Goffman (1963); the *cultural* dimension refers to symbolic reality, as embodied in, for example, science, religion, and art, and has been explored by scholars such as Pitrim Sorokin (1937) and Talcott Parsons (1951); while the morphological or *horizontal* dimension refers to the arrangement of social ties and has been emphasized by Émile Durkheim (1893), Georg Simmel (1908), and network analysts (see, e.g., Granovetter 1973).

More dimensions of social space may be discovered in the future. Moreover, several of the existing dimensions have subdimensions. For example, the morphological dimension includes both relational distance (how intertwined two actors' lives are) and radial status (an actor's degree of social participation), and these can, and will in this book, be treated as separate dimensions.

Individuals and groups occupy a position in each dimension of social space at any one time. All social interaction between them therefore has distance, direction, and elevation. When a poor man steals from a rich man, the theft has an upward direction in vertical space, and the greater the difference in wealth between them, the greater its vertical distance. Peace talks between two powerful nations take place at an elevated location in organizational space. An airport conversation with a visitor from a foreign land spans large expanses of cultural space. A complaint of child neglect filed by a law-abiding teacher against a mother with a criminal record has a downward direction in normative space. And so on. These elevations, distances, and directions do not just describe social behavior, however: they explain it.

Pure sociology explains behavior by formulating testable statements of some generality, or propositions, that link the behavior to be explained with its social geometry. One such proposition, for example, states that *downward law is greater than upward law* (Black 1976: 21). This proposition explains a host of facts, including, for example, why a study of the New Haven Colony court of seventeenth-century America found that, even though the poor greatly outnumbered the wealthy, far more cases were brought by wealthy individuals against poor individuals than the other way around. Moreover, wealthy litigants were more successful than poor litigants, whether they brought the case or it was brought against them and whether it was a civil or a criminal matter (Baumgartner 1978). The proposition also predicts many facts yet to be discovered. It predicts, for example, that a researcher who conducts a study of rape cases—in a modern or an ancient society—will find that since the direction of law is the opposite of the direction of crime, downward rapes will attract less law than upward rapes. Thus, a wealthy man who rapes a poor woman should be less likely to be arrested, indicted, tried, convicted, and sentenced severely than a poor man who rapes a wealthy woman (holding constant the parties' conduct and the other spatial characteristics of the case).

All of this implies a wholly new understanding of law. Instead of being a universal—applicable to all cases—law fluctuates with the social geometry of the conflict. Equality before the law—one of modern society's most treasured ideals—becomes a mirage. Indeed, to speak of "the law" is misleading. In reality there is no single law of rape, homicide, contract, or property. There are many laws of rape, homicide, contract, and property, and they are sociological or geometrical. Black (2007) calls this theory "legal relativity."

THE THREE P'S

Pure sociology, then, explains behavior in an innovative way—geometrically, or with its location and direction in social space. But its radical originality does not end there, for it also explains behavior without invoking a trinity of features found in virtually every other social science theory—the three P's: psychology, purposes, and people (Black 1995: 847–70).

Psychological or mental states are not relevant to pure sociology. It proceeds entirely without reference to the thoughts, feelings, or motives of the actors, focusing instead on the social geometry of their behavior. In creating it, Black finally achieves something many sociologists have long aspired to—making sociology a field of science wholly independent of psychology (1995: 848–50). An independent sociology is a notable accomplishment in itself, but it also has desirable methodological and theoretical consequences. It allows all sociological variables to be observed and measured directly—as they outwardly appear in the world of human action. And because the content of the human mind is virtually unknowable (until we develop mind readers), pure sociology avoids the uncertainty lurking at the center of psychological theories. But there may be other grounds for bypassing psychology as well. Black (2008) questions whether psychological theories can truly and precisely explain outward behavior at all, as distinct from opinions, attitudes, beliefs, and other psychological phenomena. The reason is that statements about the mind are logically separate from statements about behavior. As he states, "Psychology only explains psychology" (2008: 12). Mental states such as frustration or anger, for example, do not logically imply any action. Still less do they imply one course of action rather than another (for example, bringing a lawsuit versus throwing a punch versus going for a long walk). We can only explain specific forms of human behavior, he argues, with social variables such as those featured in pure sociology. As noted earlier, in pure sociology those variables are geometrical.

Similarly absent is any concern with purposes. To explain something with its purposes or goals is known as teleology. Ancient and medieval thinkers often explained the natural world teleologically, arguing that plants, animals, and other objects behave in accordance with their God-given purposes. Natural scientists have long since abandoned teleology. But the ends of people are equally elusive. As Black remarks, "The ends of humans are no more knowable than the ends of God or planets" (1995: 862). Even so, virtually every social science explanation invokes individual or group purposes, such as the maximization of wealth, the pursuit of happiness, the struggle for dominance, and the like. "Teleology," Black observes, "is the superparadigm of sociology, its fundamental logic, the logic of human behavior itself" (1995: 861). Only pure sociology moves beyond teleology.

Finally, and surely somewhat surprisingly to many readers, even people are absent from pure sociology. In pure sociology, social life, not people, behaves (Black 1976: 1). When a judge sentences a man to prison, pure sociologists do not see an official making a decision; they see law itself behaving. When a woman kills her husband, they do not see a violent individual but a violent structure (Black 2004a). When a celebrity sings the national anthem or a guitarist plays a solo, they do not see individuals behaving musically but music behaving individually. People are the agents of social life, not its masters.

The absence of the three P's gives pure sociology a strange, even bizarre, quality. New readers sometimes feel that something vital is missing. But nothing is. Pure sociology's theoretical principles fully explain the facts. Why is a poor man more likely to get the death penalty for killing a rich man than a rich man is for killing a poor man? Because that is what the principle "Downward law is greater than upward law" predicts. But why is law greater in a downward direction? That is just the way law behaves, always and everywhere. Until we find a still more general principle, we cannot take the explanation any further.

The explanations of pure sociology are not necessarily incomplete, then, but they are unfamiliar. And hard to grasp. All of us, professional sociologists included, are accustomed to thinking about the psychology and purposes of specific people. Thinking differently does not come easily, and it makes some who encounter pure sociology uncomfortable, even hostile. They fail to appreciate that pure sociology seeks to explain something new, an unprecedented subject matter in science: the behavior of social life.

Social life is a separate and distinctive realm of reality (Black 1995: 848–50; 2000b: 705–6). It is not a person, and it has no psychology or teleology. Its laws are independent of the laws of the mind or the body. Pure sociology seeks to discover those laws, to explain the behavior of social life itself. Black's theory of law therefore addresses the behavior of legal life, its fundamental principles—the laws of law (2000b: 707).

As a subject matter, social life offers several clear scientific advantages. For one thing, statements about the behavior of social life are highly testable, a characteristic of the best scientific ideas. Testability means that an idea can be falsified by inconsistent evidence (see Popper 1934). A testable proposition makes a prediction about what will occur (Black 1995: 831). To predict in this sense is not necessarily to prophesy the future, but rather to deduce from a theory the pattern of facts that will be found, such as when the police are more likely to make an arrest or a court is more likely to impose a death sentence. A principle of legal life such as "Downward law is greater than upward law" is highly predictive and, hence, highly testable. Its testability is made all the easier because all its variables can be directly measured and observed. No longer is there any need to refer to the contents of the actor's psychology. Law has no mind. Nor must we speculate about law's purposes or goals.

A focus on social life yields more parsimonious or simple theory as well. A central goal of science is to reduce the complexity of the world to a smaller number of ideas. Scientists therefore prefer simpler theories, as long as they can explain the facts as well as other theories. Simplicity can be measured by brevity (see Black 1995: 838). Black notes that "the elimination of people radically simplifies human reality. . . . Whereas the explanation of legal behavior such as calls to the police, arrests, lawsuits, verdicts, and remedies previously required an understanding of the behavior of particular citizens, police, lawyers, judges, and juries, for example, now it requires only an understanding of the behavior of law—a single phenomenon that everywhere obeys the same principles" (1995: 860). The principle that "downward law is greater than upward law" illustrates the simplicity that pure sociology can achieve: a small number of words explain an immense number of facts about an immense number of actors.

Social life also made possible a major advance in generality—the diversity of social facts a single theory could address (Black 1995: 833–37). As Black comments, it "led to a new discovery: Law behaves according to the same principles everywhere—across all legal cases, all stages of the legal process, all societies, all times" (2000c: 347). As long as a theory orders the facts equally well, a more general theory is always scientifically preferable to a less general theory. Since people's psychology and purposes likely vary considerably across different societies (although since they cannot be entirely measured, we cannot be sure), general theory invoking them is difficult, perhaps impossible, to attain. What motivates a man to bring a lawsuit in a West African tribal court may be quite different from what propels his counterpart in sixteenth-century China or twenty-first-century America to do so. However, once these actions are all seen as aspects of a single phenomenon—the behavior of law—it becomes possible to explain them with a single theory.

But law is only one form of social life, and pure sociology has much broader applications. "The theory of law is an example and not the ultimate concern of this work," Black wrote in the preface to *The Behavior of Law* (1976: x). The meaning of this statement soon became clear when he extended the approach to aspects of the behavior of science, art, religion, and medicine (Black 1979a). Pure sociology is therefore more than a theory. It is a paradigm capable of yielding scientific—testable, general, simple, and highly original—theories of any and all forms of social life (Black 1979a; 1995; 2000c).

In short, Black's pure sociology abandons the starting point of all other social sciences—psychology, teleology, and people. It identifies a new subject matter and offers a new strategy of explanation: the geometry of social life (Black 1995: 848–50; 2000c: 347; see also Horwitz 2002). In doing so, it reinvents sociology, creating a new science with a new mission.

BEYOND *THE BEHAVIOR OF LAW*

For all its prominence in the modern world, law handles only a tiny fraction of all conflicts today. Even in the most litigious societies, the great majority of disputes are managed without the intervention of legal officials. Following the publication of *The Behavior of Law,* Black (1984) turned his attention to this larger world of social control (the management of conflict), extending pure sociology beyond law to subjects such as moralism and partisanship.

MORALISM AND PARTISANSHIP

Moralism is the tendency to treat people as enemies. Its more extreme forms include denunciation, punishment, and execution. Black's theory of moralism embraces at least two subtheories: the theories of settlement and popular justice (1993: chap. 8). The theory of settlement explains when and how judges, jurors, and mediators intervene in cases, whether they are strict or lenient, formalistic or equitable, and given to compromise or winner-take-all decisions. The theory of popular justice addresses the handling or management of conflict through nonlegal means, such as self-help (aggression) and toleration (inaction) (Black 1990).

Partisanship is taking sides in a conflict. Legal partisans include lawyers and witnesses; popular partisans include allies and advocates (Black and Baumgartner 1983: 88–97). Black's theory of partisanship predicts who supports whom and what effect that has on the conflict itself (1993: chap. 7). Since partisans can be crucial to a party's success, adding these third parties to the case geometry considerably boosts the theory's ability to explain the outcome of conflicts.

Black's theories of moralism and partisanship have been applied and extended by other scholars to explain the management of conflict across a diversity of social settings, including suburbia (Baumgarter 1988), the international political system (Borg 1992), child day care (Baumgartner 1992b), twelve-step therapeutic groups (Hoffmann 2006), and corporations (Morrill 1995; J. Tucker 1999). Other topics explained with Blackian principles include interpersonal violence (see, e.g., Cooney 1998; Peterson 1999; Phillips 2003; Michalski 2004; Jacques and Wright 2008), therapy (Horwitz 1982), immigrant conflict

(Baumgartner 1998; Cooney, 2009), and collective violence (Senechal de la Roche 1996, 2001; Black 2004b; Campbell 2009). Black's formulations along with these applications and extensions are collectively known as Blackian theory.

The Blackian theories of law, moralism, and partisanship provide a powerful and novel explanation of the handling of conflicts in legal and nonlegal settings alike. Combined, they explain a larger subject matter: morality.

MORAL RELATIVITY

Morality refers to what is right and wrong, good and bad. For the pure sociologist, morality resides in what people do, not what they think they or others ought to do. The morality of an action is therefore known by the response to it. Morality embraces all responses to behavior that may be defined as deviant—expressions of social control as well as social approval. Morality in this sense is a quantitative variable that can be measured by its location on a spectrum of severity.

Viewing morality in this way departs significantly from traditional ways of thinking about right and wrong. Morality has long been the domain of philosophers and theologians who see it as a system of rules or principles that address the question "How should we act?" Are there universal principles of good and evil, of right and wrong, that bind all humanity, or is morality relative to particular cultures or even individuals? No consensus has emerged, and the nature of morality remains unsettled. As the great world religions spread across large sections of humanity, the answer to this question seemed clear to most people: Morality is absolute. The coming of modernity weakened that conviction. Growing social diversity within and across societies, now intermingling at a greater rate, drew attention to the diversity of moral conduct, highlighting local beliefs and undermining confidence in a constant set of standards. Moral absolutism came to be seen as anachronistic and even pernicious, a means by which a few wealthy societies dominate many poorer ones. Yet even as relativism thrived, absolutism refused to die. Absolutism has reappeared in the guise of the popular modern notion of human rights, which holds that all people have certain inalienable rights that they enjoy irrespective of who they are, what they believe, or where they live.

The debate goes on. Philosophers continue to develop sharp and subtle arguments for and against relativism (see, e.g., Hollis and Lukes 1982; Moser and Carson 2001). Taking a different route, social scientists explore not what is good or bad but what people treat as good or bad: how social groups define and handle wrongful or deviant behavior. The evidence reveals ample variation. The Gebusi of New Guinea, for example, believe that all deaths, whether arising out of accident, sickness, or old age, are caused by sorcery, and they go to considerable trouble to discover, kill, cook, and eat the sorcerer (Knauft 1985; compare Knauft 2002). The Eskimos of northern North America are one of many groups to practice selective female infanticide (see, e.g., Balicki 1967; Freeman 1971; Riches 1974). The Jívaro of the Amazon encourage the taking of hallucinogenic drugs, even giving them to infants and children (Harner 1972). Deviance would therefore appear to be culturally variable (see, e.g., Curra 2000).

But perhaps not. Cross-cultural contrasts in the handling of deviant behavior may be due to differences in factual beliefs (for example, which substances are harmful) or to practical necessities (for example, which societies can support large numbers of infants and elderly people) or to relatively trivial social conventions (for example, on which side of the road traffic should travel). On the issues that really matter, there may not be much cultural variability (see, e.g., Hauser 2006). In all societies it appears to be a grave wrong to kill leaders—chiefs, kings, presidents, and the like. There may well be limits to what is labeled deviant and nondeviant after all. Moreover, within all societies the same conduct can evoke very different responses or sanctions. Killing a leader may be wrong, but killing a serial killer may be a cause for rejoicing. The culture may not be the best unit of moral analysis.

Black (2000a) has sketched a new theory of morality in which right and wrong are neither absolute nor relative but both together. Black's theory of moral relativity holds that moral evaluations vary across individual disputes or cases, but the principles that explain case-by-case contrasts are universal across human societies. It diverges from traditional absolutism in granting that morality varies: conduct condemned in one context may be commended in another. It differs from traditional relativism in that cases, not individuals or cultures, are the axis of variation (Black 2000a: 113). Regardless of time or place, certain kinds of cases are treated as more or less immoral. Again, though, the conduct complained of cannot explain the variability of case outcomes. To kill with intent will not always elicit a more severe sanction than to kill without intent; to assault with more violence will not necessarily result in greater severity than to assault with less violence. For the same conduct, pure sociology holds, severity varies with the social structure or geometry of the case. Right and wrong are geometrical.

In sum, Blackian theory embraces a theory of law and popular justice and, more generally, of morality. The theory is testable, general, simple, and original. But the history of science is littered with brilliant failures—dazzling new ideas that failed to pan out. Is Blackian theory among them? Or is it actually valid?

THE HANDLING OF HOMICIDE IN HUMAN SOCIETIES

Recall the striking variation in how homicide is handled in human societies. The only theory to address that variation in full is Blackian theory. It alone promises to explain the severity of sanctions, legal and popular, evident across time and place imposed on men and women who take the lives of others. But does it deliver on its promise? Is there even enough information to allow us to judge?

THE RESEARCH LITERATURE

No form of deviance has been researched more often and more extensively than homicide. Many scholars over many years pursuing many projects have reported on the handling of lethal violence. These include anthropologists studying preindustrial peoples, historians investigating old archives, journalists reporting on newsworthy cases, criminologists statistically scrutinizing trial dispositions, lawyers reflecting on their court battles, human rights workers pursuing justice, missionaries seeking converts, and sociologists analyzing sentence patterns. Between them, these researchers have built a rich, detailed, and instructive informational edifice that spans diverse societies and historical eras.

For over twenty years I have been conducting research on the handling of homicide, gradually assembling all of the available information. My research has taken several forms:

- Reading all relevant reports of the handling of homicide in the anthropological, historical, and criminological literatures.
- Undertaking a quantitative cross-cultural study of the response to homicide in ten relationships in thirty preindustrial societies.[1]
- Conducting interviews with seventy-five men and women incarcerated for murder and manslaughter in Virginia and with forty-two of their relatives.[2]
- Observing the preparation and presentation of murder trials in a district attorney's office.[3]

Putting together these sources, I have accumulated a large body of information that, I believe, covers all the major English-language sources. The great bulk of this information consists of what Black (1995: 843) calls "naive evidence"—evidence gathered by researchers unaware of the theory (mainly because it did not yet exist). Because such evidence is not tilted either for or against the theory, it provides a particularly good basis for a scientific test. Moreover, because homicide is perhaps the single gravest offense known to law and morality, it is the one most likely to be handled equally across the cases—and thereby to contradict the theory. This corpus provides a unique opportunity to test Blackian theory.

COMMON ERRORS

Testing a theory involves confronting it with evidence that falls within its logical terrain. Since the data on the handling of homicide clearly fall within the purview of Blackian theory, the more inconsistent they are, the more they will falsify the theory. On the other hand, the more the evidence conforms to the theory, the more its validity will be confirmed.

Theories are most rigorously tested through experiments: the researcher takes some action (in a laboratory or the real world) and observes whether the results are consistent with hypotheses derived from the theory (see, e.g., Sherman 1992). Experimental tests have the great advantage of allowing the effect of a variable to be examined while all others are held constant. They have a major limitation, however: limited generality; they can only address parts of a theory at particular points in time. A theory such as Black's that orders facts at all times and places cannot, realistically, be fully tested through experiments. To circumvent these limitations, some sociologists conduct a second kind of test, based on statistics. The researcher finds a set of cases, reduces them to numbers, and carries out a statistical analysis to see whether the Blackian variables explain the outcome (for example, arrest or sentence length). Work of this kind can be very illuminating, shedding light on parts of the theory that fare well and other parts that may need to be developed or discarded (see, e.g., Baumgartner 1978; Phillips 2008b). Despite their popularity, statistical tests have at least four severe limitations:

- The omission of crucial variables. The police and court records on which the tests are usually based contain far more information on defendants than victims. Hence, important aspects of victims' characteristics are often missing from the analysis. Worse, official records often contain little or nothing at all on the third parties, such as witnesses, lawyers, and judges. Yet both victims and third parties are a critical component of the social geometry of the case.
- Poor measurement of the variables that are included. Vertical status, for instance, is best measured by a person's wealth, yet the most usual measure is income. Wealth and income are typically correlated, but not perfectly: owning much property does not always mean earning much money, while earning a large income may result in little property being accumulated. Even more questionably, some researchers measure vertical status with gender. While gender is correlated with wealth in the United States (and many other societies), it is also correlated with other social characteristics (such as social integration) that have effects opposite those of wealth (see Cooney 2002: 659). The outcome or dependent variables have also been shortchanged from time to time. Since Blackian theory explains variation over the life of a case, it is best tested with data from the commission of the offense through to its final resolution. Many studies, however, focus on just one or two stages of the legal process, such as arrest or conviction.
- Failure to hold the parties' conduct constant. Blackian theory does not deny that the conduct of the parties—how the killing was committed, for instance—may affect case outcomes. What the theory proposes is that, for the same conduct, cases' outcomes vary with

their case geometry. This requires holding constant the parties' conduct, which can be challenging. Studies based on ethnography or firsthand observation and in-depth interviews typically do not so, but they have offsetting compensations, yielding high-quality, in-depth data on real-world cases. Statistical tests founded on official records, however, typically lack these advantages; and failure to control for conduct, at least in part, becomes a more egregious breach of their greater purported rigor.[4]

- A narrow focus on just a single society at a single time. Research in other areas of sociology reveals how misleading it can be to rely exclusively on a single society or even a single type of society. For example, in every modern nation—whether the United States, Britain, Japan, or New Zealand—severe interpersonal violence, such as homicide, is strongly concentrated in low-status locations—among the poor, unemployed, poorly educated, minorities, and those with criminal records. But go back just a few hundred years and a strikingly different pattern emerges. Then, and for most of human history, homicide was found at all status levels: at the top, bottom, and middle. Modern violence is therefore a historical peculiarity (Cooney 1997a; 2003). Perhaps aspects of modern law and popular justice are too—in ways not immediately apparent.

At best, these limitations undermine statistical tests of the theory. At worst, they render them useless. I therefore propose to conduct a different kind of test. I call this a meta-test.

A META-TEST

Scholars confronted with a large number of studies on a particular topic (such as the effect of family structure on juvenile delinquency) will sometimes carry out a meta-analysis, an inquiry that aims to specify the empirical patterns that exist within a body of research as a whole (see, e.g., Wells and Rankin 1991).[5] By analogy, a meta-test seeks to determine whether an even more substantial and varied body of research conforms to a theory's predictions. Naturally, there are differences: meta-analysis is a sophisticated statistical method that seeks to quantify the results of a corpus of studies. A meta-test cannot do that, because it seeks to draw out the results of very different kinds of empirical inquiries—detailed firsthand observations, experimental manipulations, statistical analyses, historical narratives, in-depth interviews, and the like—that span many temporal and spatial contexts and have not, in many cases, been systematically quantified. Yet these studies are extremely valuable. Limited and even flawed as they may be individually, collectively they yield a substantial amount of pertinent data. The object of a meta-test, then, is not so much to determine whether any particular study or even line of studies is consistent with the theory as to assess whether the findings of the empirical literature as a whole supports the theory's propositions: it addresses the evidence in totality.

Given the several hundred articles and books that contain information on the handling of homicide, the different audience for which they were written, the diversity of settings to which they pertain, and the variability of the type and quality of research methods they embody, a meta-test is the most appropriate way to approach the validity of Blackian theory. This book proceeds, therefore, by isolating each major variable in Black's theory and comparing it to the totality of the relevant evidence, anthropological, historical, and modern. Although Black has not systematically extended his theory of law to popular justice as a whole, he argues that all social control can be explained geometrically (Black 1993). I assume, then, that popular justice obeys the same principles as law, and I examine the evidence, qualitative and quantitative, on the impact of case geometry on both forms of social control. In the interests of readability, I largely confine questions of evidence quality, empirical qualifications, and other technical scholarly concerns to the endnotes and final chapter. I focus on a single question throughout: Can Blackian theory, as laid out in *The Behavior of Law* and other publications, explain the severity of sanctions, legal and popular, across homicide cases, as reported in the research literature?

The Behavior of Law delivers the first and still the only general sociological theory of legal conflicts. Behind the theory lies a leap of imagination that conceives of law obeying the same geometrical principles at all times and places. The theory itself consists of a series of propositions that link variation in the quantity and style of law to variation in the parties' objective social characteristics. But Black's book goes further, making an even more fundamental contribution to knowledge by presenting a radically new theoretical paradigm with a distinctive subject matter and a distinctive explanatory strategy: pure sociology. Pure sociology has since sired several offspring, including a theory of moralism, which explains the hostility directed against others in conflict by principals (popular justice) and by third parties (settlement). A second progeny is the theory of partisanship, which explains who sides with whom and how that shapes conflicts and their outcomes. Combined, these three theories yield a new theory of morality: moral relativity.

This book aims to present a full and accurate statement of the Blackian theory of moral relativity, and to assess whether that theory can explain the available evidence on the handling of homicide in human societies. The book, then, is part exposition and part test. The test is the greater part, as it should be: ultimately, the theory lives or dies by its ability to explain the facts. Black himself cites a considerable amount of evidence—modern, historical, and cross-cultural—for his propositions. Other scholars have done likewise in applying and extending his ideas (see, e.g., Horwitz 1990; Morrill 1995; J. Tucker 1999; Michalski 2008). But work of that kind does not seek to confront the theory with the evidence in its entirety. The preliminary testing it provides is not definitive. Only with broader and deeper testing can the global validity of Blackian theory be assessed. What follows represents the most appropriate test of the theory to date. Far from being confined to a single society at a single time, it extends to all societies at all times for which there is information. Far from dwelling on the social characteristics of the killer or victim alone, it includes all the participants, both principals and third parties. Far from being restricted to legal outcomes, it extends to the popular handling of cases, the application of social as well as legal sanctions. Far from concentrating exclusively on severity, it addresses the full spectrum of outcomes, from hateful vengeance to worshipful praise. And far from ranging over a potentially confounding broad swath of behavior, it addresses just a single type of deviant conduct: homicide. Now consider the first dimension of social space, the vertical.

3 THE VERTICAL DIMENSION

The wealthy pass through life differently. They enjoy more desirable food, clothing, and shelter. They can devote themselves to the pursuit of leisure and luxury. They are healthier and live longer (see, e.g., Gilbert and Kahl 1993; Williams and Collins 1995). They receive more education, and are enriched by a wider variety of ideas and art forms. They experience more of the world's wonders, and escape more of its horrors. They demand and are granted more deference and attention. Even their jokes are funnier.

But law promises to treat everybody equally. Do the advantages of wealth stop at law's door or do they cross its threshold too? Some years ago a researcher conducted an experiment that investigated whether wealthy defendants receive the same outcomes as their less wealthy counterparts in legal trials. In order to hold all other factors constant, the researcher constructed a hypothetical criminal case in which a man was accused of murdering his wife *(uxoricide)* under ambiguous circumstances. The case had two conditions. In one condition, the defendant was identified as "Dr. Williams," a physician. In the other condition, the defendant was identified as "Mr. Williams," a member of a less prestigious profession. Undergraduates were asked to rate the legal guilt of one of the defendants (Rosoff 1989).

Taking the inquiry a step further, the researcher then looked at what happens when both defendants are of high economic status, though one is higher than the other. Using the same ambiguous case of uxoricide, the researcher constructed another two conditions. The first condition identified the defendant as a surgeon, the second condition as a dermatologist. The researcher chose those specialties because in earlier work he had established them as "the alpha and omega in the status hierarchy of medicine." The case description was read by undergraduates who were asked to render one of four verdicts: guilty of first-degree murder; guilty of second-degree murder; guilty of involuntary manslaughter; and not guilty. The verdicts were all defined in a manner consistent with the law.

If legal advantage is defined as the probability of not being convicted or being convicted of a lesser offense, then each of these experiments has three logical outcomes:

1. The wealthier defendants were more advantaged.
2. The less wealthy defendants were more advantaged.
3. Neither the wealthier nor the less wealthy defendants had systematic advantages over the other.

Before turning to the results of the experiments, let us see which result Black's theory predicts.

BLACK'S THEORY OF LAW

Wealth and its distribution constitutes the vertical dimensions of social space (Black 1976: chap. 2). Social interaction, including homicide, has a location, direction, and distance in vertical space, as measured by the relative wealth of the participants. Upward homicides, recall, are those committed by poorer against wealthier people, and downward homicides are those committed by wealthier against poorer people. The greater the wealth disparity between the parties, the greater the vertical distance of the homicide. Since the direction of social control is the opposite of that of the offense, upward homicides give rise to downward law and popular justice, while downward homicides elicit upward law and popular justice.

For law, Black posits four broad principles, each encapsulated in a testable proposition (1976: chap 2). The first three are variations on a common theme: downward law is greater than upward law; in a downward direction, law increases with vertical distance; in an upward direction, law decreases with vertical distance.

The fourth principle is that law is greater at high-status than low-status elevations. Hence, the higher the status of the principals, the more likely the defendant is to be prosecuted, convicted, convicted of a legally more serious degree of homicide, and to receive a severe sentence.[1]

How do the four principles combine? Black predicts that the quantity of law will evince a systematic, hierarchical pattern. Holding constant the conduct of the parties, upward offenses should attract the most law, followed by high lateral offenses (among the wealthy), followed by low lateral offenses (among the poor), followed, finally, by downward offenses.

Applying these principles to the uxoricide experiments yields a clear prediction: Since people generally marry within their social class, and since spouses share each other's wealth and social standing anyway, the killing of a wealthy doctor's wife should attract more law than the killing of a less wealthy person's wife. That is indeed what the researcher found. In the first case, the "jurors" convicted Mr. Williams in 11 percent of cases but Dr. Williams in 39 percent. Moreover, they were ten times more likely to find Dr. Williams guilty of first-degree murder (Rosoff 1984, cited in Rosoff 1989). In the second case, the researcher assigned a score of 3 to a verdict of first-degree murder, 2 to second-degree murder, 1 to involuntary manslaughter, and 0 to acquittal, and found that the mean score for the surgeon (2.06) was significantly higher than the mean score for the dermatologist (1.58) (Rosoff 1989).

What the experiments show, then, is that wealthy defendants may be legally disadvantaged. A wealthy individual accused of murder sometimes attracts more legal severity than a less wealthy individual. Moreover, even among the wealthy, the wealthiest may attract the most severity. The researcher argued that this is because high-status individuals are subject to a "status liability" effect—they are held to higher standards of conduct. However, there is much evidence that contradicts a status liability effect. For example, while crime occurs among all social classes, the prison population is drawn overwhelmingly from the ranks of the poor. Blackian theory tenders a different answer: the vertical structure of the case. It is the status of defendants relative to that of their victims that explains when wealthy defendants will and will not be advantaged. Wealthy defendants accused of killing wealthy victims will be treated more severely than poor defendants accused of killing poor victims. Case outcomes cannot be predicted with the status of one party alone.

Black's principles linking law and wealth can be generalized to all of social control. Specifically, regardless of whether homicide is handled by legal officials or private individuals, its immorality—as measured by the severity of sanctions it attracts—exhibits the same four general patterns. These four patterns or status effects will appear again in future chapters, applied to other dimensions of case geometry. (Hence, overlaps between wealth and other social statuses in this and later chapters do not undermine the validity of the analysis.) But are they true? Do they in fact explain case-by-case variation in legal and popular severity? And how does wealth affect the behavior of third parties, including judges, lawyers, and jurors, allies and enemies? Consider, first, the handling of homicide by legal officials.

LAW

Societal inequality—the degree to which the wealth of a country is unevenly distributed—does not, in itself, predict which homicide defendants will receive the most severe sanctions. Still, the more unequal a society's distribution of wealth, the greater the possible inequality at the case level, between killers and victims. Hence, disparities in case outcomes tend to be most pronounced where wealth disparities are most pronounced, as in slave societies.

SLAVE SOCIETIES

In most slave societies, the killing of slaves by masters is legally trivial. "Why, sir, I wouldn't mind killing a nigger more than I would a dog," an Alabaman slave overseer remarked to a Northern visitor in the late 1850s (quoted in Aptheker 1983: 139). The law echoed his insouciance. A slave may be a person but is also a possession. The latter tends to overwhelm the former: if somebody wants to destroy his own property, that is generally his own business, not the state's. A review of some forty-five slave-owning societies found that in 62 percent a master could kill his slave with impunity, and in another 13 percent he could do so with no greater risk than having to pay a small fine (Patterson 1982: 193).

South Carolina was one of the jurisdictions that provided slaves with some legal protection, though not much: not until 1821 did the written law allow a master to be convicted of the murder of a slave (Morris 1996: 173). Consequently, few cases brought by or on behalf of slaves reached a courtroom, but even if they did, the risk of punishment ranged from zero to slight, no matter how unprovoked, premeditated, or violent the killing. In an 1806 case, for instance, John Slater, a ship's captain, became angry with one of his slaves who was working on the dock at Charleston. Slater ordered the slave bound hand and foot, and directed another slave to chop his head off. The victim's remains were then thrown into the harbor. In accordance with the written law, Slater was merely found guilty of a misdemeanor and fined (Dale 2006).

Even after the change in the formal law, successful prosecutions were rare as the law's protection was more nominal than real. Thus, "South Carolina tried to protect its slaves in cases of wanton cruelty or murder by providing that the master had responsibility for their condition, so that physical evidence on a body or the condition of a corpse could constitute circumstantial evidence adequate for conviction. What the law gave, the law took away, for it also provided that a master's oath of innocence had to be respected" (Genovese 1972: 39–40). If the oath of innocence did not protect the master, the law in any event forbade slaves to testify against whites, thus providing another layer of legal protection (32, 38). Consequently, most killings of slaves went unpunished: "arrests, convictions, and punishment never remotely kept pace with the number of victims." In the odd cases that were prosecuted, the defendants were typically not of the highest status. They were more likely to be "overseers or small slaveholders than . . . gentleman of standing" (39).

The rest of the American South was little different. Although the formal law provided more protection in the post-Revolutionary era, few masters were ever punished for killing slaves. Even if cases made it to court, juries were sympathetic to defendants. For example:

> In Lowndes County, Alabama, Malachi Warren faced two charges. In the first, that of cruel and unusual punishment, he was accused of putting "divers iron rods and bands" around [his slave] Dick's belly, chest, and neck—all held together by an iron rod up and down the slave's back. It was also alleged that Dick was "bruised wounded and cut." The verdict was not guilty. The next charge repeated those facts but added that the punishment lasted for ten days (November 1–10, 1842) and Dick died. Warren was charged with murder but was again acquitted by the jury in Hayneville. (Morris 1996: 179–80)

Leniency is not inherent in the law of slave societies. Far from it. A homicide in the opposite direction—by a slave of a master—invariably elicits the gravest of penalties (Morris 1996: 275–86). An ordinary death sentence is often deemed insufficient (see, e.g., Dean 2001: 128). The killer may be hanged in chains—in effect, slow death by starvation—where others are merely hanged (see, e.g., Morris 1996: 277). He may be burned alive at the stake (Banner 2002: 71). He may be tortured before being executed and his corpse hacked apart afterward (see, e.g., Schwarz 1988: 141). His entire family may be held collectively liable and put to death. If his killing is part of a larger revolt against slavery, he may be executed in a mass public execution (Blackman and McLaughlin 2003: 245–50). Regardless of the society in which he lives, the harshest sanctions await him:

> The Romans prescribed that a slave who contemplated any action against his owner was to be burned alive. The slave who was so bold as to ask a fortune-teller about the health and life of his master was to be crucified. Moreover, the entire family of a slave was to be put to death if one of its members killed their owner. That terror was the purpose of this edict is clear from the inclusion even of minors among the proscribed if they were suspected of having participated in, or had been present with the master, at the time of the murder. The rest of the victim's slaves were subject to torture, as were slaves belonging to the spouse of the deceased. . . .
>
> Middle and late Muscovite law recognized little ceremony for slaves who killed their owners: they were put to death without any mercy. . . . The Lithuanians specified that the slave was to be hanged . . . and then drawn and quartered. (Hellie 1982: 120–21)[2]

Slaves who kill free persons other than their master are also treated with conspicuous severity: for example, execution in the Islamic world and the American South, castration, mutilation, and slow death in Latin America. By contrast, when a free person kills a slave, the typical sanction is merely to require the killer to compensate the master for loss of property (Hellie 1982: 154–62).

Slaves who kill other slaves are guilty of destroying property and hence may be strictly punished (Hellie 1982: 170–71). But their sanctions are generally less severe than those for slaves who kill nonslaves other than their master. A study of four rural counties in rural Virginia, 1785–1829, found, for example, that all of the eighteen slaves convicted of murdering whites received the death penalty, while only half of the fourteen slaves who murdered other slaves did so (Schwarz 1988: 231–34).

ARISTOCRATIC SOCIETIES

Outside of slave societies, wealth inequalities between killers and victims are often greatest in advanced agricultural, or agrarian, societies (Lenski 1966). Among agrarian people, a small, landowning hereditary elite—the nobility or aristocracy—typically dominates a large population of poor peasants who work the land. Eventually, an intermediate class of merchants and professionals emerges, but it remains a small minority. Sharp social class boundaries, apparent to all, are a striking feature of every agrarian society (see, e.g., Crone 1989).

Agrarian aristocrats enjoy a battery of legal advantages unavailable to the ordinary person. Among these are the right to own land, to collect some taxes and to be immune from others, to vote and hold office, to bear arms and use titles, to trade certain goods, to hunt, as well as the right to make important life decisions for subordinates, such as when and whom they can marry (Bush 1983). Not surprisingly, aristocrats sometimes enjoy explicit rights in legal conflicts, such as homicide cases. In Lithuania, when a band of peasants murders an aristocrat, all are liable to be put to death, but when a band of aristocrats murders a peasant, only the actual killer is liable to execution (Bush 1983: 66). Additional privileges reflect the rigidity of the stratification system, exempting the aristocracy from the more painful and humiliating forms of punishment. In many countries they are spared either the death penalty or the most degrading forms of it (see, e.g., Farr 2005: 179–80, 186). In Poland an aristocrat who murdered a peasant before 1768 was exempt from the death penalty, paying only a fine instead. In France and Spain the aristocracy was long exempt from hanging. English aristocrats convicted of murder were customarily beheaded; only in especially aggravated cases were they hanged like commoners (Durston 2004: 672–76). When breaking on the wheel was finally authorized for the Portugese aristocracy in 1758, they considered the new law to be a "massive insult" (Bush 1983: 66). Immunities of this kind extend beyond Europe: in ancient India, for instance, "a Brahmana [highest caste] murderer enjoyed a privileged position in society . . . [and] was generally spared from the death sentence" (Das 1977: 39).[3] And in Imperial China, high-status offenders sentenced to death were sometimes granted the special dispensation of killing themselves (van der Sprenkel 1962: 63).

Despite these privileges, aristocrats are subject to the formal law of homicide. Legal rules no more allow them to kill than anybody else. But theory is one thing, practice another (see, e.g., Ylikangas 2001: 47–50). Especially in early times, when the gap between nobles and commoners was especially yawning, aristocrats could—and often did—kill their social inferiors with impunity (see, e.g., Dean 2001: 31–34). A study of thirteenth-century England describes such a case:

> On December 3, 1274, John of Rushall, a knight, and his squire Henry of Hastings were entertained at the parson of Melchbourne's house in Bedfordshire. Henry took provisions for his lord from several men in the vill (i.e., village). When they came to demand payment, John and Henry answered that they had no cash with them and asked the townspeople to send a man with them to Cambridge to be paid there. The villagers elected to send Ellis of Astwood. Outside Melchbourne, the knight and his household cut Ellis's throat. It appears that John and his retinue never suffered any inconvenience for this act. (Given 1977: 88–89)

Upward killings of aristocrats, on the other hand, are a very serious matter indeed. The same study recounts the following incident:

> Sometime in the first quarter of the thirteenth century the people of the village of Sandford in Somerset combined to kill their lord, Nicholas de Arundel. According to the report of the jurors . . . the entire population of the vill, with the exception of four men, chased Nicholas through the town to the church, where he tried to take refuge. The chaplain slammed the door shut in his face. His pursuers killed him, carried him to his house, and set fire to the building to make it appear that he had died in the blaze. For this deed, fifteen men and women were drawn and hanged.

> Six others fled and were outlawed by order of the king's courts. (Given 1977: 89–90)

Wealth may even affect the handling of homicides committed within the household. In England, the Treason Act of 1351 defined certain upward domestic killings, such as the killing of a master by a servant, as "petty treason." Ordinary murderers were hanged; those found guilty of petty treason were burned at the stake (see, e.g., Beattie 1986: 100).

Over time, the simple contrast between the rich and poor gave way to a more gradual and complex pattern of agrarian stratification (Nolan and Lenski 2004: 174). As it did, the sharp inequalities in the handling of upward and downward homicide became a little more muted. Blatant downward murders came to be prosecuted, though conviction was still rare enough to cause surprise. For instance, several centuries later in England, "the marquis of Paleotti was hanged in 1718 for running his valet through with his sword for impertinence. Paleotti went to the gallows still incredulous that he could actually be executed for such a 'peccadillo'" (McLynn 1989: 46).

Despite the greater equality inscribed in the written law, aristocratic privilege remained entrenched. Elites could still get away with murder, especially when the circumstances were ambiguous. Again, an English example:

> In 1747 a coroner's court brought in the verdict that a servant found in an Oxford college with his skull fractured had been murdered "by persons unknown." In fact it was known that when last seen the murdered servant had been made drunk and was being used as a plaything by a quartet of young "bloods". These were Lord Abergavenny, Lord Charles Scott, Sir Francis Blake Delaval, and the Reverend Sackville Spencer. The murdered servant was found in the morning at the foot of Lord Abergavenny's staircase. All the circumstantial evidence pointed in the same direction. But clearly indictments against such a powerful quartet were out of the question. (McLynn 1989: 148)

By the nineteenth century the economic dominance of the aristocracy was in decline, but social class divisions, now derived from industry and commerce as much as land ownership, remained sharp and severe. The handling of homicide followed the contours of the new class system. A study of Kent, a county in the southeastern corner of England, notes that the relative social class of the killer and victim strongly affected whether the killing was ruled to be a murder or a manslaughter, and how severely it was punished (Conley 1991: 59). Most vulnerable to severe treatment at the hands of the law were those who killed victims of a higher social station. In several cases, for example, soldiers killed their superior officers, offenses that involved not just a breach of authority but, at a time when officers were recruited from higher and soldiers from lower social ranks, an infringement of class boundaries as well. They and civilian workers who killed their class superiors received harsh treatment: "One hundred percent of those accused of killing an employer or superior officer were executed. In six of these cases there had been no immediate provocation and a deadly weapon had been used, hence showing intent to kill; but the same factors were present in some other cases in which no death sentence was issued" (Conley 1991: 59).

COLONIAL SOCIETIES

The nineteenth century witnessed the intensification of an ancient social pattern—the subjugation, occupation, and exploitation of foreign societies, or colonialism. As industrialism surged at home, European nations expanded abroad, acquiring colonies that yielded cheap raw materials and labor. Colonial societies are always highly unequal, with especially wide wealth cleavages separating settlers from natives, the conquerors from the conquered. Violence tends to thrive under colonialism (Banivanua-Mar 2007). The legal ramifications of violent conduct vary drastically, however, with its vertical direction. On the Caribbean island of Trinidad, for example, a small European, plantation-owning class held sway in the latter half of the nineteenth century over a large indentured labor force, many of whom were Asian or East Indian. Downward homicides were, at most, venial offenses: "The authorities considered East Indian life to be cheap. East Indians could be whipped, kicked, and beaten to death with impunity. There was no recourse to the law, since the courts invariably released the aggressor with ridiculous fines and warnings" (Trotman 1986: 140).

Over in East Asia itself, life was little better for those who toiled under colonial masters. In the Dutch colony of Sumatra, downward killings of Chinese plantation laborers by planters or their agents were either handled leniently or ignored altogether. Upward homicides, however, attracted the utmost legal severity (Breman 1989). Likewise, in India: the relatively rare killing of British planters by their native laborers or "coolies" typically elicited grave legal penalties, while the far more numerous cases in the opposite direction usually wound up with light legal charges and mild or no punishments (Kolksy 2007). The occasional exception only confirmed the link between personal status and punishment, as any Britons punished were likely to be of low social origins (e.g., soldiers) and their Indian victims of high standing (e.g., professionals) (Bailkin 2006: 464; Wiener 2007: 260).

Southern Rhodesia (now Zimbabwe) yields a particularly well-documented case of colonial justice. It provides additional evidence that, regardless of the law on the books, the law in action did not conform to the observation made by Lord Mansfield, a famous English judge, that "an Englishman in Ireland, Minorca, or the Plantations has no privilege distinct from the natives" (quoted in Wiener 2007: 258). At the beginning of the twentieth century, native labor was in great demand in the fledgling Rhodesian mining industry. To ensure a steady supply of cheap workers, the British authorities taxed the native population heavily, restricted movement so that people could not seek work elsewhere, and sent police to round up tax defaulters for the mines. The mining companies routinely misled the workers about their conditions and length of service. When a worker's contract came to an end, the company manager might refuse to sign his papers, thereby leaving the worker vulnerable to being arrested as a "deserter." Not surprisingly, the workers despised this system, which they referred to as "chibaro" or forced labor (van Onselen 1976).

Within the mines, discipline was severe. Workers who were considered tardy or negligent, disobedient or insolent were liable to be beaten or even killed. Their deaths carried few legal consequences, no matter how unprovoked the killing or brutal the manner of its perpetration. In one case, four miners who flogged two black workers to death over a period of three days were acquitted on the grounds that the victims were suspected thieves. A few other examples:

- When African miner Sulman could not find the spanner that miner Samuel Hodgkins wanted in a hurry, Hodgins pushed him down a mine shaft. A jury acquitted Hodkins of murder.
- An African worker named Umdarra dropped a valve into a bucket of hot water. Enraged, Gustav Peer, a miner, pushed Umdarra's head into the water, and held it there. Umdarra died as a result. Peer was sentenced to a $50 fine or six months' hard labor.

If miners were charged with murder, they were often acquitted on the basis of medical evidence. For instance, after the jury heard that the worker whom Neil Griffin had kicked to death in 1907 was suffering from an enlarged spleen, it immediately acquitted the defendant. Such testimony was common: "In a part of Africa where malaria was epidemic, members of all races tended to develop slightly enlarged spleens. If medical evidence—usually provided by the district surgeon—could testify to the presence of an 'enlarged spleen' much of the reason for the fatality could be explained away. For at least two decades 'enlarged spleens' were regularly made to account for deaths following assaults on native miners" (van Onselen 1976: 146).[4]

Occasionally, the workers rebelled against their masters. When they did, management invariably moved quickly to quash the disturbance, typically with a show of force. If one or more workers were killed in the process, so be it: no legal culpability attached. Judges and juries inevitably saw management violence inflicted in the course of quelling riots as necessary and justified (van Onselen 1976: 149–50).

THIRD WORLD SOCIETIES

As colonialism gradually retreated in the twentieth century, new nations came into being around the globe in Africa, Asia, and South America. These third world societies began the process of industrialization as the wealthier nations were leaving it. They bore the imprint of their past, continuing to exhibit pronounced economic inequalities. To this day, a small elite typically controls a very large percentage of national wealth. The elite enjoy many privileges, among them a degree of protection from legal sanctions. A case from Saudi Arabia exemplifies the immunity from law that high economic status can bring: "In October 1998, a member of the royal family shot and killed two members of the religious police who entered his property without permission. The killer was allowed to pay compensation to the family of the victims instead of being charged with murder" (U.S. Department of State 2000, vol. 2: 2210). Similar results are possible in Pakistan, where a 1990 law gives the victim's heirs in most murder cases a choice as to whether the killer should be criminally punished or made to pay compensation. The victim's family can accept compensation and terminate the criminal proceedings at any point in the case, even after a sentence of death has been imposed. In a 1994 case, for instance, a convicted murderer who was on his way to the gallows had to wait with the noose around his neck for thirty minutes while his family and the victim's family haggled over the amount of compensation to be paid. When the two sides failed to reach an agreement, the luckless offender was hanged. The wealth of the defendant is not recorded, but he was more than likely poor. A law giving a veto power of this kind to the victim's family "makes it likely that a compromise settlement may be less frequently found with a poor convict than a rich one" and that "poor people sentenced to death [are] more likely to be executed than those who are rich" (Amnesty International 1996a: 13).

The wealth gap between rich and poor engenders a considerable amount of collective tension in many industrializing nations. In rural areas, landless peasants and small landholders seeking land may clash with large landholders. In urban areas, where wealthy, cosmopolitan elites maintain luxurious, well-guarded mansions in neighborhoods surrounded by a sea of shanty towns, conflict often revolves around wages, conditions of employment, and the right to form and join trade unions. Regardless of where it occurs, the response to homicide varies sharply with its location and direction in vertical space. Lateral killings among poor people are a low priority, often ignored or glossed over quickly by the police (see, e.g., Nash 1967: 461). Downward killings are especially likely to be tolerated. In the Indian state of Andhra Pradesh, for example, killings of lower-caste individuals have few repercussions: "Upper caste groups have launched armed attacks in which *dalit* (i.e., those formerly known as 'untouchables') and tribal villagers have been murdered, assaulted and raped. Such attacks have been carried out in order to terrorize the villagers and prevent them from asserting claims to land and other social and political rights. Police, who sometimes assist in the attacks, seldom investigate the crimes and almost never prosecute those responsible" (Gossman 1992). Similarly, in the eastern state of Bihar, legal officials have been known to turn a blind eye to downward killings committed by high-status militias while vigorously pursuing upward killings. Thus, while members of high-status militias are rarely prosecuted, members of low-status militias are routinely detained and charged by the police, and many are killed in encounters that the police claim are shoot-outs but are in fact, some believe, executions (Narula 1999: 44, 57, 65).

MODERN SOCIETIES

Wealth continues to influence the handling of homicide in modern, industrial societies such as the United States. Data on the point are not as plentiful as in many previous societies, in part because the rise of the middle class blurs the absolute contrast between rich and poor and in part because wealthy people rarely kill or are killed. In the great majority of modern homicides, one poor person kills another (see Cooney 1998: 25–31). Police seek to solve these cases and will often go to some lengths to do so. But on the relatively rare occasions in which a wealthy person is killed, the drive to make an arrest is all the greater, especially if the suspected killer is impoverished (see, e.g., Simon 1991: 19–20). In these "big cases," the police tend to pull out all the stops and to "interview large numbers of potential witnesses and informants, and conduct extensive interrogations, polygraph ('lie detector') tests, and 'line ups' (sessions at which suspects are viewed by victims or witnesses through a one-way mirror)" (Black 1980: 16).

As the victim's economic status declines, the police may be less thorough in their investigation. And when the victim is of decidedly low status, they may not pursue even the most obvious investigative leads, regardless of the legal gravity of the incident. The killing of another poor person in a poor neighborhood is not the kind of case that lingers at the center of detectives' radar screens, especially when many other cases remain to be solved.

Later decisions in the criminal justice system also reflect the relative wealth of the parties. Thus, one study examined the fate of more than four hundred randomly selected individuals arrested for homicide in a "large urban jurisdiction in Northeastern United States." The researchers ranked the defendants in terms of the legal gravity of the crime of which they were eventually convicted (that is, from first-degree murder to dismissal of the charges). They found that less wealthy defendants (as measured by the prestige of their occupations) who killed wealthier victims were convicted of more legally serious types of homicide than wealthy defendants who killed wealthy victims, and they in turn received more serious convictions than less wealthy defendants who were convicted of killing less wealthy victims (Farrell and Swigert 1978: 572–73; 1986).[5]

Wealth effects are manifest in sentencing decisions as well. In Florida during the 1970s, defendants represented by privately retained attorneys—typically better-off defendants—were less likely to be indicted for first-degree murder and, if convicted, less likely to be sentenced to death than defendants represented by attorneys paid by the state, holding constant the race of the parties (Bowers 1983). In Georgia, after being convicted of murder, poor defendants were more likely to be sentenced to die than their wealthier counterparts. Additionally, defendants convicted of killing poor victims were significantly less likely to receive the death penalty (Baldus, Woodworth, and Pulaski 1990: 157–60, 588–90). In Philadelphia, 1983–93, the killing of a poor victim had "the substantial and statistically significant effect of reducing a defendant's likelihood of receiving a death sentence" (Baldus et al. 1998: 1715). In Nebraska, 1973–99, defendants accused of killing wealthy victims faced an elevated risk of being sentenced to death (Baldus et al. 2002).

Somewhat surprisingly, the Georgia study also found that wealthy defendants convicted of murder were more likely to be sentenced to death (1990: 588).[6] The finding held up in some of the analyses, but not in others (see, e.g., 1990: 620–29). The relatively weak nature of the pattern is probably explained by the strong effect exerted on death penalty decisions by another variable in the study: race. In America race and economic well-being are strongly correlated. The typical African American family, for instance, earns only sixty-two cents for every dollar earned by the typical white family.[7] African Americans also own considerably less property—land, houses, stocks, bonds, and other valuables—than whites (see, e.g., Oliver and Shapiro 1995). Hence, race effects are partly wealth effects. And because race and wealth are closely correlated, only rarely will they both strongly predict the legal response to homicide (see, e.g., Farrell and Swigert 1986).[8]

Race is not a pure economic status effect, however. Black and white Americans are further separated by contrasting histories, traditions, customs, linguistic patterns, and interactional styles. For that reason, a consideration of race differentials in legal outcomes will be deferred until issues of culture are discussed in a later chapter.

Finally, it is worth noting that in civil lawsuits arising out of homicides, the killing of a poor person attracts less law than the killing of a rich person. In actions for wrongful death, the amount of money the victim's relatives can expect to receive is directly tied to the economic status of the victim. Since damage awards are based in large part on lost future earnings, the greater the income of the victim, the more his or her relatives will be awarded by the law. Killers of men, for example, generally pay more than killers of women (see, e.g., Goodman et al. 1991). Thus does the civil law value the life of a wealthy victim more highly than that of a poor victim.

THIRD PARTIES

Wealth helps to explain the behavior and effect of third parties—persons other than the principals who know of the conflict (Black and Baumgartner 1983; Black 1993: 126). Third parties are of two main types: partisans (on one or both sides) and settlement agents (such as judges and jurors) who are significantly nonpartisan at the outset but who may ultimately take one side or the other when they decide the case.[9] Both types of third parties are important: they explain some of the paths by which the parties' social characteristics get translated into different outcomes, and they add additional explanatory elements to a case. Consider, first, partisans.

PARTISANS

Partisans may commit strongly to one side, or only weakly so. The strongest do all they can to help; the weakest, very little. Black views the nature and degree of partisanship as a form of "social gravitation" that obeys geometrical principles (1993: chap. 7). He proposes that the strength of partisanship is "a direct function of the social superiority of one side and the social inferiority of the other" (1993: 127). Thus, third parties are more likely to side with a wealthy party over an impoverished one, and the greater the disparity in wealth between the parties, the more strongly partisans are attracted to the wealthier party.

Partisanship, it should be noted, is itself a kind of status (see Campbell 2008). Consequently, those who have stronger partisan support are more likely to win. They also attract more partisanship: "Partisans themselves add social stature to an adversary, and so each partisan increases the likelihood of more partisans in the manner of a bandwagon. Partisanship begets partisanship" (Black 1993: 127).

Partisanship therefore illustrates the "Matthew effect": social advantages accrue to those already advantaged; or, more simply, the rich get richer and the poor get poorer (Merton 1968).[10] Moreover, wealthy litigants appear more likely to attract wealthy (and other high-status) partisans.

High-status partisans are, all else the same, more valuable—their testimony is more convincing, their backing more compelling, their support more fateful. They are especially valuable to low-status parties (Black 1989: 13–14). Lawyers, for example, vary in status, but most are at least moderately wealthy. Hence, acquiring a lawyer can give a considerable status boost to an indigent client. But high-status partisans can assist wealthy parties as well, as the O. J. Simpson case demonstrates.

O. J. Simpson

In June 1994, O. J. Simpson was accused of murdering his ex-wife, Nicole, and a young man, a waiter friend of hers, Ronald Goldman (who was returning a pair of spectacles left at a restaurant) at her home in Los Angeles. Things looked bleak for Simpson: a formidable body of evidence pointed to him as the killer (see, e.g., Toobin 1996; Rantala 1996). He had, for example, a documented history of violence toward Nicole, and tensions between them had mounted in the weeks prior to her death. His blood was found at the murder scene. Also found at the scene was a footprint from a pair of expensive Italian shoes in Simpson's size sold by a store at which Simpson had bought shoes, a cap with hairs matching his, and one glove, the partner of which was found outside his home holding strands of the victims' hair and traces of their blood and his. The gloves were of a relatively rare kind, two pairs of which the defendant's ex-wife had bought for the defendant several Christmases previously. Simpson's car contained his blood and that of the two victims, and a trail of blood led from his car to his bedroom. His socks were spattered with his blood and that of his wife. Simpson had cuts on his arms the day after the murders. Finally, while he had an alibi for the hours leading up to and following the murder, he had no alibi for the hour of the murder itself.[11]

Although the legal case against Simpson was strong, the sociological case was weak. "O. J.," as he was universally known, was rich, famous, and popular. A nationally known ex-football player, he appeared regularly on television and in the occasional movie. He was a spokesman for several major corporations, had a large income, and owned an expensive home in Los Angeles and property in other locations. He and Nicole had been married for seven years, but after the divorce Nicole found herself in reduced circumstances and at the time of her death was arranging to sell her townhouse because she could no longer afford to live in it. Ron Goldman worked as a waiter at a local restaurant. In short, Simpson was charged with double downward murder.

The partisanship Simpson attracted further boosted the stature of his side over those of his opponents. With the enormous amount of publicity devoted to the case, lawyers, many of them in high demand and far too busy to take on most clients, were soon queuing up trying to join the defense team (Toobin 1996: 3–12). The final defense roster came to be known as "the dream team," and included nationally known lawyers from Los Angeles, New York, and Florida, as well as a professor from Harvard Law School, perhaps the preeminent center of legal education in the world. They were assisted by experienced investigators from Los Angeles, Florida, and New York. Eminent expert witnesses rounded out the team. They included the former chief medical examiner of New York City, a forensic scientist from Connecticut, and a pathologist from New York State, individuals at the very top of their professions (Toobin 1996: 86–87; Schiller 1996: 100; Petrocelli 1998: 437).

Simpson's defense team went all out to acquit their man. Poring over every detail, they devised a "judo defense," turning the very strength of the state's case against it (Toobin 1996: 154). They argued, in effect, that the state's case was suspiciously strong, and that when closely scrutinized it was vitiated by a mixture of ineptitude and dishonesty

(Dershowitz 1996). Their expert witnesses criticized how the police had gathered and analyzed the physical evidence, arguing, for example, that the blood collected at the crime scene had been contaminated in laboratory analyses by the defendant's blood. And the lawyers contended that a detective with a demonstrated history of racial bias had planted the glove found at Simpson's home.

Arguing police incompetence and malevolence is a risky strategy. Few mount this defense, and fewer still succeed with it. Yet the stature of Simpson's partisans, together with his own status advantage, combined to make this a plausible interpretation of the events. When leading experts in the nation consistently cast doubt on the prosecution's case, jurors take notice.

Contrast Simpson's potent legal army with the haphazard platoon of partisans that the typical low-income murder defendant can muster. The average impoverished suspect could never begin to put together a "dream team" of top lawyers, investigators, experts, and medical allies. But Simpson did, and managed to eke out an improbable acquittal.

(Unfortunately for Simpson, the legal proceedings did not end there. He was later sued in civil court by the families of the victims and lost heavily. Why he won the criminal and lost the civil case is largely explained by the cultural geometry of the case, discussed in chapter 7.)

SETTLEMENT AGENTS

Settlement agents are typically wealthier than the disputants who appear before them: as M. P. Baumgartner notes, "There is generally an upward drift of disputes in which higher-status people are invoked to settle the affairs of those beneath them" (1985: 22). Even so, cases vary: some settlement agents are much wealthier than the principals, others less so. The settlement agents' relative status or superiority is an important factor. The greater the superiority, the more severe the settlement tends to be (Black 1993: 146–47). In addition, the more superior the settlement agent, the more decisive—less apt to involve compromise—and more formalistic—more apt to be based on explicit rules—the settlement tends to be (Black 1993: 145–46).

Wealthier juries are therefore more likely to convict (Adler 1973). And wealthier judges are more likely to sentence convicted defendants to prison than to probation and for longer periods (Levin 1972).

But consider another application of the principle: the greater leniency of jurors compared to judges.

Judges versus Jurors

Judges, in general, are considerably wealthier than jurors. Where judges are typically recruited from the ranks of affluent professionals, jurors are usually drawn from an average cross-section of the population. Consistent with the superiority principle, judges have long been known to be harsher than jurors on defendants (see, e.g., Wiener 1999). Indeed, the clemency of juries is sometimes a cause for complaint. Nineteenth-century French juries, for example, were often faulted for being too prone to find murder defendants not guilty, a tendency some attributed, in the words of one critic, to their lack of "elevated personages . . . [,] that is to say the elements which constitute the richness of society" (quoted in Harris 1989: 136).

Modern American juries are more lenient toward defendants accused of murder or manslaughter than are judges. In one classic study, researchers sent out more than 3,500 questionnaires to judges who presided over jury trials, asking them whether they would have reached the same decision as the jury and, if not, how they would have decided the case differently. They found that the judges disagreed with their jury's verdict 40 percent of the time in murder and manslaughter cases. When they did, the judges would nearly always have been more severe on the defendant. In 35 percent of the cases, the juries either acquitted where the judge would have convicted, or convicted on a lesser charge than the judge thought warranted (Kalven and Zeisel 1966: 69).[12]

The basis of juror leniency varies. Sometimes they take a different view of the evidence. Thus, they may be more open to the testimony of defendants who have no criminal record, requiring somewhat more proof of guilt before they will convict (Kalven and Zeisel 1966: 168–90). At other times, they take a different view of the appropriate punishment, for example, believing that a defendant who accidentally killed his uncle who had tried to intervene in a tavern brawl had suffered enough already (Kalven and Zeisel 1966: 301–12). At still other times, they take a different view of the law. In particular, jurors tend to have a broader conception of self-defense than judges do (Kalven and Zeisel 1966: chap. 16). Where the law requires the defendant to have been in imminent danger and to respond only with enough force to repel the attack, jurors are less punctilious. Although juries sometimes treat the victim's aggression as reason to acquit outright, more commonly they reduce the defendant's level of conviction. Some examples from the research:

- The defendant is severely beaten up by his son-in-law in a fight that breaks out when they are drinking. The defendant goes home and arms himself. When the son-in-law enters the house, the defendant kills him. The judge opts for murder in the first degree; the jury, murder in the second.
- The defendant is thrown out of a bar after a brawl. He returns some time later, fires a shot into the bar, and kills the man who ejected him. The judge finds murder; the jury, manslaughter.
- A woman shoots and kills her husband after he comes across her taking a ride with another man. The husband had been violent toward his wife over a seven-year period. The judge thinks this a second-degree murder; the jury brings in a second-degree manslaughter verdict.
- During a quarrel between his stepfather and his mother, a son shoots and kills his stepfather. The victim has a history of abusing his wife. The judge finds manslaughter; the jury acquits.

POPULAR JUSTICE

The state's dominance of modern homicide cases makes it easy to forget that things were not always so. For most of human history, there were no police, courts, lawyers, or prisons. Justice was entirely popular. Even today, most justice remains alegal, although this is less true of homicide than just about any other form of conduct.

For all its numerical supremacy, however, popular justice is much less well explored than state justice. The golden age of popular justice preceded the birth of the state, but writing was not invented until about the same time as the state. Consequently, there are fewer recorded examples of pure popular justice than of law. Yet herein lies a paradox: although less is known about popular justice than law, what is known is often known more thoroughly. The data on popular justice are less extensive than on law, but they are often fuller and richer. This is largely due to the efforts of anthropologists who, while living among stateless people, have often observed or reconstructed individual conflicts in more detail than modern researchers have done by relying on police or court records.

Blackian theory predicts that these data will reveal a statistically improbable fact: popular justice obeys the same geometrical principles as law. If the theory is valid, the fourfold Blackian status pattern should hold for the full range of popular sanctions: from praise, through toleration, shunning, and compensation, to self-help. Does it?

WEALTHY VICTIMS

Evidence from across human societies reveals that the killing of wealthy people usually triggers severe popular sanctions, particularly when perpetrated from below. Upward homicides are nearly always more serious, eliciting comparatively severe penalties. Both lynching by a community and vengeance at the hands of the victim's relatives, for example, are more likely following the slaying of a victim possessed of wealth.

Lynching occurs in many human societies (Senechal de la Roche 1996; 2001). One of the best-known instances is the spurt of communal killings that claimed several thousand lives in the southern United States, the majority of them African American, in the half-century beginning around 1880 (Tolnay and Beck 1995). Homicide was the most common trigger of a southern lynching (Tolnay and Beck 1995: 92, 96). But only some homicides led to a lynching. Much depended on their vertical direction (Senechal de la Roche 1997: 56–58). Penurious killers were more likely to be lynched than affluent killers. And the wealthier their victim, the greater their risk of being lynched. Among the cases most likely to incite a lynching party, then, was the killing of a well-to-do employer by a poor worker.

Vengeance displays the same sensitivity to victim wealth. The slaying of an affluent herder or a rich landowner is more likely to spur the victim's relatives to inflict deadly violence on the killer's family. Lower the victim's status, however, and the chance that the victim's family will pursue vengeance drops accordingly (see, e.g., Hasluck 1954: 239).

Wealth influences the targets of vengeance as well. When vengeance is exacted, only the death of a person of similar social rank will usually suffice to restore the honor of the victim's family (see, e.g., Oberg 1934: 146–47; Hasluck 1954: 43). If there is no target of equal standing to the victim, as, for instance, when the wealthiest man in a region is murdered, the avengers may seek to take more than one life. In Albania, for example, a high-status victim's avenger (usually his closest male relative) "would not make peace till he had killed two of the other's men" (Hasluck 1954: 239). But extra targets come with a cost. Losing two or more members is liable to anger the original killer's group, who feel that they have paid too heavily. The likely result is more violence: a chain of killings and counterkillings, or even an explosive, all-out war with the two sides seeking to inflict as many casualties as possible. Thus can murders at the top of social hierarchies have far-reaching social consequences, their reverberations being felt even by people only remotely connected to the original protagonists.

When wealthy families deign to accept compensation, they usually insist on having their social standing acknowledged by demanding or receiving greater-than-normal amounts (Black 1987: 566). Among groups as diverse as medieval Icelanders (Miller 1990: 27), medieval and early modern Irish (Nicholls 1972: 54) and Scots (K. Brown 1986: 52), Tibetan pastoralists (Ekvall 1968: 77), the Ifugao of the Philippines (Barton 1919: 60, 74–75), the nomads of Somalia (Lewis 1961: 164), and the Mae Enga of New Guinea (Meggitt 1977: 139), the wealthier the victim, the more compensation the killer must pay.

Like their modern counterparts—perhaps even more so—women in those premodern societies that produce surplus property typically command less wealth than men. Hence, sex is often a crude indicator of economic status (see, e.g., Blumberg 1978, 1984; Chafetz 2004). Female victims tend to generate less compensation than male victims, for a variety of reasons (Black 1987: 565–66). Their deaths may be a lower priority than those of men, the case pursued less vigorously and more likely to lapse with time (see, e.g., Meggit 1977: 140).[13] Or the amount payable may be lower. In Somalia, for example, 100 camels are payable for the killing of a man, 50 for a woman (Lewis 1961: 163; see also Hasluck 1954: 239; Peters 1967: 270). Among other groups the male-female differential is not quite as great: the Kipsigis of eastern Africa, for instance, prescribe the payment of 10 cattle and 50 goats for the death of a man, and 9 cattle and 40 goats for the death of a woman

(Peristiany 1939: 194–95; see also La Fontaine 1960: 97–98). Only relatively seldom do male and female victims attract the same amount of compensation (see, e.g., Howell 1954: 57).

POOR VICTIMS

Poor victims, by contrast, attract considerably less popular justice. Their killers generally run less risk of being lynched by the community or avenged by the victim's relatives (see, e.g., Malinowski 1926: 118–19). If pressed, they can often settle the matter by paying compensation (Black 1987: 569, 572). Poor families are more likely to be mollified by an offer of cattle, sheep, or other valuables. Unlike the wealthy, they do not tend to look down on compensation, seeing it as beneath their dignity, its acceptance a sign of reduced social standing, and therefore to be sedulously avoided (e.g., Barton 1938: 242). In a case among Israeli Bedouin, for example, a member of a low-status group was shot and killed by a high-ranking sheik under ambiguous circumstances. Guns are often fired in the air at Bedouin weddings to signal happiness, and the killing may or may not have been an accident. Either way, revenge was an option for the victim's group. But rather than risk the permanent enmity of the influential killer's group, the victim's group agreed to forgo retaliation and accept compensation instead (see Ginat 1997: 35–36).

If vengeance is associated not just with wealthy victims but also with poor killers, compensation is associated with poor victims and wealthy killers. The Tlingit of Alaska illustrate these principles at work:

> Immediately after a murder was committed spokesmen from both clans met to decide who was to die in compensation for the murder. If the murdered man happened to be of low rank and of poor reputation, a payment of goods could satisfy the injured clan. But if the murdered man was of high rank, a man of equal standing was demanded from the murderer's clan. . . .
>
> The actual murderer, if a man of great wealth and rank often went free, but if the man was of low rank and came from a poor house he went as a slave to that house in his clan which had given up a man in compensation for the murderer. (Oberg 1934: 146–47)

Increase the vertical distance between the parties, and a downward homicide may not even be compensated. Aristocrats who kill peasants, for example, may suffer few consequences. In a case from eleventh-century France:

> Acharias of Marmande was feuding with three other aristocrats who destroyed his castle and seized his land. In retaliation, Acharias launched a nocturnal attack in which he burned down a house and killed its occupants. Among those killed were two noblewomen, one of whom perished alongside her young sons. Acharias chose to make peace with the victims' families. He approached the abbot of a local monastery who persuaded the victims' families to reconcile with Acharias provided Acharias pay to have 200 masses sung for their slain relatives (thereby relieving the families of the expense). The agreement took no account, however, of the peasants who had also been killed in the raid: no masses were to be sung for their souls, nor did their families receive any other compensation. (see White 1986: 214–21)

THIRD PARTIES

Downward homicides generate less popular severity, in part because the killer's side typically enjoys more partisanship. Third parties are drawn to wealth. In medieval England, to cite just one example, seldom did the wealthy have any trouble assembling a group of supporters in times of conflict: "The rich tend to have more friends than the poor. Their resources give them many ways to attract retainers. . . . A French romance writer said of his villain around 1170 that because of his wealth he had many knights. . . . Money talked, won friends, and so conferred power in the twelfth and thirteenth centuries. It was ever so" (Hyams 2003: 31).

Having partisan backing is particularly helpful in systems of popular justice because there are no judges with ultimate decision-making authority over homicides. At most, popular justice involves arbitrators who judge the merits of cases, but have no power to enforce their decisions (see Black and Baumgartner 1983: 102–4). Consequently, the side that amasses the greater number of partisans often prevails in popular conflicts. Thus, as the partisanship of the killer's side grows relative to the victim's, so does the likelihood that the killer will escape sanctions altogether, no matter how intentionally and aggressively he acted. Conversely, as the victim's side enjoys an ever-greater imbalance of partisanship, the odds of a lynching rise, regardless of how little intent or aggression the killer displayed (Senechal de la Roche 2001: 129).

Strong partisanship on both sides elevates the chance of a cycle of vengeance. Feuding typically occurs when the opposing sides are groups of approximately equal size and strength (Black 2004a: 153). If one side is appreciably larger or stronger, a cycle of tit-for-tat counterkillings is unlikely to develop. In Montenegro, for example, a small victim's clan opposing a large victim's clan will usually forgo vengeance and accept compensation instead. On the other hand, a small killer's clan opposing a large victim's clan will typically flee to avoid annihilation. Its abandoned property will be destroyed, and the clan will be forced to seek refuge with another tribe for whom it may have to take an enemy head in order to gain acceptance, thereby exposing it to a new risk of attack (Boehm 1984: 107–8). Less partisanship is less status, and a considerable handicap. Like its legal counterpart, popular partisanship tends, then, to augment the core case geometry.

There are two commonly held views on the relationship between wealth and legal sanctions—the idealistic view that wealth is irrelevant, and the cynical view that wealthy defendants always do better than poor defendants. Blackian theory adopts a third position: Wealth is relevant, but wealthy defendants do not always come out on top. They only do so when other factors are held constant, including the wealth of the victim (Black 1989: 9–10). Indeed, of the two, the wealth of the victim more strongly predicts how the case will be handled.

The research evidence is supportive, indicating that, in diverse places and at diverse times, legal sanctions for homicide vary with the vertical status of the parties. So do popular sanctions. Thus, the advantages enjoyed by the wealthy in today's legal system cannot be attributed primarily to factors peculiar to modern law, such as professional lawyers. Rich people today have better access to experienced and effective attorneys, and that undoubtedly strengthens their cases. But the popular justice data show that the wealthy do better when there are no lawyers or even no law at all. Regardless of the form social control takes—imprisonment, vengeance, compensation, or toleration—the severity of homicide sanctions fluctuate with the relative location of the parties in vertical space. Homicides at higher elevations are more serious or immoral than those at lower elevations, and upward homicides are more immoral than downward homicides.

Third-party geometry generally augments the core case geometry. Partisanship is greater in an upward than a downward direction. Consequently, wealthy killers are better able to surround themselves with allies of all kinds, whether lawyers or warriors, than poor killers. And downward settlement is more severe, decisive, and formalistic, whether it involves a judge, jury, or community arbitrator.

Thus are the wealthy advantaged. We do not know for certain in which system of social control—law or popular justice—their advantages are most pronounced. But it may well be in law. Wealth effects are greatest where wealth inequality is greatest. And wealth inequality tends to be greatest in agrarian and early industrial societies, both of which have legal systems that handle most homicides. Moreover, in systems of popular justice, the fact that vengeance is obligatory for wealthy families who wish to maintain their status means that well-to-do individuals often have to become embroiled in bloody and potentially lengthy feuds to secure justice. The advent of law may render some wealthy killers newly vulnerable to sanctions, but it also absolves the relatives of wealthy victims of the obligation to put their own lives on the line in pursuing vengeance. And while law is more rule-bound than popular justice, and rules typically stipulate equality of treatment across similar categories of defendants, formal rules rarely prevent people's social characteristics from impacting case outcomes, a recurring theme throughout this book.

In short, homicide sanctions vary with the wealth of the killer and victim and their partisans, as and how Black's theory predicts. But the theory also states that wealth is far from being the only component of social geometry that shapes the handling of homicide. The outcome of cases should also respond to the organizational status of the parties, the subject of the next chapter.

4 THE ORGANIZATIONAL DIMENSION

> As he enters the room, he knows what awaits him. Resistance is useless. He cannot escape; there are simply too many of them, and there is nowhere to hide anyway. Hands take hold of him and strap him tightly. Now he cannot move. They have total control over him. They set to work quickly, efficiently, and without malice. They follow a strict protocol, their actions being exquisitely coordinated toward a single end. They begin to kill him, deliberately and methodically. This is not their first time to take life. They make no attempt to conceal their intentions or their actions. On the contrary, they do everything in public, before an audience who watch as his life ebbs away.

If premeditation is central to the handling of homicide, this killing ought to evoke considerable severity. (The case itself is a fictional composite of actual cases; see R. Johnson 1998: chap. 7). But it does not. In fact, the law tolerates it, and some people even praise it highly. The words "homicide" or "killing" are rarely used to describe it. Instead it goes by another name: "capital punishment." Capital punishment—state execution of convicted criminals—illustrates the power of a key variable in Blackian theory: organization.

LAW

Organization, or "the capacity for collective action," is an autonomous dimension of social space, and can be measured by "the presence and number of administrative officers, the centralization and continuity of decision making, and the quantity of collective action itself" (Black 1976: 85). Organization is a type of social status. As such, it operates like other social statuses, exhibiting the fourfold Blackian status pattern (Black 1976: 86–97). Thus, homicides committed upward in organizational space ought to attract greater sanctions than homicides committed downward in organizational space. In an upward direction, sanctions increase with organizational distance; in a downward direction, sanctions decline with organizational distance. And sanctions ought to be greater at higher than lower elevations of organizational space.[1]

Organizational status is enjoyed not just by organizations themselves but by the individuals who act on their behalf. Consequently, it is more serious to kill a store worker employed by a large corporation than a self-employed vendor (see Lundsgaarde 1977: 134–36). And the higher the office individuals hold in organizations, the greater their vicarious organizational status. Accordingly, it is more serious to kill a corporate executive than a factory worker. The same is true of officials of the state.[2]

THE STATE

The most organized organization is the state. Hence, the killing of state officials is and has long been a particularly grave crime (see, e.g., Lane 1997: 338). Among the gravest of all is the assassination of a monarch, president, or prime minister. Those who do so are more likely to be sentenced to death (see, e.g., Amnesty International 1989). Sometimes this is written into the law itself. An international review of capital punishment law conducted in the mid-1990s found that in Thailand, for instance, the death penalty was mandatory for regicide, or the murder of a state official on government business. In Egypt offenses carrying death included political murder, and armed attacks on law enforcement authorities. Similarly, in Indonesia the list of capital crimes included the assassination of senior state officials (Amnesty International 1997a; see further "Use of Capital Punishment" 2007).

Some states are more organized than others, however. A key indicator of state organization is centralization, the concentration of decision making. The most centralized states invest a single individual with control over the entire apparatus of government; the least centralized disperse it among different institutions and groups, including the citizenry at large. A state's degree of centralization depends in part on its political structure and in part on its environment. All polities tend to centralize in times of national crisis, such as war, natural disaster, or terrorist threat (Black 1976: 86). Even the least centralized states in normal times may act like centralized states in times of emergency.

Centralization, whether rooted in structure or circumstances, is sociologically significant because it widens the status gap between the state and the citizenry—in Blackian terms, it increases the organizational distance or superiority of state officials over citizens. Although the empirical possibilities are many and varied, three broad types of state can be distinguished on the continuum of centralization: democracy (rule by the many), oligarchy (rule by a few), and autocracy (rule by one). Since the theory predicts that severity varies with organizational superiority, there ought to be considerable differences across the three types of states in the handling of homicide committed by and against state agents. That is indeed what the research discloses.[3]

DEMOCRACY

Democracy disperses political rule across a variety of actors and institutions. The populace elects political leaders with some regularity, decision making is divided among several branches of government, and state institutions are open to some degree of citizen inspection, review, and influence. Although democracy has the lowest level of organizational superiority, the state is still a substantial and potent social actor. Consequently, the handling of homicides by and against state officials can be expected to display considerable contrasts. Consider the most likely parties to official homicide in a democracy: police and citizens.

CITIZEN-POLICE HOMICIDE

The killing of a police officer by a citizen invariably triggers a heavyweight legal response. On learning of the incident, police departments make immediate and "extraordinary efforts" to capture the killer (Rubinstein 1973: 336). The slaying of an officer in New York in 1984, for instance, led the police to cordon off three square blocks—creating the largest crime scene in the history of the city to that point (Jackall 2005: 309). After another New York police officer was killed in 1988, over two hundred detectives were working the case at the height of the investigation (McAlary 1990: 87).

Once a suspected killer is arrested, he can expect little mercy from the prosecutor, who will likely maximize the charges and move the case forward aggressively. When the case reaches court, the likelihood of an acquittal is slight and that of a severe sentence considerable.

Nationwide, some 1,536 persons were involved in killing 1,094 law enforcement officers in the United States, 1968–77. Those arrested and charged numbered 1,280 (the others were killed, committed suicide, or became fugitives). Of the arrestees, 63 percent (802) were convicted of murder (a further 16 percent were convicted of lesser offenses). Of those convicted of murder, 13 percent (107) were sentenced to death, and 51 percent (407) to life imprisonment. The remainder received prison terms of varying lengths; only 2 percent were not punished (Bedau 1982: 46, 55).

Of the 1,280 persons arrested and charged, then, 40 percent (514) wound up being sentenced to death or life imprisonment. (The percentage sentenced to death would have been even higher had the death penalty not been constitutionally suspended from 1972 to 1977.) That is markedly higher than in comparable studies of citizen victims—nine times higher than the percentage in Houston in 1969, for instance, where only 4.5 percent of persons arrested for homicide received sentences of death or life imprisonment (Lundsgaarde 1977).

The high proportion of death sentences is consistent with the written law of most states that lists the killing of a police officer as an aggravating factor in weighing whether a death sentence should be ordered (Baldus, Woodworth, and Pulaski 1990: 22). In Georgia, for instance, one of ten statutory aggravating circumstances occur if "the offense of murder was committed against any peace officer, corrections employee, or fireman while engaged in the performance of his official duties" (Ga. Code Ann., cited in Baldus, Woodworth, and Pulaski 1990: 35). Two Georgia studies confirm that killing a police officer elevates the risk of a sentence of death (Baldus, Woodworth, and Pulaski 1990: 157, 657). A police victim also affects the final stage of death penalty cases: the decision to execute or commute the sentence. In Texas, 1924–70, defendants convicted of killing police officers were only about one-half as likely to have their death sentences commuted by the governor as all other persons sentenced to death row (Marquart, Ekland-Olson, and Sorensen 1994: 15–120). But the privileged position of police officers in homicide cases goes well beyond their elevated victim status in capital trials. It extends to officers who kill citizens.

POLICE-CITIZEN HOMICIDE

Switch the organizational direction of police killings and conspicuous severity gives way to marked leniency. In the American West of the late nineteenth and early twentieth centuries, for instance, the law was highly tolerant of police officers who killed citizens (McKanna 1997: 30–35). Today, the vast majority of such cases are deemed to be within departmental guidelines and legally justifiable, and neither discipline nor punishment results (Klinger 2004: 205). The best evidence comes from the United States (although a small study from France tells a similar tale: see Amnesty International 1994). A survey of police departments in seven American cities reports: "Most shootings are called 'justified' by departments, and very few are referred for criminal charges. When an officer is formally charged in connection with an incident occurring in the line of duty, juries generally do not convict. . . . Departmental discipline in such cases rarely goes beyond a verbal or written reprimand to the officer involved" (Milton et al. 1977: 11).

These findings are borne out by a nationwide study of 1,500 police-citizen killings, 1952–69. Only three officers were convicted of any crime. Compare that to the 1968–77 national study described above in which 1,007 people were convicted in 1,094 homicides of police officers. The killing of an officer by a citizen was therefore over forty times more likely to result in a conviction than the killing of a citizen by an officer (0.92 compared to 0.02). Moreover, of the three officers punished, one was sentenced to five years to life, a second to five years, and the third to one day (Kobler 1975).

EXPLORING THE CONTRAST

An alternative explanation for the sharply contrasting sanctions in homicides involving citizens and police is that most police-citizen killings are legitimate, while most citizen-police killings are criminal. In other words, police typically kill in circumstances permitted by the law, while citizens do not.

Whether any given homicide is legally permitted or prohibited is not a factual issue, and hence beyond the scope of this book.[4] However, the contrasts in the outcome of homicides involving civilians and police are so pronounced that they can only be explained by legal rules if the rules are markedly different for officers who kill than for citizens who do so, a pattern that would itself reflect the organizational status of the parties.

Regardless of what the formal law states, it is clear that, for the same conduct, police officers who kill are treated more leniently. Consider, for example, the following case, one of the three from the national study to result in a conviction:

> Patrolman S.S. was charged with first-degree murder, accused of deliberately shooting C.H., a 27-year-old fugitive, from a distance of four feet with a 12-gauge shotgun while H. was crouched on his knees and elbows in a bush where he hid while trying to elude the police. The shotgun S.S. used was an unauthorized weapon. S.S. had deliberately traveled some seven miles out of his district to serve the felony warrant on C.H., and it was alleged at the trial that S.S. was having a sexual affair with the wife of C.H.
>
> The jury was instructed it could return one of four verdicts: first degree murder, second degree murder, manslaughter, or acquittal. They found S.S. guilty of manslaughter. He was sentenced to five years on that charge and three years for perjury to be served concurrently. (Kobler 1975: 178–79)

Reverse the parties in this case—the citizen kills the officer under the same circumstances—and a manslaughter conviction and a five-year sentence are virtually unimaginable.

The key to the lenient treatment of police-citizen killings, then, is their organizational geometry. Indeed, such cases illustrate several of the mechanisms by which higher social status gets translated into more advantageous outcomes, and for that reason warrant a closer look. Consider several ways American criminal practice and procedure favors police offices accused of killing citizens:

- The killing must first be ruled a homicide by the coroner or medical examiner, both of whom work closely with the police. Their close professional ties predispose them to view the event favorably to the police. All presumptions therefore run in favor of the officer. A sociologist who observed a medical examiner's office over a three-year period noted: "Whereas an evidentiary standard of 51 percent is sufficient to declare a suicide, the standard for a death to be classified as a homicide in cases involving police seems close to 99 percent. In such cases, forensic pathologists rely on ultraconservative standards of evidence. If any natural disease might allow for an alterative explanation, it will likely weigh heavily. Unless there are extraordinary circumstances, law enforcement officials will receive a generous benefit of the doubt" (Timmermans 2006: 183). Consequently, some cases that might be categorized as homicide are classified instead as self-inflicted fatalities effected by provoking the police to lethal violence, or "suicide by cop" (Timmermans 2006: 183–85).

- Once ruled a homicide, the case is usually investigated by members of the same department and always by members of the same profession, who are also inclined to construct the event favorably to the killer. A reporter who spent a year observing the Baltimore homicide detective squad put the point succinctly when he said that "inside every major police department, the initial investigation of any officer-involved shooting begins as an attempt to make the incident look as clean and as professional as possible" (Simon 1991: 377).
- In many jurisdictions, police officers are able to delay making a statement to investigators, allowing ample time for them to formulate, rehearse, and perfect a credible justificatory story (A. Collins 1998: 74–75).
- Most police departments compel officers involved in shootings to provide a statement as a condition of their continued employment. The law forbids these compelled statements from being used in criminal prosecutions. Compelling a statement therefore effectively ties the hands of the prosecutor (A. Collins 1998: 75–76).[5]
- Only the strongest legal cases are likely to make it to trial, but even then a conviction is far from inevitable, since those deciding the matter tend to be understanding of officers. As one writer has observed:

> Juries are naturally sympathetic to an officer, who, after all, became involved in the incident as part of his or her duties. They are reluctant to brand the officer a criminal and find beyond a reasonable doubt that he or she committed a crime. Jurors usually see the victim as unsympathetic, as contributing to the event, or a criminal who deserved what he or she got. Jurors may worry that a criminal conviction will send the wrong message to other officers, lower morale, or encourage officers to be less aggressive. They may also worry that a convicted officer will face retaliation from prisoners if sent to jail. (Cheh 1996: 253)

The end result is that very few officers are punished for killing civilians, despite a tightening of the written law since the 1970s and a reduction in the number of such homicides (see, e.g., Brown and Langan 2001). Many cases fail to get off the ground at all, even when the facts appear damning:

> In the 1980s, Dallas County grand juries refused to indict officers who shot seventy-year-old Etta Collins, an unarmed black woman, through the front screen door of her house; Larry Brice, an unarmed twenty-year old white, who was shot nine times; David Horton, an eighty-one-year-old black man who, as a crime watch coordinator for his neighborhood, had phoned in a burglary report; and Sammy Stone, a black burglar who was shot to death after he had been handcuffed. (Swindle 1993: 85)

If there is an indictment, conviction is rare. In New York, for example, "despite scores of fatal shootings," not a single on-duty police homicide resulted in a conviction between 1977 and 1995 (A. Collins 1998: 87). In Los Angeles charges were filed in just one of the 174 fatal shootings that occurred between 1979 and 1991 (Katz 1991). No criminal charges were filed against any of the 77 San Diego police officers who killed citizens from January 1, 1985, to December 20, 1990 (Petrillo 1990).[6]

The contrasts, then, in the legal response to police-citizen and citizen-police homicides are considerable in democratic states. However, as a considerable body of human rights research attests, they are even more considerable in oligarchic states.[7]

OLIGARCHY

Oligarchy hoards political authority at the center. The state is not controlled by a single individual, yet the populace has comparatively little influence either. A small elite, usually wealthy, perhaps hereditary, monopolizes the higher reaches of government. Leaders stay in power a long time; elections, if held, are frequently accompanied by corruption, intimidation, and violence; and state officials are subject to little civilian control. Police departments tend to be shielded from effective public influence and scrutiny, operating under a militaristic and centralized model of organization. Today, many third world countries fall into this broad category, to a greater or lesser degree.

Relatively little information exists on the legal response to citizen killings of state officials in oligarchies, although it is likely to be severe. What is clearly known is that oligarchy expands the boundaries of legal toleration of killings committed by officials. The presumption of legitimacy found in democracies anneals into something close to an axiom of legitimacy. State officials can therefore commit more and more blatant killings without fear of penalty (see, e.g., Weitzer and Beattie 1994). Consider some of the ways oligarchies are more tolerant of killings by officials:

- More victims: Rates of official homicide are high, but rates of official conviction for homicide are low. In the early 1990s, for instance, a comparison with New York City showed that the number of homicides committed by the police per capita was 3.5 times higher in Buenos Aires, 5 times higher in Mexico City, over 10 times higher in São Paolo, and almost 20 times higher in Jamaica (P. Chevigny 1995: 224; see also Mars 2002: 138). Very few of these killings were punished; some were even officially praised. One São Paolo officer who was involved in forty-four homicides received a promotion (P. Chevigny 1993: 11). A police lieutenant in Rio de Janeiro who led or participated in eleven police operations that resulted in eighteen deaths was promoted in 1996 (Cavallaro 1997: 27–28). Others have received pay increases for their killings (Cavallaro 1997: 15–16). Still others have been awarded citations and medals, at the conferring of which the number of people they have killed is proudly announced (Amnesty International 1996b).

- More groups of victims: Not only do the police and military in oligarchies kill more citizens, they massacre them in larger groups and still walk free. Colombia, for example, had sixty-eight massacres in which 589 people were killed over a sixteen-month period (January 1990–April 1991), according to a government report. All of the massacres in which the identity of the perpetrators was known were committed by members of the police or military. In three out of four of the massacres, the case was dismissed after a preliminary inquiry (see Méndez 1992: 32–33). In an infamous incident, Brazilian military police stormed a São Paulo prison (popularly known as the Carandiru) in October 1992 to quell a riot. By the time they left, 111 prisoners were dead. Investigations revealed that "the police summarily executed dozens of their victims, many after they had been forced to strip naked and return to their cells" (Cavallaro 1997: 14). No charges were brought until five and a half years later when over eighty officers were indicted (Amnesty International 1999a). Twelve years later, however, not a single officer had been imprisoned (Amnesty International 2004a).
- More violence: When officials kill, they often do so with more violence than is necessary to eliminate the victim; they "overkill" (see, e.g., Amnesty International 2007). In Colombia, for instance, soldiers indiscriminately attacked and killed civilians, including six elementary school children on a field trip, in August 2000, shooting at the group for forty minutes (Human Rights Watch 2001). In Brazil, after four police officers were killed by drug traffickers in a *favela* (squatter settlement) in Rio de Janeiro in August 1993, a group of hooded and heavily armed men entered the *favela* and shot indiscriminately at local residents for two hours, killing twenty-one people. Intensive publicity and several investigations led in 1996 to the rare spectacle of two military policemen being convicted and sentenced to long terms of imprisonment (Amnesty International 1997b). However, the sentences were reduced considerably on appeal. (A third policeman was eventually convicted and sentenced in 1998 to a combined term of 204 years for his part in the massacre [Amnesty International 2003: 11].) Police also torture and mutilate with some regularity. In many countries the corpses of people killed by the police or military bear marks of

beating, often severe in nature (see, e.g., Méndez 1992; Amnesty International 1993; P. Chevigny 1995).

- More premeditation: Police shootings have high levels of fatality, suggesting high levels of intent to kill. In the early 1990s, for example, 65 percent of police shootings in Jamaica, 70 percent in São Paolo, and 85 percent in Guyana were fatal compared to just 30 percent in New York and 35 percent in Los Angeles (P. Chevigny 1995: 46, 67, 148, 212; Mars 2002: 139). Less effective emergency medical care explains some of the difference. But by no means all. Individual case histories reveal significant premeditation in many police shootings in São Paolo, Jamaica, and Guyana, with police targeting individuals for execution (P. Chevigny 1995; Mars 2002: 158–64). Tellingly too, data from Jamaica show that while police kill more civilians than they wound, civilians wound more police than they kill, again suggesting that many police homicides are not occurring in shoot-outs but in deliberate executions (P. Chevigny 1995: 212).[8]
- More blatant manipulation of the law: The greater organizational status of oligarchical officials enables them to employ a wider variety of tactics to manipulate the legal process to their own advantage, including:
  - Claiming self-defense. Police who kill regularly claim that the deceased fired on them first and that a shoot-out followed in which they prevailed (see, e.g., Penglase 1994: 49; P. Chevigny 1995: 147–48; Amnesty International 2003: 9). On the Indian subcontinent these homicides are so familiar that they even have their own name: "encounter killings" (see Gossman 1992: 27, note 73; Eckert 2005). When outsiders manage to investigate encounter killings, they commonly discover that the victims were already in the custody of the security forces when they were killed (Gossman 1992: 27).
  - Stigmatizing the victim. Many industrializing countries are plagued by high rates of violent, property, and drug-related crime, and the public often favors stern measures against criminals (see, e.g., Penglase 1994). It is not unusual for thieves and other criminals to be lynched (see, e.g., P. Chevigny 1995: 157). Aware of the popular feeling, police routinely claim that their

homicide victim was a criminal. If pressed, they will often devote considerable energy into uncovering a criminal background. Should they find one, the investigation is effectively closed. As one writer notes, "Implicit in this procedure is the idea that the police may kill criminals without fear of consequence" (Cavallaro 1997: 24; see also Brinks 2003).

— Disposing of the corpse. Political suspects picked up by police have disappeared in a variety of countries, including Guatemala (see, e.g., Manuel 1991), India (see, e.g., Gossman 1992: 24), Morocco (Amnesty International 2004c), and Algeria (Amnesty International 2000). Even ordinary criminal suspects are sometimes never seen again after they enter police custody (Cavallaro 1997: 44–47).

— Intimidating witnesses and officials. Individuals who participate in cases against police officers are often threatened, beaten, or killed (see, e.g., Amnesty International 2005b: 39–41). For instance, the trial of a Mexican police officer in 1990 for the killing of a prominent human rights lawyer led to the murder of six prosecution witnesses (P. Chevigny 1995: 244–45). In Argentina police officers who were accused of killing four youths and planting weapons on them, a claim supported by five eyewitnesses, had their cases dismissed after the witnesses withdrew their testimony and one of the judges left the country following multiple threats on his life (Chevigny and Chevigny 1991: 14–15, 34–35). In Brazil a judge who refused to drop her investigation into police homicide after being threatened by heavily armed and hooded men was then summoned to a prison by a police lieutenant where she was locked in a cell with 130 inmates. When she complained to an external agency, she was charged with libel (Jahangir 2004: 10).

— Co-opting the medical profession. Police may get doctors to write false medical reports to back up their claim that the person they murdered committed suicide, a practice that has been found, for example, in Pakistan (see, e.g., Amnesty International 1993: 14–16). Or the state may underfund and undertrain its forensic doctors to the point that they cannot conduct proper investigations, a pattern documented in Guatemala (Manuel 1991). Or the authorities may employ doctors who are routinely prepared to cover up official violence: for instance, in 1992 a leading South African pathologist came forward and admitted that 90 percent of the two hundred deceased detainees on whom he had performed autopsies under the Apartheid regime had been murdered by police (see Weitzer and Beattie 1992: 102).

— Delaying the case. If all else fails and police are prosecuted, the passage of time can shield the defendants. Cases against police officers may take years to come to trial, by which time the chance of conviction, never very high, has dwindled to minuscule proportions (see, e.g., U.S. Department of State 2000, vol. 1: 612). Mexico provides one of many possible examples:

> Time plays an important role in impunity in Mexico because the justice system's slowness in prosecuting perpetrators allows them to flee, valuable evidence is lost, or family members and human rights groups pushing for justice are forced to give up. In the Guadarrama case, for example, the officer responsible for the "disappearance" was able to watch without fear as the judicial process went nowhere; despite detailed information indicating that he was responsible, authorities did not act against him until Mexican and international human rights groups took up the case. When authorities finally indicted the suspect seven months after the "disappearance," and long after sufficient evidence existed to move against him, the officer slipped away. (Solomon 1999: 105)

Oligarchies thus provide a safe haven for officials who kill civilians. But not all oligarchies are the same. The weaker they are, the less pronounced the above tendencies will be. In Brazil, for example, the decline in centralization brought about by the fall of the military regime (1964–85) saw the occasional police officer being prosecuted for killing a citizen (Huggins, Haritos-Fatouros, and Zimbardo 2002). Equally, the more oligarchies centralize, the more they tolerate state killing. Oligarchic regimes experiencing civil wars, insurgencies, and other armed political conflicts typically kill large numbers of citizens. Virtually no one is ever punished for these killings (see, e.g., U.S.

Department of State 1998–2007; Human Rights Watch 1998–2007). In that way they resemble autocracies.

AUTOCRACY

Autocracy "works on the theory that all conduct should emanate from a single will" (Walter 1969: 258). As such, it evinces the highest level of organizational superiority. The autocratic leader—the emperor, absolute monarch, dictator—controls all political decisions. He rules a highly repressive state that restricts personal liberty, curtails political speech and travel, and prevents its citizens from freely expressing themselves religiously, sexually, and artistically. The state controls mass communications, gathering information on its citizens while remaining remarkably secretive about its own affairs. Consequently, comparatively little information leaks out about the handling of homicide by and against state officials. Still, the broad pattern is clear: officials who act in the name of autocracies are virtually exempt from law.

KILLERS

Autocracies are notoriously harsh and punitive toward their own people (see, e.g., Courtois et al. 1999; Applebaum 2003). The most extreme kill citizens in large numbers (see, e.g., Cooney 1997b). On countless occasions throughout human history, autocrats have exterminated entire segments of their own populations with impunity. In the fourteenth century, the Sultan of Delhi, Muhammad bin Tughlak, slaughtered so many Hindus that "there was constantly in front of his royal pavilion a mound of dead bodies and a heap of corpses, while the sweepers and executioners were wearied out by their work of dragging" the victims and "putting them to death in crowds" (quoted in Rummel 1994: 48). The Aztec emperors had their priests perform mass human sacrifice, including ripping open and plucking out the heart of the victim (see, e.g., Berdan 1982: 111–18). The Spanish Inquisition, initiated in 1480 by King Ferdinand and Queen Isabella, executed several thousands of people in the name of religion, many of them "burnt alive . . . by a slow fire . . . after their constancy had been tried by the most excruciating agonies that minds fertile in torture could devise" (quoted in Rummel 1994: 62). Emperor Kangxi ruled a state that massacred some 700,000 people in putting down a rebellion in the Chinese province of Kwangtung in 1681 (Rummel 1994: 52). Shaka, the nineteenth-century Zulu King, slaughtered thousands of victims—at least seven thousand in one session alone—for displaying insufficient grief on the death of his mother (Walter 1969: chap. 7). His victims of this and other homicidal episodes often expired in excruciatingly painful ways. An eyewitness reported that "the means of killing varied: strangling seems to be reserved for royal persons, and sometimes warriors could claim death by the spear in preference to more lowly forms. For the rest, victims were dispatched by dislocating the neck, clubbing, stoning, various mutilations, or pounding sharpened stakes through the rectum" (Walter 1969: 136).

Twentieth century autocracies were just as lethal. Communist regimes, such as the Soviet Union, China, and Cambodia, and fascist regimes, such as Nazi Germany, exterminated millions of their own citizens (Rummel 1994). Very few of the victims had attacked, sabotaged, or undermined the state. Most were killed because they were members of social categories suspected of disloyalty: Quondam patricians, carriers of heterodox ideologies, members of ethnic minorities, and the like. Only in the most exceptional cases were their killers punished.

Autocracies, then, are the most murderous of regimes. They commit more multiple victim homicides, up to and including massacres and even genocides, than oligarchies, and vastly more than democracies (see, e.g., Rummel 1994). Again, these killings virtually never carry any legal penalties. The written law is largely irrelevant: in autocracies mass official slaughter is, in effect, legitimate.

VICTIMS

In stark contrast, homicides directed upwardly against autocratic regimes are deeply and profoundly illegal. One example of such regimes is found in the absolute monarchies of early modern Europe, whose autocratic nature is captured in a remark, perhaps apocryphal, attributed to King Louis XIV of France: "L'état, c'est moi" (I am the state). To kill or even attempt to kill an absolute monarch—the very embodiment of the state—was a monstrous crime. If the offender were caught, he could expect to die slowly and agonizingly. Robert-François

Damiens was one such unfortunate. He was convicted of attempting to assassinate Louis XIV's great-grandson, Louis XV, in January 1775 and was sentenced thus:

> To be taken and conveyed in a cart, wearing nothing but a shirt . . . to the Place de Grève, where, on a scaffold that will be erected there, the flesh will be torn from his breasts, arms, thighs and calves with red-hot pincers, his right hand, holding the knife with which he committed the said parricide, burnt with sulphur, and, on those places where the flesh will be torn away, poured molted lead, boiling oil, burning resin, wax and sulphur melted together and then his body drawn and quartered by four horses and his limbs consumed by fire, reduced to ashes, and his ashes thrown to the wind. (quoted in Foucault 1975: 3)

The prisoner endured this torment for four hours before expiring. After his death, his house was destroyed, his siblings were forced to change their names, and his father, wife, and daughter were expelled from France.[9]

In modern times dictatorships are among the most autocratic states. To kill—or even attempt to kill—a dictator, especially while his country is at war, is to strike at the highest peaks of organizational status, and ranks among the gravest of all offenses. In July 1944, in the midst of a global war, a group of German army officers attempted to assassinate Adolf Hitler and senior members of his military staff. Hitler survived the bomb planted in a briefcase underneath a conference table, but four officers did not. In a radio address to the German public the next morning, Hitler called the conspirators "a gang of criminal elements which will be destroyed without mercy." He was as good as his word. The celebrated history *The Rise and Fall of the Third Reich* reports that in the days and weeks that followed, "the barbarism of the Nazis toward their own fellow Germans reached its zenith. There was a wild wave of arrests followed by gruesome torture, drumhead trials, and death sentences carried out, in many cases, by slow strangling while the victims were suspended by piano wire from meathooks borrowed from butchershops and slaughterhouses. Relatives and friends of the suspects were rounded up by the thousands and sent to concentration camps, where many of them died." All told, as many as five thousand people may have been killed (Shirer 1959: 1069–70, 1072).

CIVIL SUITS

Criminal sanctions, then, are largely a dead letter in official killings, especially when officials enjoy vast organizational superiority over citizens. Yet the story does not end there. Organizational misconduct is less often defined and treated as a crime to be punished than a debt to be paid off, reflecting the principle that "cases against groups are more compensatory than cases against individuals" (Black 1987: 572). Police officers are therefore more vulnerable to civil than to criminal litigation.

In the United States a civil suit typically names the officer as defendant, but individual officers are rarely forced to pay damages, responsibility falling on the city that employs them. Damage awards and out-of-court settlements against cities are "common," according to one expert (Klockars 1996: 4). Just how common is unclear in the absence of statistics (but see Pate and Fridell 1993). But some indication can be gleaned from the large amounts of money paid by cities to plaintiffs in damage awards, or settling cases of improper police actions: The city of Los Angeles paid just short of $80 million in civil actions against police officers between 1991 and 1996. Between 1994 and 1996, New York paid about $70 million (although this figure also includes traffic accidents). Detroit paid $72 million between 1987 and 1994. Many of these awards were for lethal violence (A. Collins 1998: 76–85).

To say that homicides perpetrated by police never have legal repercussions would, therefore, be inaccurate. But the repercussions are typically civil rather than criminal, and visited on the employer city rather than the employee officer. Moreover, only in more democratic polities are police consistently vulnerable to civil actions. In oligarchic states, such as Brazil, successful civil actions against police are rare (though not unknown) (Penglase 1994: 52). But in autocratic states, such as Maoist China or Stalinist Russia, civil suits against police are unthinkable. The more centralized the state, the more remote the likelihood that a citizen will bring, let alone win, a civil action against state officials.

One puzzle remains, however: why are successful civil suits against cities more frequent than successful criminal prosecutions against officers? After all, Blackian theory would, on its face, suggest otherwise:

in civil cases individual plaintiffs (usually the victim's family) sue an organization; in criminal cases an organization (the state) sues an individual who represents an organization. The geometry of the civil case is, in theory, less conducive to legal success yet, in practice, civil cases consistently enjoy more success. We shall return to this anomaly in a later chapter.[10]

THIRD PARTIES

Organizational variables help to explain the behavior of third parties. Partisans as well as settlement agents respond to the organizational geometry of the case. Consider, first, partisans.

PARTISANS

Organization is attractive to third parties. Partisanship behaves in accordance with Black's status principle (1993: 127), increasing with the organizational inferiority of one side and superiority of the other side. Hence, informal groups attract more partisans than individuals do; formal organizations attract more than informal groups; and states (and their officials) attract more than any other organization.

Organizations appear to attract greater partisanship from other organizations and high-status individuals. As partisans, organizations and their officers are, all else equal, more valuable than individuals. Testimony is more credible when given by an on-duty police officer than by an officer in his capacity as a private citizen.

These principles help to explain why the state wins so many of its criminal cases. The more witnesses the prosecution and defense call, the more successful they are (Calder, Insko, and Yandell 1974; Wolf and Bugaj 1990). But the state typically has twice as many witnesses as the defendant (who is typically an individual): 11.3 compared to 5.7 (Kalven and Zeisel 1966: 141). Moreover, the prosecution has higher-status witnesses: police appear for the state in nine out of every ten homicide trials, and experts in almost six out of every ten. The typical defense witnesses, by contrast, are the defendant (79 percent), and his or her family and friends (57 percent). Experts appear for the defense in only one out of every four homicide trials (Kalven and Zeisel 1966: 142–43). Thus, by comparison with the defense attorney, the prosecutor generally "does not face a problem of credibility with respect to his evidence since most of his witnesses are agents who are higher in the hierarchy of credibility" (Ericson and Baranek 1982: 206). Perhaps realizing this, about one-half of all homicide defendants facing a trial plead guilty. Of those who stand and fight, four out of five go on to lose at trial anyway (Baumer, Messner, and Felson 2000: 296).[11]

SETTLEMENT AGENTS

Organized settlement is more severe, decisive, and formalistic (Black 1993: chap. 8). The higher the organizational status of judges, for example, the more punitive, one-sided, and rule-bound their decisions tend to be. But consider another application of the principle: the contrasts between state and nonstate settlement. Popular settlement agents, such as mediators and arbitrators, may represent the local community and speak in the name of public opinion, but, unlike judges, they do not have the backing of the state. The decisions of a tribunal in the highlands of Montenegro, known as the Court of Good Men, nicely illustrate how settlement agents dispose of cases in the absence of the state's organizational superiority.

The Court of Good Men

A Court of Good Men is convened to decide a particular case, its task being to find a solution acceptable to both sides. While the court's decision carries a considerable amount of moral authority, it is not backed by force. The court arbitrates rather than judges cases.

As an example of the court's work, consider the following case in which a father sought compensation for the slaying of his son, Milós. A court consisting of two dozen respected men selected by the two families in dispute met outside a church. The arbitrators swore to hear each side and decide the case fairly with the aid of God.

> The killer presented his case first. He told the assembly that he and his wife had warned Milós to stay away from their unmarried daughter, Savica. However, Milós had continued to seek her out. When Savica became pregnant, he denied being the father. Worse, he said that even if he were, it was Savica's fault: "It is fit for the falcon to go hunting," he said, "and for the prey to take care of itself." At this insult, her father said, his blood boiled. The following day, he went with his brother and son and shot Milós.

> In response, Milós's father argued that Savica had encouraged Milós. When her father learned of the pregnancy, he should have come to him instead of killing his only son and extinguishing his family line. He now asked to be compensated for the death.
>
> After discussing the case among themselves, the arbitrators agreed that both sides were at fault, though Milós was at greater fault because he refused to marry the girl he had shamed. But the greater problem was what to do about the child. It would not be fair for Savica's father to have to pay for the upkeep of another's illegitimate child. In their written judgment, they therefore recommended that if Milós's father elected to adopt the child as his own, Savica's father would have to pay for a woman to nurse it and pay 100 sequins as compensation for the man's death. If, however, Milós's father did not take the child, he would receive no compensation. Moreover, he and Savica's father would have to split the cost of keeping Savica and her child in food and clothing until the child died or she married. (see Boehm 1984: 123–31)

The settlement of the case provides a study in contrasts to the trial of homicide in modern countries, such as the United States. For one thing, the proceedings were markedly less formalistic. While the arbitrators took an oath and followed the accepted procedures for conducting a case, they did not limit the parties to narrowly defined issues, heard no technical legal arguments presented by lawyers, and justified their decision with appeals to indigenous notions of right and wrong rather than written rules. The homicide occupied just part of their deliberations, most of their attention being given to how the parties might live in peace once the case was over. Tribal societies are often thought to be obsessed by the past. But when it comes to settling conflict, nothing could be further from the truth. Arbitrators such as these are much less concerned with establishing a definitive view of the facts, or how similar cases have been decided previously, than with finding a workable solution for the future.

The settlement, moreover, was not directed toward declaring a single winner or loser. Indeed, the very idea was anathema to the arbitrators, the eldest among them remarking, "Never is judging going to be, for one side or the other, exactly what they want. . . . It would be an evil thing if one party to a legal case were to go home singing and the other lamenting" (Boehm 1984: 127).

The court's decision clearly represented a compromise. Adoption would reduce the stigma that the child would face, and remove the burden of upkeep from Savica's father. Yet the arbitrators did not mandate that outcome, because they knew they could not force the child on Milós's father. Instead, they used the homicide compensation as an incentive for the adoption.

Not only was the outcome a compromise, it was not severe. The arbitrators displayed no interest in rhadamanthine justice. They did not pronounce on guilt or innocence. They neither punished nor coerced the parties—at no point was the killer ever in danger of being imprisoned or executed, for example. While they encouraged the victim's father to adopt the illegitimate child as his own, they acknowledged that the decision to do so was his alone.

The relative lack of formalism, decisiveness, and severity is typical of tribal settlement. This should not be taken for granted. Popular mediators and arbitrators are not inherently or personally incapable of decisive, formal, or severe decisions. Many of the settlement personnel described so well by anthropologists, such as the *monkalun* of the Ifugao (Philippines) (Barton 1919), the Arab *wasita* (Ginat 1997: chap. 3), and Tibetan mediators (Ekvall 1964), belong to societies in which people commonly respond decisively and aggressively to insult and injury. They are no strangers to severity. But without the organizational superiority of the state, they do not settle cases in a severe manner.

POPULAR JUSTICE

Blackian theory proposes that popular justice, like law, varies with the location and direction of a homicide in organizational space. Popular justice should therefore be greater at higher elevations of organizational space. And, indeed, in my thirty-society cross-cultural study, some form of retaliatory killing (self-help) is the typical response to homicide in 80 percent of cases with groups present on both sides, compared to only 10 percent of cases where they were absent. In modern society the absence of organized groups of partisans means that vengeance is rarely pursued following a homicide (see Cooney 1998:

73–95). Gangs are the main exception—their presence greatly increasing the likelihood of retaliatory homicide (e.g., Shakur 1993). In general, more organization means more severe popular sanctions. But what about cases between parties of different organizational status?

HIGH-STATUS VICTIMS

When kings, presidents, and other high-ranking state officials are killed, the law typically snaps into action, taking full control of the case. But should the victim's supporters get there first, they are likely to treat the killer harshly:

> In 1330 the king of Hungary, Charles, and his wife, Elizabeth, were murderously assaulted by a baron named Felician as they dined in their castle at Wischegrad. Neither intended victim died, though the queen lost four fingers of her right hand. The royal servants managed to overpower Felician and kill him on the spot. They also seized Felician's son and several other accomplices, whom they tied to horses' tails and dragged through the streets until they died. Their bodies were then cut up and fed to dogs. Felician's head was sent to the capital where it was impaled on the city gates as a reminder to all of the gravity of his crime. (see Dean 2001: 118)

Many centuries later, and a continent away, official victims continued to evoke stern responses from the populace. In the American South after the Civil War, the killing of a police officer raised the odds of a lynching (Brundage 1993: 76–77). Moreover, the lynching was often especially violent: "torture as well as execution of the offender often resulted" (Senechal de la Roche 1997: 57). In one such instance Stephen Bowers, a black man who killed a white sheriff in Seymour Texas in 1916, was hunted down by a posse. An eyewitness reported that "the posse had him in the little square near the jail in the center of Seymour. As we watched, they hung him with a rope, making a terrible racket as he was choked to death. It was a pretty grim sight. But that wasn't enough for them. They then gathered a lot of wood, put it under the Negro man, and set fire to it. He was literally burned to a crisp as he hung there, although he was already dead from the rope" (quoted in Neal 2006: 228).

In parts of the Arab world, where political parties are based on ethnic, tribal, and religious affiliations, the assassination of a member of a leading family puts pressure on his group to exact vengeance or be dishonored. In such cases honor demands blood:

> Suliman Franjiyya was president of the Lebanon between 1970 and 1976 and now leads a Maronite faction in northern Lebanon. In 1978 fighting took place between rival factions and in the affair Franjiyya's son Tony, his wife and their 3-year-old daughter were assassinated. Franjiyya accused Bashir Jamaiel as being responsible for the murders. Franjiyya not only deposed that he would take revenge, but built a special chapel to house the coffins, proclaiming that he would bury his kin only after he had taken revenge.
>
> In 1982 Bashir Jamaiel was elected president of the Lebanon, but was killed one week before his inauguration. In an interview, Franjiyya stated that he was happy that Bashir was dead, but that his joy was not complete as he himself was not responsible for the killing, and that he was still determined to take revenge by killing other members of the Jamaiel family. Because of their high status the two families cannot allow themselves to settle their dispute though a *sulha* (peace agreement) and payment of *diyya* (compensation). If they take money it will affect their long-term status—people will use it against them in other disputes and will be wary of entering alliances with them. For their honor to be effected, revenge is the only solution. (Ginat 1997: 49–50)

Most cases of popular justice, however, do not overlap with the state but arise outside, or even in opposition to it. Still, the same principles apply: victims of high organizational stature evoke more popular justice. In Los Angeles the shooting of a leading gang member—a "ghetto star"—elevates not just the probability but the scale of vengeance: the survivors are more likely to kill and kill several times than they would be for the homicide of a rank-and-file member (Bing 1991: 231; 237–58). In premodern societies too, the killing of group leaders is more serious. Among the Kiowa of North America, for instance, the killing of a chief is the only offense that might elicit vengeance (Richardson 1940: 40–41). In New Guinea, chiefs can kill low-status Tauade victims and expect just to pay compensation; the killing of a chief, on the other hand, is "sometimes followed by the massacre of the entire hamlet responsible" (Hallpike 1977: 151). In Pakistan, among the Swat peoples, "clients and tenants accept blood money; chiefs are forced . . . to pursue revenge" (Barth 1959: 85; see also Lindholm 1982: 74–75).

When a victim's group is prepared to accept compensation for the death of a leader, it will usually demand and receive more than it would for the slaying of an ordinary member. Among the camel-herders of Somalia, for instance, the killer's group must pay over and above the standard one hundred camels in compensation when the victim is a tribal elder (Lewis 1961: 164). Leaders' lives are worth more.

LOW-STATUS VICTIMS

The killing of individuals attracts less severe popular sanctions than the killing of organizational officials, especially when perpetrated by officials. Organizationally downward homicides are less likely to be avenged or compensated, and more likely to be tolerated and praised. When the state executes criminals, for example, crowds outside the prison celebrating the event are a common sight (see, e.g., McFeeley 2000: 35–39). When nonstate organizations kill, the deed may similarly be popularly lauded, and those in charge may be treated as moral heroes. Consider, for instance, vigilante groups.

Vigilante organizations established to fight crime have sprung up at various times in many parts of the world. One particularly hospitable setting was nineteenth-century America. From the 1770s to the 1890s, Americans formed several hundred organizations dedicated to combating murder, theft, cattle rustling, and other iniquities. While some groups had as few as a dozen members, the largest, and best known, was the San Francisco Vigilance Committee of 1856, which boasted as many as eight thousand members. All told, vigilante groups are believed to have killed over seven hundred individuals. Virtually none of these homicides was prosecuted, and many who perpetrated them wound up bathing in the warmth of their fellow citizens' praise (R. Brown 1975: chaps. 4–5). For example:

> Following the assassination of the chief of police in 1890, the mayor of New Orleans formed a Committee of Fifty to tackle

> the problem of ethnic Italian secret societies, widely believed to have been responsible for the murder. After nine of the nineteen Italians accused of the murder were acquitted by a jury, a huge crowd, said to consist of 12,000 to 20,000 people, gathered and stormed the jail where all nineteen defendants were still being held. Eleven Italian prisoners were found and shot. Two were handed over to the sanguinary crowd outside and hanged.
>
> Nobody was ever arrested for the lynching. Instead, those who participated were lauded for the resoluteness and justice of their actions. Nor was the praise confined to New Orleans. Fifty percent of the newspapers across the country that commented on the case supported the action, including the *New York Times* and the *Washington Post.* Even the *Times* of London voiced its approval. The *American Law Review* published a paper by a local judge that described the incident as "a movement conceived by gentlemen and carried out by gentlemen—men who were led by what they conceived a solemn and terrible duty. . . . Every exchange and commercial body in New Orleans on March 14th endorsed what had been done that morning." (see Gambino 1977)

Even today, homicides committed downwardly in organizational space may garner popular praise. In Brazil, for example, police officers are often respected, admired, and honored for their killings. For instance, the officer who commanded the 1992 raid on the Carandiru prison in which 111 prisoners were killed, the great majority after already surrendering, stood for political office, choosing the number 111 as his electoral ticket. He was elected (Amnesty International 1999a, 2001).[12]

THE EVOLUTION OF JUSTICE

Organization, finally, helps to explain certain key facts in the evolution of social control, including the now widely accepted idea that homicide is a criminal act deserving of punishment. Recall that for most of human history, people have lived without organized government. In such societies some individuals—headmen, elders, chiefs—might possess more authority than others, but lacking is any state—any "autonomous political unit, encompassing many communities within its territory and having a centralized government with the power to collect taxes, draft men for work or war, and decree and enforce laws" (Carneiro 1970: 733).

Justice in stateless societies tends to be collective rather than individual. Groups, usually kin-based, act in most conflicts, especially among farming and herding peoples. Thus, when A kills B, the case is typically conducted by B's kinship group against A's kinship group. Over time, though, organizations gradually give way to individuals as the targets of social control. The resulting shift in the structure of cases from organization versus organization to organization versus individual brings with it several important evolutionary changes.

- Liability becomes more individualized: When groups prosecute conflicts, any member of the group may be held responsible for the killing, not just the killer. This is known as collective liability (see, e.g., Senechal de la Roche 1996). Thus, when a homicide triggers vengeance, it is the group that is the target of (and seeks) lethal violence. Which member winds up being killed is often a matter of chance. Finnish Gypsies, for example, call all the relatives of the perpetrator, and any one of them can be slain in requital (Grönfors 1986: 113). When compensation is sought, all members of the killer's kinship group contribute to the payment and all members of the victim's group receive a portion of the payment (see, e.g., Howell 1954). By contrast, in modern society individual rather than collective liability prevails. It is the killer alone who is arrested, tried, convicted, and sentenced. His family and friends are not formally blamed or punished.
- Liability becomes more subjective: Group involvement also influences the subjective dimension of liability—the state of mind that must be present before sanctions are imposed. Black proposes that the liability of organizations is greater than the liability of individuals (1987: 576). Thus, where organizations are the parties to homicide cases, the killer's state of mind when killing is often irrelevant, and accidental killings may trigger sanctions every bit as severe as intentional killings. Among the Tlingit Indians of the Northwest Coast of North America, for example, "if a man was injured or accidentally killed while out hunting with the members of another clan, this clan would have to compensate the dead or

injured man's clan by a payment of goods" (Oberg 1934: 150). As societies modernize and cases come to be brought against individuals rather than groups, full legal responsibility usually requires that the defendant intentionally killed the victim. In the absence of intent, a defendant can only be found guilty of a lesser crime, such as manslaughter.

- Compensation gives way to punishment: Black argues that where cases against groups tend to attract the compensatory style of social control, cases against individuals tend to attract the penal style (1987: 572). The facts bear this out. In many preindustrial societies, killers are not punished but must pay for their lethal actions, and they do so with the help of their family members. But kinship groups eventually shrink in size and weaken in strength, in part because the growth of law means that people can rely on the state rather than their kinfolk in times of conflict. With the state now pursuing individual defendants, social control acquires a new penal emphasis. Killers are no longer asked to compensate their victims, even when they can well afford to do so. Instead, they are accused, tried, convicted, and sentenced. (Only when an insurance company stands behind them, as in many civil actions for wrongful damages, are compensatory damages sought and paid.) Punishment becomes the normal and accepted way of responding to those who kill. Homicide becomes a crime.

There are two species of social beings—Homo sociologicus: individuals and organizations. True, organizations are made up of and by individuals, but organizations have emergent properties of their own. Individuals must die; organizations need not (as long as people in general exist). Individuals are physically located in one place at any one time; organizations can be physically present and active in many places at the same time. Individuals can touch, taste, smell, speak, and hear; organizations, as such, cannot. Consequently, individuals are much more obvious in the social landscape, even as their actions are less far-reaching. Most everyone knows that the earth's human population grew rapidly over the course of the twentieth century; fewer realize that the organizational population increased even more swiftly over the same period (Coleman 1982: 9–12).

Social control clearly illustrates the importance of distinguishing individuals from organizations. Organizations attract a different style of social control—the compensatory—and different types of liability—strict and collective. Conduct treated as clearly immoral when committed by individuals may not be immoral at all when committed by an organization. Blackian theory posits that organizations attract more partisanship and less social control as offenders, and more partisanship and more social control as victims. The homicide data are consistent with this. Across diverse settings, the response to homicide varies with its location and direction in organizational space. Hold constant the parties' wealth and conduct, and downward killings (for example, police-citizen) attract less law and popular justice than upward killings (for example, citizen-police). And the greater the distance in a downward direction, the less social control attaches to a homicide. Thus, in oligarchies and, especially, autocracies, with their greater organizational superiority, killings by officials of citizens are tolerated, even when they involve multiple victims, clear premeditation, and little or no wrongdoing on the part of those killed. For upward homicides, law and popular justice increase with organizational distance: it is more serious to kill a member of a group than an individual, a group leader than a rank-and-file member, and a leader of a more centralized organization than a less centralized one. While the killing of a police officer, a soldier, or, especially, a political leader in a democratic polity is indubitably serious, even more serious is the assassination of an absolute monarch, dictator, or other autocrat. Alter the organizational geometry of a homicide, then, and its immorality alters as well. The same is true of its radial geometry, addressed in the next chapter.

5 THE RADIAL DIMENSION

> Gilbert, or "Beto" as he was widely known, began living on the streets of Rio de Janeiro at the age of four. By the time he was sixteen he was a leader among the homeless kids. The police harassed him constantly. Following his arrest one day, representatives from a church organization went to the police station and demanded that he be released, claiming that he was being illegally detained in the same place as adults. After his supporters obtained a warrant, the police chief reluctantly let the boy go, saying, "You got him out of prison but you haven't saved his life. . . . I doubt he will survive a single week."
>
> Several months later, Beto's bullet-ridden body was found under a viaduct, bearing signs of torture. Nobody was prosecuted for the murder. (see Dimenstein 1991: 49–50)

Here is a textbook example of the toleration of homicide. A violent killing goes completely unpunished. Indeed, the killing was probably not even investigated. If the police did launch a probe, they likely did so perfunctorily, quickly dropping the case after it began to snake back close to home. After all, the victim was of little importance in the eyes of the world: he had no family, no job, no home, no future. His friends were mostly people like himself, adrift from the social mainland. Living nomadically on the perilous streets of a huge city, he suffered the liability of a social disadvantage that influences law, popular justice, and the behavior of third parties alike: a lack of social integration, or, in Blackian terms, low "radial status" (1976: 48).

LAW

Think of society as a circle. Some people exist on the margins while others—the socially integrated-occupy the center of things. Marginality and integration represent the low and high ends of radial status, itself known by the degree to which people participate in social life. Measures of radial status include working, marrying, parenting, owning property, soldiering, volunteering, and other forms of altruistic giving. Radial status is a distinct form of social status. Although low radial status is often coupled with poverty, the two do not automatically go together: Jane might be poor but is highly integrated through marriage, employment, and charitable work, while John, a recluse, is wealthy yet marginal.

Groups too vary in their radial status—some participate energetically in the activities of the larger community; others withdraw. Even genders may have different overall degrees of marginality: women are often more integrated than men into family life, itself a central social institution.

Radial status is an important and independent component of the social geometry of a case. Blackian theory proposes that it exhibits the fourfold status pattern (Black 1976: 48–54). Thus, centrifugal law (directed from the center to the margins) is greater than centripetal law (directed from the margins to the center); centrifugal law increases with radial distance; centripetal law decreases with radial distance; and law increases with the radial status of both principals. These propositions, it turns out, are supported by a broad band of evidence on the handling of homicides that cuts across time periods and societal types.

INTEGRATION AND MARGINALITY IN HISTORY

It is, and always has been, more serious to kill a socially integrated person. Conversely, killings by such individuals—by those who have a spouse, children, relatives, friends, a job, and a home—often elicit considerable understanding, sympathy, and leniency from legal officials.

The advantages of the integrated are mirrored by the disadvantages of the marginal. Their handicaps are more apparent at some times than others. Periods of large-scale social change, for instance, often trigger surges in marginality that render those caught up in it more visible. Wars, plagues, revolutions, the growth of cities, the arrival of industrialism, and other social upheavals typically dislodge considerable numbers of people from their customary ways of life, shifting many of them from the center to the periphery. When several of these causes combine, the effect may be to marginalize entire sections of society. The decline of feudalism in Europe was one such episode, with hordes of people finding themselves displaced from their ancestral lands. Most had no choice but to take to the roads and look for work in cities and towns. Not long afterward, landowners began to enclose their estates, replacing crop cultivation with the raising of livestock, which required less labor. Periodic outbreaks of plague and warfare brought further instability. A spike in population exacerbated all of these trends, putting further pressure on the existing stock of land, home, and jobs. The net result: an increasingly detached, mobile society (Durston 2004: 78–79).

Governments responded harshly to the growing rootlessness of the populace. They enacted a series of vagrancy statutes, making transience a criminal offense (Chambliss 1964). The new laws prescribed severe penalties for vagrants, including public flogging, branding, and forcible repatriation to their place of birth or last permanent residence (see Black 1976: 52–53). A way of life became a crime.

The law was powerless, however, to halt the tide of transiency. As one contemporary Englishman noted, "The punishment that is ordeined for this kind of people is verie sharpe, and yet it can not restrain them" (quoted in Durston 2004: 77). Early modern Europe remained replete with the itinerant, the idle, and the isolated. Some could eke out a living by working odd jobs or trading part-time, but many had to depend on the charity of churches and their fellow citizens. The largest city in Europe at the time was Paris. At the beginning of the fourteenth century, it probably had about two hundred thousand inhabitants, of whom somewhere between eight thousand and twenty thousand were beggars (Geremek 1971: 7, 193–94). This group formed a kind of floating underclass, marked off from the settled population, even the settled poor, by their detachment from the stable forces of job, family, and home (Geremek 1971). Like the socially unattached everywhere, they were believed to harbor strong criminal tendencies. Blamed for much of the crime, they became the object of suspicion, surveillance, and, once in the clutches of the law, severity. Their persistence as a social category ensured that much thought was given to neutralizing them. A pamphlet published by "a gentleman" in London in the middle of the eighteenth century, for example, attributed to the idle a love of "gaming, drunkenness, and debauchery" that leads them to commit robbery and murder, for "the dead tell no tales." He proposed a series of measures to combat the problem, including establishing a "Vagrant Constable" in each parish who would compile a list of all those not gainfully employed and a "Vagrant House" for confining those who persisted in idleness: "Any Nobleman, Gentleman, Farmer or other, having any Work to do, and there are not Hands sufficient in the Neighborhood for the Work, [would] have Liberty to take any Number of Hands from the Vagrant-house . . . and employ them in such Work, paying what is reasonable for their Labor" (*Public Nuisance* 1754: 63).

Despite the picture this anonymous writer painted of a hedonistic existence free of the burdens of work, family, and communal responsibilities, the reality was far bleaker. Many marginals inhabited a Hobbesian world in which life was nasty, brutish, and often short. Living largely outside mainstream social institutions, they received little or no protection from the state. Crimes against them were of little moment. Should one of them be killed, the incident would often not have been even recorded as a homicide. Were the corpse of a vagrant to wash up on the banks of a river bearing signs of violence, for example, little official action was likely to ensue. Even if it did and a perpetrator was charged, he was unlikely to suffer sanctions of any great gravity. On the other hand, when a socially integrated individual was found murdered, marginals were often the first to be suspected. A homeless, single transient accused of killing an employed, familied, and settled member of the community ran a high risk of being convicted and sentenced to death. He was also more likely to be executed. A man with a wife and family stood a much better chance of being pardoned (Geremek 1971: 275, 254).

Even the possession of a single marginal characteristic, such as being single or unemployed, could make a difference in early modern Europe. In England, for example, the written law of infanticide differed after 1624 for married and unmarried women. A married woman could only be convicted under the regular law of homicide if the prosecution could prove that she had intentionally killed the baby. An unmarried woman, however, was guilty of the offense of concealment of birth unless she could prove that the child had been stillborn (Beattie 1986: 113; McMahon 2004: chap. 8). In nineteenth-century France, when men were accused of violent crimes, "Two central issues were probed to determine whether they deserved indulgence. A good and diligent work record, for example[,] was almost always noted by the investigating magistrate and often mentioned by the President [i.e., head judge of the superior or Assize Court] during his interrogation. On the other hand, evidence of past unemployment . . . or a bad word from the boss in the workshop was often sufficient to prejudice the outcome of the case" (Harris 1989: 276).

Elsewhere, marginality had similar impacts. Early colonies, for example, were often sharply divided into two social spheres, one recently arrived, the other long present, living side-by-side but with little mutual interaction. The newcomers controlled the legal system, and it was integration into and marginality from their group that helped to dictate how severely the law responded to the taking of human life. In nineteenth-century Australia, for instance, many Aborigines in the northern part of the state of Queensland lived wholly separately from the whites who staffed the legal system. They had little contact with the newcomers or their society. When these Aborigines were assaulted or killed by white settlers, little or no punishment typically resulted. Their lives counted for little.

Yet not all Aboriginal victims were as marginal—or as quickly forgotten. Some Aborigines did participate in the white world. Those who did so—through being adopted by a white family or employed by a white business or farm, for instance—and suffered physical attacks could sometimes attract the protection of prosecutors and courts (Highland 1994: 132–33). Their lives counted for something.

THIRD WORLD INTEGRATION AND MARGINALITY

Radial status continues to display its effects today, nowhere more so than in the industrializing or third world. The killing of integrated victims remains more serious. In Laos, for example, "when homicide comes to the attention of the central government authorities, the suspected murderer is jailed. Then a hearing occurs before a government official. If the suspect is declared guilty, then a *khaa hua* (head price) is set. The head price varies according to the age and social status of the victim, whether he was married or had children. If the head price is paid to the victim's survivors, the murderer may be in prison for a few months to a few years. If it is not paid, he will spend ten to twenty years in prison" (Westermeyer 1971: 566).

Third world countries provide a glimpse of the effects of extreme marginality under more modern conditions. Most of the industrializing nations of South America, Asia, and Africa have large populations of landless peasants, beggars, vagrants, alcoholics, and drug addicts, rootless people drifting from one desperate situation to another. Many of these individuals suffer from multiple counts of marginality: homelessness, joblessness, and perhaps friendlessness as well. Their lack of attachments arouses suspicion and, sometimes, fear among the integrated population. In some countries, many regard them as social vermin, and the law effectively welcomes their elimination. In Colombia, marginals are know as *descehables*—disposable people. The killing of *descehables,* far from being treated as criminal, is commonly regarded as a form of "social cleansing":

> Victims of "social cleansing" murders frequently are discovered without identifying documents, and are registered at the morgue as "NN" (no name). No one appears to claim their bodies or protest their deaths. Often, the authorities charged with collecting evidence fail to investigate properly. For instance, after the rash of "social cleansing" killings in December 1993, the Bogotá Personería discovered that the coroner had not gathered forensic evidence from bodies in the morgue, but instead had washed, shaved, and cut their hair, making identification nearly impossible. (Kirk 1994: 14)

Case statistics bear out this general picture. In the capital, Bogotá, eighty-one street people were known to be killed in 1993: not a single person was arrested (Kirk 1994: 14). Similar patterns have been observed elsewhere as well: In Brazil, for example, seven homeless men were beaten to death in São Paolo in a two-day period in 2005, apparently by death squads. "Two military police officers and a private security guard were subsequently charged with the killings. However, the charges were dropped on grounds of insufficient evidence" (Amnesty International 2005a).

The killing of marginals is especially likely to be tolerated when the offenders are themselves integrated members of the community with jobs, families, and records of civic participation. Colombian social cleansing killings are usually the work of "death squads," composed of more socially integrated individuals (e.g., business owners, security guards) whose clandestine lethal activities are rarely investigated, still more rarely prosecuted, and even more rarely punished (see, e.g., Kirk 1994).

Death squad killings are symptomatic of the open distaste of marginals on the part of the integrated population and their legal agents. Not just the police but large segments of the public blame marginals for most of the many thefts, robberies, assaults, homicides, and other crimes that make daily life so difficult and dangerous. Being the object of much suspicion, marginals quickly become accustomed to being stopped and questioned, harassed and arrested by the police. Should a homicide (or other crime) occur nearby, they can expect to come under scrutiny. Once taken into police custody, they may be beaten or tortured. The police may even target them for extrajudicial executions. These killings, though often highly premeditated and violent, typically have, like death squad killings, no criminal consequences. But then the line between police and death squad homicides is often quite blurred. In Colombia, for instance, off-duty police officers are one of the main sources of death squad members. In 1991 death squads committed close to four hundred social cleansing killings: virtually none resulted in any official actions (Méndez 1992: 5–6). In Brazil, too, death squads have operated with impunity for many years in the major cities (see, e.g., Huggins 2000; Amnesty International 2005b: 46–47, 50).

Despite their frequency, death squad executions have attracted relatively little attention in the English-speaking world. The one exception is the killing of street children. The issue first came to international attention in Brazil, which, ironically, has some of the most pro-child legislation in the world. Most of the victims are young men, aged between fourteen and seventeen years old. Some have committed crimes; others are suspected of having done so. Regardless of what they have done, their very marginality is an offense to many. One nine-year-old boy was found strangled to death on a beach in Rio de Janeiro with a note on his body that read, "I killed you because you didn't go to school and had no future" (quoted in Dimenstein 1991: 31). Killings of this kind, whether carried out by death squads formed by local merchants to protect their businesses or by police officers, typically have slight or nonexistent legal repercussions: the child disappears, never to be heard from again; end of case (see, e.g., Amnesty International 2005b: 46–47; Scheper-Hughes 2006: 173). Investigations are rare and usually peter out anyway. Asked to describe how police investigate these murders, a priest replied: "The way an investigation works for us is this: we bring a boy who has witnessed or been the victim of violence to the police to file a complaint; the kid disappears; the investigation never occurs" (quoted in Penglase 1994: 40–41).

Brazil is not alone. The execution of street children has also been documented in Guatemala (see, e.g., Manuel 1991; L. Tucker 1997). There too the marginal status of the victims virtually assures that most cases will not be vigorously investigated or prosecuted. Still, there are exceptions. Occasionally, the killers are apprehended. Very occasionally, they are even convicted. But even then there is no guarantee they will be punished. For instance, in one case two private security guards killed a fourteen-year-old and a ten-year-old boy and wounded a third. The boys were shot multiple times from behind. The men admitted the killing and were convicted of murder. They appealed. As the date of the appeal approached, the victims' family members, their supporters, and their lawyers began receiving death threats. The appeals court upheld the appeal and nullified the conviction, a result that surprised many observers and led them to speculate that the judges had been threatened or bribed (see L. Tucker 1997: 40–41).

In India, too, unpunished killings of street children while in police custody have been documented. Most of the deaths arise out of beatings that went too far. Regardless of how they occur, these homicides typically generate little or no response on the part of the authorities. In one case, for example, the police took a fifteen-year-old rickshaw puller named Sudhakar into custody after a customer of his jumped out of his rickshaw and fled from approaching policemen. The police questioned Sudhakar about the customer. After four days of torture, Sudhakar was sent home unconscious. He died five days later without ever regaining consciousness. The police, who said he died of natural causes, were never prosecuted (see Ganesan 1996: 86).

MODERN INTEGRATION AND MARGINALITY

Marginality continues to be a legal handicap in modern societies. The killing of a vagrant, for example, is not the kind of case that excites much investigatory zeal. Should the police stumble upon the body of a homeless, unemployed, single alcoholic, an inhabitant of "skid row," bearing signs of violence, they may not even bother to register it as a homicide (Black 1989: 6–7).

Still, marginals in modern society are generally less disadvantaged than their counterparts in third world societies or at earlier times. The gulf between the legal experience of the marginal and the integrated has narrowed somewhat. The homeless in America, for example, appear to be less vulnerable to the sharp end of the law than their counterparts in earlier societies or in poorer countries today. This is not because of the growth of formal rules requiring legal officials to decide cases equally, according to what people do and not who they are. Third world countries do not want for written rules mandating equal treatment of accused persons. Rather, the change is due to a drop in the intensity of marginality itself in modern societies. Modern governments fund a series of programs that serve to reduce marginality, including welfare payments for the poor, unemployment benefits for the jobless, publicly subsidized housing for the homeless, and universal compulsory education. All of these help to bring the outer edge of marginality closer to the center of social life, as do the altruistic activities of many private groups operating locally, regionally, nationally, and internationally. Overall, modern marginality is considerably less frequent and extreme than at earlier times or in contemporary poorer countries: marginals today have more radial status, and that mitigates the harshness of legal officials toward them.

Marginality has not disappeared, however, and data on its effects can still be found, even if they are less frequent and less extreme. The handling of homicide continues to illustrate the importance of social involvement and withdrawal. For example, in America unemployed persons charged with murder are more likely to be incarcerated before and after trial than employed persons (Chiricos and Bales 1991). They are also less likely to have the charged dropped at the preliminary hearing (which determines whether there is probable cause that the defendant is guilty of the offense charged and so results in a decision either to prosecute or to dismiss the case). A study of the preliminary hearing of homicides committed in the course of another crime in a large northern industrial city found that the strongest predictor was the employment status of the parties. Unemployment on the part of the defendant increased the chance that the case would be prosecuted, while unemployment on the part of the victim reduced it (Boris 1979: 152–53).

Unemployment affects the later stages of homicide cases as well. In a California study defendants convicted of first-degree murder who were unemployed at the time of the killing experienced a three-fold increase in their odds of being sentenced to death. In addition, those who had a history of low job stability (meaning that they held no job or more than four jobs in the last five years) experienced a further two-fold increase in death penalty odds (Baldus et al. 1980: 27–28; see also Judson et al. 1969: 1337).[1]

Being single and childless are further indicators of marginality that operate to a litigant's disadvantage. Conversely, marriage and parenthood increase social integration and provide a layer of legal protection. It is more serious to kill a familied victim, and less serious for a familied person to kill. A study of California capital cases found that juries sentence defendants to death more often when the victim is married rather than divorced or single (85 percent compared to 33 percent) and a parent as opposed to being childless (60 percent compared to 27 percent) (Sundby 2003: 358).

Since women tend to have more family responsibilities, especially the care of children, than men, they tend to benefit from greater leniency in the aggregate within the criminal justice system (Daly 1987; H. Allen 1987a, 1987b). The same reasoning extends to victims. The slaying of somebody who takes care of children or elderly people is more serious than the slaying of somebody not so integrated into family life. Because women perform these services more often than men in modern societies, they typically attract less severity when they kill and more severity when they are killed (see, e.g., Farrell and Swigert 1978: 574; 1986; Baldus, Woodworth, and Pulaski 1990: 588–90, 661; Langan and Dawson 1995).[2]

In any given study of real world cases with many factors working simultaneously, the effects of radial status may be more visible at one stage of the criminal justice system than another. An analysis that stretches over several stages will therefore usually be more revealing than an analysis that stretches over just one. The fact that most of the studies of radial status (and indeed other variables as well) that find a significant effect are confined to a single stage is testament to its power as a predictor of legal decisions.

THIRD PARTIES

Blackian theory holds that radial status influences the behavior of third parties as well as the principal parties. Partisanship and settlement alike vary with the location and direction of a homicide in radial space. Although many patterns await empirical confirmation, the theoretical predictions are clear.

PARTISANS

Third parties are drawn to integrated parties over marginal ones. And the greater the difference in radial status between the principals, the stronger the partisan attraction. In homicide cases, the greatest partisanship is found when a highly integrated killer (or victim) opposes a highly marginal victim (or killer).

Just as third parties are attracted to socially integrated killers and victims, so they are repelled by socially marginally principals. Marginals appear to be particularly unattractive to the socially integrated and other high-status partisans. Seldom do socially integrated lawyers and witnesses flock to the defense of a marginal accused of murder. Homeless men facing murder charges do not put together an O. J. Simpson–like "dream team" of famous lawyers, expert witnesses, and investigators. Yet it is marginals who would benefit the most from the support of the socially integrated. Integrated partisans give a greater boost to the radial status of a marginal party than an integrated party. Marginal partisans, by contrast, do not appreciably elevate their side's social standing. Indeed, they may reduce it. Drawing attention to an opposing witness's status as a welfare recipient can therefore be an effective trial tactic (see, e.g., Comack and Balfour 2004: 87).

Overall, partisans tend to reinforce the core case geometry. Just as the socially integrated repel law, so they attract partisanship. And as the marginal attract law, so they repel partisanship. When both parties are integrated, their case attracts law and partisanship alike; when both are marginal, the case attracts less law and less partisanship.

Partisanship may extend to legal officials. Police officers, prosecutors, judges, and jurors frequently side with one party over the other. Because their partisanship takes more time to manifest itself and is more considered than most, Black dubs it "slow partisanship" (1993: 138–39). Fast or slow, legal partisanship falls within the purview of the Blackian principle that partisans tend to side with higher-status over lower-status parties.[3] This is one reason why persons of higher radial status enjoy more success than persons of low radial status both as defendants and as victims in homicide cases.

SETTLEMENT AGENTS

Settlement agents tend to possess high radial status. Modern judges are typically selected from the ranks of the married, employed, and property-owning. They have ties to the community, and perhaps a record of voluntary service as well. Jurors too usually exhibit some degree of social integration. Juries may not always be composed of the most socially integrated individuals, but they are rarely composed of the least integrated actors either. Very few juries are drawn from the ranks of the single, the homeless, and the unemployed.

Centrifugal settlement is more severe than centripetal settlement. The most severe settlement—with a high probability of conviction and long sentence—should therefore be found in cases decided by highly integrated judges against marginal defendants (Black 1993: chap. 8). Conversely, the least severe settlement is likely to be found where the settlement agents are not radially superior to the person accused of homicide.

Since judges are more integrated, on average, than jurors, they are more severe as well. Their greater radial status (along with other factors, such as their vertical status) helps to explain the pattern noted earlier: that judges are more likely to convict than are jurors. It also helps to explain their greater penchant for legal rules and for all-or-nothing decisions. Lawyers who tie their arguments closely to the substantive and procedural rules of homicide ought generally to do better with judges than with jurors. And lawyers who seek all-out victories—such as a complete acquittal—should be more likely to earn them from judges than from jurors.

POPULAR JUSTICE

Beyond the realm of judges, lawyers, and legal officials of all stripes, radial geometry continues to be crucial to how cases are handled. Popular justice responds, it appears, in the same way as state justice to the integration and marginality of the parties. Thus, severe popular sanctions, such as feuding or lynching, or even sizeable compensation payments, are not as likely to follow in the wake of outward homicides (or inward cases) as inward homicides. These contrasts in popular severity are found in stateless societies and state societies alike. In urban America, for example, "gang members pursue offenses committed by the members of other gangs less vigorously when a peripheral rather than a core member of the group reports that he was attacked or insulted" (Horowitz and Schwartz 1974: 239).

As with gangs, so with all groups. The less integrated the victim, the more lenient the popular sanctions.

MARGINAL VICTIMS

Even in so-called vengeance cultures, only some homicides are, in fact, avenged (Gould 2004). Relatives and neighbors are slower to put their own lives on the line for the slaying of a marginal. And the more marginal the victim, the less popular justice of any kind is to be expected. The killing of isolates, loners, and drifters will often be tolerated. Indeed, when the killers are socially integrated, they even may be praised for their services to the community. In Brazil, for instance, where death squads made up of the socially integrated typically target marginals, such as the single, the homeless, and the unemployed, their killings are often received favorably, many people admiring and applauding them, some openly. Not only are their perpetrators seldom prosecuted, they sometimes become folk heroes. The 1984 arrest in São Paolo of a man believed to have killed seventy-two people triggered a public protest in the center of the city by residents of his neighborhood. Another well-known death squad leader was awarded an honorific title by his city for his services and proudly stood as a candidate in local elections (Dimenstein 1991: 45–46).

Lynching, too, is less likely to follow in the wake of outward homicides. Marginal victims attract less partisanship, integrated killers more partisanship. These conditions are the exact opposite of those required for lynching: "Lynching is a joint function of strong partisanship toward the alleged victim and weak partisanship toward the alleged offender" (Senechal de la Roche 2001: 129). Thus, in the postbellum South, the killing of an isolated outsider by a socially active insider was very unlikely to result in a lynching. This was true even if the victim was white and the killer black: radial status could negate race (132–33).

INTEGRATED VICTIMS: PREINDUSTRIAL SOCIETIES

Integrated victims evoke more popular justice. In the postbellum South, for example, the killing of a person on whom family members were dependent was particularly likely to heighten community ire. The 1903 murder of a young man in Houston County, Georgia, led to the lynching of Banjo Peavy. According to the local newspaper, the murder victim "had won the respect and esteem of the entire community, not only by his big heartedness, but by his constant attention and devotion to his widowed mother and sisters, who had learned to depend on him entirely." A few weeks later, three men were lynched in Baker County, Georgia, for the murder of F. S. Bullard, a farmer. The murder, the local paper explained, "left the Bullard family in a sad condition, his wife being a hopeless invalid and his several small children dependent" (quoted in Brundage 1993: 74).

Popular sanctions are severe when the victim is integrated and the killer marginal: centrifugal popular justice is greater than centripetal popular justice. They are especially severe when the victim is highly integrated and the killer highly marginal: centrifugal popular justice increases with radial distance. Contributing to the 1896 lynching of two marginal killers in Texas, for example, was not just that their victim was familied and employed but that his employment as a bank teller put him at the center of a large informal network of people:

> Two out-of-town drifters, Elmer "Kid" Lewis and Foster Crawford, held up a bank in Wichita Falls. The robbery went awry, and they wound up shooting and killing a cashier, Frank Dorsey. Dorsey was a pillar of the community, married, a father of three children, and a long-time and respected employee of the bank. On the day he was to be buried the local school was dismissed so that everybody could attend the funeral. The church in which the memorial service was held was not large enough to accommodate all who attended. Feelings ran high. After the funeral, a large group of people assembled and marched to the jail where the killers were being held. They quickly overpowered the deputy in charge, seized Lewis and Crawford, tied their hands behind their backs, and hanged them from a telegraph pole in front of the bank. (see Neal 2006: 49–62)

Occupational integration increases the probability and severity of sanctions in other settings as well. In Gila County, Arizona, 1880–1920, only three homicides resulted in the lynching of the killer by a group of citizens. One case involved the murder of a Wells Fargo coach driver, an individual who, again, by virtue of his job came into contact with many people. Three men were arrested for the crime. As they awaited their legal fate, the three were seized from jail by a mob and hanged from a nearby tree (McKanna 1997: 147–48).[4] A somewhat similar case in Nebraska in 1916 had a better outcome for the killers, though it was a close call: "Three men suspected of killing a street car conductor were being held in jail. As word spread of the men's presence, a noisy crowd assembled outside the jail. Some members of the crowd found a large utility pole and began to batter down the outer door of the jail. After they had succeeded, they went to work on the inside door only to be repulsed by a group of police officers who waded into them. The crowd scattered and the accused men were saved" (McKanna 1997: 72).

INTEGRATED VICTIMS: MODERN SOCIETIES

Most killers today are not subject to severe popular sanctions. Penalties for taking human life emanate primarily from the state, not society. Still, many killers and their families experience some shunning at the hands of others. With the loose social ties of modern societies, it is easy for the victim's friends and relatives to cut off contact, to snub the killer and his relatives. Shunning may occur at various points: before the defendant is arrested; while the defendant is in jail, out on bond, in prison following conviction; or after his release. Since incarceration by necessity involves a curtailment of interaction, not all reductions in contact following a homicide can properly be deemed "shunning." Some ties weaken simply because the defendant is no longer in circulation. Shunning, by contrast, is a moral reaction that expresses disapproval of the defendant's actions. To distinguish shunning from mere relational mortality, I asked the defendants in the Virginia sample why they felt the other person had reduced contact with them. Only when the defendant stated that the reduction was related to the killing did I consider it to be shunning.

Forty-five of the seventy-five defendants (60 percent) experienced some shunning, so measured. Most (twenty-four) were avoided by no more than two people, but as many as nine were shunned by more than ten people. One of the best predictors of which killers were shunned was the social integration of the victim.

Victims who left behind a spouse and children, for example, evoked more shunning of the killer and the killer's family. So did occupationally integrated victims, such as storekeepers in small towns. Whether they are wealthy or not, storekeepers, like their counterparts of old, are often among the best-connected members of their communities in modern America. They meet and chat with large numbers of people every day, often dealing with the same individuals over and over again, especially in rural areas where stores are not plentiful. Widely known for miles around, they are relied upon not just for material goods but for news and gossip. They are friends to many and acquaintances to even more. A storekeeper's murder will therefore reverberate widely, touching a large circle of people. The killer—even if from the same community—will rarely be extended much sympathy or support. Most likely he will quickly become persona non grata. Four of the Virginia victims were storekeepers, and in three of the cases the defendant experienced extensive shunning. In one, for instance, the defendant was a high school student with a wide circle of friends and acquaintances. They all rebuffed him. His family also found their social ties sharply curtailed. His grandparents had been members of a church all their lives and held positions of responsibility in it. They were made to feel so uncomfortable that they eventually stopped attending. In another case, a defendant who killed a storekeeper for no apparent reason was partially shunned by his siblings and his grandmother, and totally shunned by his father (who lived elsewhere) and his friends. The slaying of an integrated member of a community remains a very serious matter.

Social withdrawal can be costly. It pays to join in, to contribute, to participate. There are many ways to participate, including going to school, getting a job, marrying, having children, paying taxes, volunteering in the community, and serving one's country. Blackian theory holds that participation of all stripes increases radial status and confers a geometrical advantage on killers and victims alike. The research evidence bears this out. In all known settings, from the highways of medieval Europe to the freeways of modern America, from the streets of vast South American cities to the pastoral landscapes of east Africa, those who possess radial status—the socially integrated—are protected by law and popular justice alike. Further, the more integrated they are, the more protection they enjoy. Thus, the killing of highly integrated victims triggers severe penalties, legal and popular. By contrast, the slaying of victims who lack radial status—the marginal—may go unnoticed. When the victims are extremely marginal, when they lack spouses and children and jobs and homes, their violent demise may even be a matter for rejoicing. Should they themselves commit homicide, however, their actions are met with a severity proportional to their degree of marginality. Conversely, the same homicide committed by one who is socially integrated stands a greater chance of being punished lightly or even being excused altogether.

Third parties too are drawn to the integrated over the marginal. Integrated killers consequently enjoy more partisanship than marginal killers. Integrated victims are similarly attractive: those who have a record of social involvement have more people clamoring for sanctions against the killer than those who remain on the margins.

Radially, then, the least immoral homicides (the most understandable and commendable) occur centrifugally or outwardly: from the center to the margins. The most immoral homicides (the most shocking and horrifying) occur centripetally or inwardly: from the margins to the center.

Criminal propensities are commonly attributed to those of low radial status. But the legal vulnerability of marginals is independent of any crimes they might commit. Even so, criminal behavior, or even a reputation for it, is fateful as it lowers an actor's standing in the normative dimension of social space, the topic of the next chapter.

6 THE NORMATIVE DIMENSION

Bob worked at the weekend in the garden of a wealthy 80-year-old lady named Mrs. Smith. Lately, a man named Danny had started to live with Bob and his wife. One Friday afternoon, as Danny was painting Bob's front porch, Bob approached him with a proposition. He knew that Mrs. Smith had money and jewelry in her house. If he kept the old lady busy, Danny could search for and take her valuables; they would split the proceeds fifty-fifty. Danny agreed to the plan.

The two men drove to Mrs. Smith's house, with Danny concealing himself by lying down on the back seat. Bob went in the front door to talk to Mrs. Smith. Five minutes later, as agreed, Danny entered the house through the garage. He searched two rooms but found nothing. While searching another, he heard Mrs. Smith and Bob coming close and had to jump under the bed until they left the room. When he emerged, Danny saw that Mrs. Smith had left her pocketbook. Danny grabbed it, exited the house, and hid in the car. Several minutes later, Bob emerged with Mrs. Smith, discussing the yard. Bob drove off with Danny concealed from sight.

Disappointingly, the pocketbook contained only $9. Bob said he knew there was money still in the house. The two drove around for a while, consumed a six-pack of beer, and decided to try again. As Danny lay on the back seat, Bob told him that if Mrs. Smith found him searching the house, he was to grab her and lock her into a closet.

When they arrived back, Bob went into the house and talked to Mrs. Smith, who was upset about not being able to find her pocketbook. Bob told her that she must have misplaced it and offered to help her find it. Danny once again went in to the house

> through the garage, but this time Mrs. Smith saw him and asked him what he wanted. Danny told her he had lost his dog. Seeming to accept this explanation, Mrs. Smith told him that she had not seen a dog. Danny thanked her, and began to walk away. After Mrs. Smith and Bob went back into the house, Bob was able to block Mrs. Smith's vision of the door. Danny slipped back inside and began to search the house, moving from room to room. Intent on his search, he failed to hear Mrs. Smith approaching. Seeing him, she screamed. Danny grabbed her by the throat—to quiet her, he said—and they struggled. Mrs. Smith fell, and did not get up. Danny felt her pulse and then ran downstairs to tell Bob that he thought Mrs. Smith was dead. The two quickly searched the house, took some jewelry, and then packed Mrs. Smith's body into the trunk of their car. They drove to an old well and pushed Mrs. Smith's body down it.
>
> Several days later, the police arrested the two men and charged them with murder and robbery. Both pleaded not guilty. They were tried separately. Both were convicted.

Given the facts of this case (from my Virginia study), surely Danny would receive the more severe sentence. After all, it was he who actually killed the elderly lady. Bob came up with the plan, participated in the theft, and helped dispose of the body, but he never struck or injured anyone.

In fact, Bob was sentenced to sixty years in prison while Danny received only twenty years. But the surprise soon disappears on learning of the criminal history of both defendants. Bob had a string of prior convictions to his name and had twice served time in prison. Danny's record was comparatively clean: he had been convicted of several minor property offenses, and had even spent thirty days in a local jail, but had never done any prison time. When it came to the murder, Bob was, in effect, punished not just for this crime, but for a lifetime of criminal behavior. In Blackian terms, Bob was handicapped by low "normative status."

Normative status or respectability refers to a person's reputation for good and evil. It is known by the amount of social control to which social actors have been subject (Black 1976: 111). The more social control people have experienced, the more unrespectable they are. The social control may be legal (e.g., a criminal conviction) or popular (e.g., acquiring a reputation for dishonesty). It may have a precise target (e.g., a sexual molestation) or be diffuse ("he's just not a nice guy"). The critical point is that the individual's reputation is compromised to one degree or another among those handling the case.

LAW

Normative status is a key component of the social geometry of a homicide case, exhibiting, Black proposes, the familiar quadripartite status effect (1976: 111–17). Offenses by unrespectable offenders against respectable victims should therefore attract the most law, followed by respectable offenders victimizing respectable victims, followed by unrespectable offenders victimizing unrespectable victims, followed, finally, by respectable offenders victimizing unrespectable victims. The evidence, it turns out, is highly consistent with these theoretical predictions.

Respectability differs from other geometrical variables in one important respect: the formal law allows it to be taken into consideration. Unlike, say, wealth or marginality, the prior record of the defendant is often a legal criterion for assessing how the defendant ought to be handled. But pure sociology holds that respectability plays an even larger role in legal cases. It matters both when it is legally relevant (e.g., bail, sentencing) and when it is not (e.g., conviction). And it matters for whom it is legally relevant (the defendant) and for whom it is not (the victim). Consider each party in turn.

UNRESPECTABLE KILLERS

Legal officials everywhere proceed more vigorously against defendants who have a record of deviance than those who do not (see, e.g., Baumgartner 1992a: 136–37). And the longer and graver the record, the more vigorously they proceed. In searching for an unknown killer, for instance, detectives will pay particular attention to persons with a criminal history, violent or not (see, e.g., Simon 1991). When the case gets to court, an unrespectable defendant faces an uphill battle. One study conducted in an unnamed northeastern city, for instance, examined the effect of a prior criminal record on conviction seriousness—the level or degree of homicide of which the defendant was found guilty. Distinguishing four levels of conviction (first-degree murder, second-degree murder, voluntary manslaughter, and involuntary manslaughter), the authors found that the more legally serious a defendant's prior criminal record, the graver the homicide offense of which he or she was convicted (Swigert and Farrell 1986: 78–81).

Studies of the death penalty powerfully illustrate the stigmatizing effect of low normative status. In San Francisco a prior conviction for a legally grave felony doubles the odds that a prosecutor will treat the case as a potentially capital case; a prior homicide conviction is even more damning, boosting the odds eighteenfold (Berk, Weiss, and Boger 1993: 101). A statewide study of California first-degree murder convictions revealed that, holding constant some 150 variables, the defendant's odds of receiving a death sentence were nine times greater if he or she had a criminal record (Baldus et al. 1980: 27; see also Judson et al. 1969: 1326–36). Several measures of unrespectability were found to increase the frequency of death sentences in a pair of Georgia studies. In one analysis, the authors report that, after adjusting for over thirty other variables, the odds of a death sentence increase fourfold for a prior violent felony conviction,[1] an additional fivefold for multiple murder convictions, and an additional sevenfold for the defendant being a prisoner or escapee (Baldus, Woodworth, and Pulaski 1990: 319; see also, e.g., Nakell and Hardy 1987; Keil and Vito 1989). As always, the precise numbers are less important than the general pattern they evince: unrespectable suspects charged with murder run a greater risk of being sentenced to death. And the greater their unrespectability, the greater their risk.

UNRESPECTABLE VICTIMS

Although researchers have studied the effect of the victim's reputation less often and in less depth, it exerts a strong influence of its own on case outcomes. Take investigation, for instance. Detectives are judged by how many cases they solve, and are therefore keen to arrest suspects (see, e.g., Litwin 2004). But some cases are a higher priority because, as one observer of police investigators notes, "in the world of detectives, some human lives are simply worth more than others"

(Jackall 1997: 114). Finding the murdered body of an upstanding citizen with no criminal history and a good reputation triggers the kind of vigorous investigation so familiar to viewers of police television shows and movies. Cases with less respectable victims—drug dealers, wife beaters, child molesters, gang members, and the like—may evoke "less investigatory zeal" (Corwin 2003: 86). "Nothing deflates a detective more than going back to the office, punching a victim's name into the admin office terminal and pulling out five or six pages of misbehavior, a criminal history that reaches from eye level to the office floor," notes a journalist who spent a year observing Baltimore homicide detectives (Simon 1991: 177). Detectives sometimes dub such killings "public service homicides" (Jackall 2005: 125). As on the streets, so too behind bars: when violent incarcerated criminals are killed, "officials often dismiss such cases as N.H.I.s—'No Humans Involved'" (Grann 2004: 167). In short, "The moral status of victims greatly affects . . . investigations" (Jackall 2005: 199).

The lack of enthusiasm that police display toward unrespectable victims can strongly influence the eventual outcome of the case. In a Georgia trial that I observed, for example,

> Marquis, a young black man whom the police strongly suspected of being a drug dealer, shot and killed a close friend, another young black male also believed to be in the drug business. Marquis turned himself in to the local jail on May 11, the day after the shooting, and told the authorities he was prepared to make a statement to the police. Seven months later, in mid-December, when the case came up for trial, the prosecuting attorney complained that the investigating officer had still not taken a statement from Marquis. Busy with other cases, the detective did not treat the killing of one street-level drug dealer by another as a high priority. Because of the lack of evidence, the assistant district attorney had to accept a plea of involuntary manslaughter instead of pursuing a murder conviction.

Situational unrespectability can also stigmatize a victim. A victim with no history of deviance but who was behaving improperly or illegally at the time of the killing attracts less severity. Should it turn out that, for example, the victim confronted or provoked the defendant, or that he was present at the scene to purchase, sell, or use drugs or to commit some other crime, the chance of a conviction, and especially a first-degree murder conviction, declines (Baumer, Messner, and Felson 2000).[2]

Unrespectable victims evoke more lenient punishment at the sentencing stage as well (see, e.g., Wilbanks 1984: 83–84). In capital cases, for instance, jurors will lean toward life imprisonment rather than a death sentence where they detect evidence of wrongdoing on the victim's part. Capital jurors in California, when interviewed by researchers, revealed themselves to be quite sensitive to the moral standing of victims. "Punks" and "low-lifes" was how one juror described the victims in a drug-related killing, stating that "I'll be honest with you, I guess they will be missed by their immediate family, but as far as I am concerned, society will not miss them." Another juror described an abusive victim as "a bitch," adding, "It makes me sick to even think about her," and concluded by saying that "I think she deserved what she got" (Sundby 2003: 365–66).[3]

As these juror quotations make clear, it is not just the victim's formal legal record that counts in homicide cases. Nor is it just the victim's informal reputation either. It is the combination of the two that really matters, as a pair of experimental studies illustrates (Landy and Aronson 1969). The researchers devised a scenario in which a drunk driver kills a pedestrian and is charged with negligent homicide. They systematically varied the social characteristics of the victim. Although the descriptions varied slightly across the two experiments, one victim was described in both as a "notorious" criminal who was currently under police investigation and who was carrying a loaded pistol at the time of the incident. The second victim, by contrast, was both respectable and integrated: he was said to be a successful professional man, with two children, who was "an active member of the community welfare board," and who at the time of the incident "was on his way to the Lincoln Orphanage, of which he was a founding member, with Christmas gifts." Students read one version of the case, and then sentenced the defendant to a term of years. Combining the results of the two experiments, the researchers found that, holding constant everything else about the case, sentences were, on average, 2.5 years shorter when the victim was unrespectable.

TRIAL TACTICS

Lawyers usually try to manipulate issues of status to the advantage of those they represent in court. Normative status is a particularly fertile source of legal maneuvering. Defense attorneys, for example, commonly seek to strengthen their case by elevating the respectability of their client, and lowering that of their opponent. They will attempt to exclude from the trial as much evidence of the defendant's criminal or violent history as possible. They will advise their client to dress conservatively, and to display a remorseful and repentant mien (see, e.g., Dunne 2001: 17). They will encourage clients with drug or alcohol issues to enter a treatment program in a bid to provide the judge with something positive to focus on at the trial (Comack and Balfour 2004: 83). They will often turn the spotlight on the deceased, effectively putting the victim on trial (see, e.g., Lundsgaarde 1977: 42). To that end, they will highlight any behavioral blemishes likely to lower the victim's standing in the eyes of the judge and jury, such as alcoholism, bad parenting, or a poor work record. Was the victim known to neglect his family? Was he a drug user? Skillful advocates tailor their arguments to the preferences and prejudices of the local community. In a rural county in which many people are known to frown upon homosexuality, for instance, the defendant's lawyer is unlikely to ignore a victim's lesbianism (see, e.g., Pohlman 1999). Whatever the prevailing norms, the more morally compromised the portrait the attorney can paint of the victim, the better the defendant's chances of a light sentence or even an outright acquittal. If the strategy works, the trial becomes a morality contest, in which the central issue is no longer the guilt of the accused but the respectability of the victim. The strategy is memorably summarized in an aphorism, perhaps apocryphal, attributed to a Houston attorney: "No property needs stealing but a lot of people need killing" (Lundsgaarde 1977: 42).[4] Or, more plainly still, "The sorry son of a bitch needed killing anyhow" (quoted in Neal 2006: 14).

Disparaging an opponent while lauding a client can extend to the trials of the rich and famous. Consider a case that attracted an enormous amount of attention in its day—the 1906 high-society killing of the famous architect Stanford White, in a building he had designed, New York's Madison Square Garden.

Stanford White was killed by Harry Thaw, with whose wife, Evelyn, a former showgirl, he was continuing to conduct a long-standing affair. Thaw was the heir to an enormous fortune, then controlled by his mother. Having become increasingly jealous of White's involvement with his wife, Thaw armed himself with a pistol and set out for the theater on a night that he knew White would be in the audience. During the performance, Thaw drew his gun and shot White twice in the face and once more as he lay on the floor.

Thaw was quickly arrested and charged with murder. His mother financed a press campaign to portray White as a morally depraved lecher and debaucher of young women. A string of scandalous stories about White began to appear in the newspapers. Thaw's mother also hired a team of well-known lawyers who devised a novel defense, claiming that Thaw had suffered from a new mental disorder known as "Dementia Americana," which afflicted only American males because of their belief that a man's wife is sacred. Doctors testified that the disease would cause a man whose wife was taken by another man to experience an irresistible impulse to kill his rival. Evelyn told the court of how White had pursued her for many years, taking her virginity while she was only seventeen, and enticing her with his money and blandishments.

The defense strategy of vilifying White while vindicating Thaw was successful. After a first trial resulted in a hung jury, Thaw was found not guilty by reason of insanity. (His mother then spent six years fighting a legal battle to have her son declared not insane. She eventually succeeded, whereupon Thaw was released from his asylum and quickly divorced Evelyn.) (see Scott 2005: 75–85)

RESPECTABILITY IN HISTORY

As the White-Thaw case attests, respectability has long made a difference to the outcome of homicide cases. Indeed, in many early legal systems, it was not a crime to kill a criminal (see, e.g., Dean 2001: 137).[5] Even after it became technically illegal to do so, legal decisions continued to be influenced by the moral standing of both parties. Juries in early modern England, for example, were "unwilling to convict men of good character unless the evidence was especially clear, sometime accepting quite far-fetched defences." By contrast, "men of bad character were less likely to get the benefit of any doubt" (Durston 2004: 601). Juries of the time responded to the victim's reputation as well. A jury at the Old Bailey (London's principal criminal court) acquitted Richard Thornhill in 1711 of murder, for example, after witnesses testified that the victim was "unwarrantably contentious" (Durston 2004: 65–66).

In Victorian England, "a woman who drank or was verbally abusive usually forfeited her right to protection." Thus, in one case, a man who beat his regularly drunken wife to death was sentenced to just six months' imprisonment (Conley 1991: 80). Women who lived on or close to the streets likewise received little legal protection. In several cases, minimal or no legal consequences befell the men suspected of the murder of street women, despite considerable evidence against the suspects (Conley 1991: 55–56). One trial, for instance, arose out of the slaying of

> Bridget Goodsall, a middle-aged woman who, according to the police, had "since the death of her husband, led a rather dissipated life." The police arrested two local laborers who gave contradictory statements. One of the men admitted raping her. The police surgeon said that the physical evidence showed she had suffocated while one man held her down for the other to rape her. The blood and hair of the victim were found on the clothes of the accused. . . . After hearing the evidence of ten witnesses, Justice James Willes directed the grand jury not to indict as he felt there was insufficient evidence that the men had killed her. The fact that one of the men had confessed to rape was ignored, as was the medical testimony regarding the cause of death. The case was closed. (Conley 1991: 55)

At about the same time across the sea in Ireland, tenant farmers were locked in a struggle with their Anglo-Irish landlords. Evictions were common. Those who aided and abetted evictions were extremely unpopular, and often the subject of scorn and social exclusion. (One landlord's agent—Captain Boycott—became the eponym for a powerful form of popular justice after he was collectively ostracized for attempting to eject tenants from land in County Mayo in 1880.)[6] Particular contempt was reserved for bailiffs who served eviction notices and writs for seizure of property. To be called a "bailiff" was a grave insult, and to be one could be extremely dangerous. Some were murdered in broad daylight. Their deaths evoked little sympathy among juries. In one case, "The widow of a Roscommon bailiff who was stoned to death by a crowd told the court his killers 'were a drunken clan, clamoring.' The three men arrested were all acquitted. When the jury announced it could not reach a verdict in another case in which a crowd had beaten a bailiff the judge asked, 'Is it that you think it lawful to assault a bailiff?' The foreman replied, 'Some of the jury think so, my lord'" (Conley 1999: 191).

HONOR KILLINGS

Respectability plays a central role in the handling of that distinctive type of homicide known as honor killing, committed in order to punish a grave affront to personal or familial reputation. Most homicides arise out of conflict—they punish, get even, or obtain justice from the other party (Black 1983, 2004a). But honor killings are especially moralistic, the killer executing a victim who has violated important rules of social morality. Honor, in the sense used by social scientists, is a key component of many cultures, including those of early modern European aristocrats, the antebellum South, the Mediterranean rim, and many pastoral societies (Stewart 1994; Nisbett and Cohen 1996; Cooney 1998: chap. 5). Honor typically demands a man be courageous and honest, and protective of the sexual purity of his wife and daughters (though particular cultures emphasize some of these elements more than others). If his honor is impugned, he is expected to take forceful action. His options included demanding an apology, challenging his opponent to a duel or fight, or launching peremptory aggression.

Honor cultures discount honor killings. Thus, when European aristocrats fought lethal duels over matters of honor, the killer could reasonably expect to suffer few, if any, legal consequences (McLynn 1991: 141–45). In nineteenth-century France, for example, if a dueling homicide was prosecuted, "acquittals were invariably brought in by juries" (Nye 1993: 175). As in France, formal English law drew no distinction between killing a man in a duel and premeditated murder, but convictions for manslaughter in dueling cases were rare and for murder rarer still (Andrew 1980; Simpson 1988: 121–33; Landale 2005: 222–24, 229–33). None of the five men tried for dueling deaths in Surrey between 1660 and 1800, for example, was convicted of murder, and just one was convicted of manslaughter (Beattie 1986: 98). As late as 1852, when Count Rice was accused of the murder of Viscount DuBarre in a duel, the judge recommended that the jury find him guilty only of manslaughter. But the jury, after deliberating for just several minutes, acquitted him of all charges (see Andrew 1980: 415–16).

Things were much the same in North America. Honor killings, whether committed in the course of a duel or otherwise, were invariably handled with leniency (see, e.g., Ayers 1984: 266–69). The Richmond trial of James Grant for the murder of Rives Pollard, described in chapter 1, is a clear-cut example: In printing his article that cast a slur on the Grant family name, Pollard issued a grave insult and laid himself open to a lethal response. Honor explains why two juries were prepared to give Grant the benefit of what most disinterested observers would surely see as a very improbable doubt.

Honor continues to flourish in some cultures today, especially in much of the Islamic world (see, e.g., Eck 2003). A woman who has sex outside of marriage disturbs the system of male sexual property rights and brings grave dishonor to her family. Mere social contact with an unrelated male may be an offense. Even rape may be no excuse. Once a public accusation of an illicit relationship is made against a woman, her male guardian—usually her father or husband—is morally obligated to restore his family's honor (Ginat 1997: chap. 5). He may kill the woman and her alleged paramour, or kill the woman and accept compensation from the paramour. In practice, many more women than men are killed. In Pakistan alone, several hundred honor killings of women occur each year (Amnesty International 1999b). Among the cases:

- In January 1999 a woman was set on fire by her brothers on suspicion of a relationship with a neighbor. Reportedly, the burned and naked body lay unclaimed on the street for two hours.
- In April 1998 a woman was axed to death by her son. The woman had left her family, supposedly with another man. Her family tracked her down.

- In November 1997 a man axed to death his sister, a mother of six children, who was suspected of an illicit relationship.

Despite the deliberate and violent nature of many of these killings, the perpetrators are seldom punished. The Pakistani police are unlikely to investigate (Amnesty International 1999b: 45). Even if they do, the victim's family has the choice whether to pursue a criminal case, an improbable decision for the family of the woman, since their honor has been restored, and for the family of the man, who can be offered compensation. If the case goes forward, the formal law favors the defendant. Pakistani law provides that although the death penalty is mandatory for murder, a maximum sentence of fourteen years' imprisonment can be imposed when the victim's heir is a direct descendent of the offender. Thus, when the killer is the husband, he cannot be sentenced to death if the victim bore him a child, because the child is the mother's heir (Amnesty International 1996a). If the couple is childless, or if the killing is carried out by her male relatives, the death penalty is usually avoided by a finding that the victim "provoked" the killing (Amnesty International 1999b: 47–49).

Pakistani law is by no means nonpareil in its treatment of honor killings. Other countries too handle them with similar laxity. In Jordan, for instance, the legal system is highly tolerant of men who kill their female relatives in the name of family honor. In practice, the man is usually sentenced to a few months' jail time against which his time incarcerated awaiting trial is credited: in effect, he walks (Peratis 2004: 18). In Egypt and Turkey, honor killers typically receive more lenient sentences than other homicide offenders (U.S. Department of State 2000: 2046; Eck 2003: 34–35, 67). Lebanese law allows a man who kills a wife or close female relative to receive a reduced sentenced if he can show that the victim was conducting a socially unaccepted sexual relationship (U.S. Department of State 2000: 2160). And several other North African and Middle Eastern countries have similar provisions in their law (see U.S. Department of State 2000; Fathi 2007).

THIRD PARTIES

Respectability helps to predict the related topic of third-party behavior. Partisanship and settlement alike respond to the location and direction of the case in normative space.

PARTISANS

Respectability is attractive. Third parties are drawn toward the more respectable side of a case. And the greater the contrast in respectability between the two sides, the more strongly they are drawn to the more respectable side (Black 1993: 127). Thus, the strongest partisanship is garnered by highly respectable parties opposing highly unrespectable ones.

Respectable partisans are, all else the same, more valuable than unrespectable partisans. A defendant accused of homicide supported by a witness of unquestioned character when the victim's side is supported by a witness with a lengthy criminal record has a considerable advantage, no matter what the underlying facts. Likewise, a defendant opposed by a morally impeccable witness while supported by a morally compromised one faces an uphill battle, no matter how weak the prosecution evidence otherwise is. Indeed, a case may fall apart if built on a foundation of unrespectable third parties. "When witnesses are themselves criminals," an observer of New York City detectives notes, "one sees in stark relief the central dilemma of criminal investigations. One of the street witnesses to the infamous 1991 quadruple murder in the Bronx's 40th precinct gave Detective Mark Tebbens a vivid eyewitness account and key identification of two of the several shooters. But he was useless in court because he made his living riding the trains in an ankle-length leather coat beneath which he carried a sawed-off shotgun to encourage people to part with their money" (Jackall 2005: 165–66).

Respectable parties appear better able to attract respectable partisans. Partisanship tends, therefore, to reinforce the original normative geometry. Normatively vertical cases—between parties with different levels of respectability—tend to acquire greater normative distance through the process of partisan attraction. Elevated lateral cases—between a respectable killer and victim—typically recruit respectable partisans and thereby consolidate their lofty position. And cases at low elevations of normative space—between drug dealers, gang members, or street criminals, for example—normally have fewer and more morally compromised partisans, further reducing their moral stature.

SETTLEMENT AGENTS

Most settlement agents occupy elevated regions of normative space. Jurors and, especially, judges are typically selected from the ranks of the morally unblemished. Judges are expected to set an example for others, and a reputation for probity is generally a prerequisite for the role. Rarely do former prisoners and other individuals with a record of deviance become judges, though they may sometimes sit on juries. It has long been so. In ancient Athens, those who judged homicide cases "were expected to be particularly upright and respectable citizens." Even minor transgressions—eating in a pub, laughing in the presence of the judges, writing a comedy—could disqualify a candidate for judicial office (Lanni 2006: 84).

Among respectable settlement agents, those of somewhat lower normative status are less severe (Black 1993: chap. 8). A jury composed of people with a record of misdemeanors, for example, is less likely to convict on a serious charge or recommend a harsh sentence (such as the death penalty) than a jury composed of people who have never been in trouble with the law.

Less respectable juries are not as formalistic or decisive either (Black 1993: chap. 8). A lawyer seeking to set aside the technicalities of the written law in favor of an equitable result is likely to meet with more success arguing in front of a jury of individuals with minor criminal records than one with no records at all. So too is a lawyer seeking a compromise outcome, such as a conviction on a manslaughter rather than a murder charge.

POPULAR JUSTICE

As in law, so too in popular justice. The elevation, direction, and distance of a homicide in normative space helps to predict the severity of its popular response. Compensation payments, for example, are typically lower in amount when the parties are unrespectable (see, e.g., Howell 1954: 48, 56; Miller 1990: 176). Other popular penalties display a similar sensitivity to the parties' respectability.

RESPECTABLE VICTIMS

Respectable victims attract stronger partisanship and more severe popular sanctions. Thus, self-help is triggered more often by the killing of morally upright victims than by the killing of persons tainted by a reputation for quarrelsomeness, unscrupulousness, dishonesty, cruelty, or other misconduct. A family prepared to risk an attack to avenge a respectable kinsman may be willing to accept compensation for the murder of a delinquent sibling, spouse, or child (see, e.g., Miller 1990: 203).

Communal self-help—lynching—is also more likely to follow the killing of a respectable person. For example, in the mining towns of the nineteenth-century American West, the so-called Wild West, lethal conflict was common. Most killings were casual affairs, the outcome of disputes between men intent on asserting themselves on the streets or in saloons. Frequent though killings were, they did not evoke a uniform response. When a violent man was killed, the public rarely reacted negatively; generally, the incident was shrugged off, most people feeling that the victim probably got what he deserved. "He who lives by the sword shall die by the sword" appeared to be a fairly universal sentiment. On the other hand, when a law-abiding, peaceful, respectable individual was killed, "the reaction of the citizens was immediate and came in the form of vigilantism" (McGrath 1984: 255).

UNRESPECTABLE VICTIMS

Unrespectable victims garner weaker partisanship and milder popular sanctions. In many tribal societies, the elimination of persistent deviants is accepted by the community and tolerated by the victim's relatives. Recorded instances include notorious troublemakers or those who violate ceremonial taboos (the Murngin of Australia), hotheaded warriors who embroil the clan too often in lethal conflict (the Mae Enga of New Guinea), repeat killers (the Bushmen of the Kalahari), sorcerers (the Shavante of Central Brazil), adulterers (the Albanian highlanders), and persistent nuisances (the Berbers of the Atlas Mountains) (Warner 1958: 162; Meggitt 1977: 79; Lee 1979: 392–95; Maybury-Lewis 1974: 186–87; Hasluck 1954: 212; Gellner 1969: 116–17).

In modern societies too, the killing of criminals, drug dealers, wife beaters, bullies, and other unrespectables continues to attract fewer and more lenient popular sanctions. Indeed, the killer's actions may be a cause for rejoicing. When Bernhard Goetz, a thirty-seven-year-old man, shot four teenagers on the New York subway in December 1984 who, he claimed, were about to rob him, he became an instant celebrity (Rubin 1986; G. Fletcher 1988). None of the victims died, though one almost did and was paralyzed for life. Goetz's shooting came after a period of high crime rates in New York in general and on its subways in particular, and was widely praised. He was lauded in the press, acclaimed when he appeared in public, and supported by a clear majority of New Yorkers in opinion polls. Many people regarded him as a hero. Signs proclaiming "God Bless You, Bernie" sprung up around the city.

Race and social class partly explain the praise lavished on Goetz. Goetz was white, educated, self-employed, middle-class; his victims were black, high school dropouts, unemployed, welfare-class. However, it was the moral standing of the parties, actual and attributed, that was the crucial factor in the popular reaction. Goetz had no criminal record, but his victims had all been arrested, and three had convictions. He became the champion of the law-abiding citizenry fed up with being victimized by predatory criminals. Although his blamelessness was diminished when it emerged that he had shot at the paralyzed victim a second time after standing over him and saying, "You seem to be [doing] all right; here's another," and although he went on to be convicted of criminal possession of a weapon, Goetz was acquitted by a New York City jury of several more serious charges, including attempted murder, and he remained a popular figure in the city and indeed throughout the country.

Killings may evoke similarly positive responses in lower-income communities when the victims are morally objectionable. In one incident in New York, "a raucous street party celebrating the death(s)" broke out in Harlem when two sixteen-year-olds, widely feared as violent bullies, were gunned down (Jackall 1997: 110). In a case that occurred among the Latino community of Chicago, "a gang member shot and killed his father after finding him a number of times with several different young girls. Not only did the father publicly flaunt his infidelities, but he was often out of work and did not support his family well. There was considerable support for the son's actions within the community and his mother fought for his release" (Horowitz 1987: 443).

Even the police may praise killers. In a New York City case, for example, a researcher recalls what happened when the detectives he was observing were called to the scene of a shooting at a bank:

> When the squad and I arrived, the uniformed police officers were cracking jokes and laughing loudly, while standing over the bullet-torn, bleeding body of the victim. The shooter, who was not in custody, was chatting amiably with the officers. Handing over his gun and his carry-permit, he explained that he owned a local business and had tailed his employee, who was carrying $30,000 cash receipts for deposit at the bank. As the employee started to enter the bank, the "victim" tried to rob him at gunpoint. The businessman said that he came up behind the robber, told him to stop, and then, when the robber turned around with a gun pointed at the owner, shot the robber in the shoulder. The "victim" turned out to be a career robber wanted for several similar heists. The detectives took the shooter back to the station house to record his statement and then congratulated him for his good citizenship. (Jackall 2005: 201–2)

Police may be the objects of criticism as well as the sources of praise. Many third world nations have high crime rates and an inefficient and sometimes corrupt legal system, a combination apt to arouse strong sentiments against dishonest police officers. In one incident, a venal officer was killed in a samba club in a Brazilian *favela* (squatter settlement). Several men stepped forward to urinate on his face. "He was a much hated figure, and there was a great sense of relief . . . after his death" (Goldstein 2003: 184).

HONOR KILLINGS

The popular response to honor killings starkly illustrate the power of differential respectability. Individuals who commit murder in the name of honor often experience a surge of social esteem (see, e.g., Gilsenan 1976: 201; Lindholm 1982: 76–77). Recall how James Grant was feted by the denizens of Richmond after being charged with killing Rives Pollard. That reaction is not unique. People frequently treat honor killers not as lawbreakers but as upholders of the moral order. Family members, friends, neighbors, and bystanders applaud the stern action they have taken to remove the taint on the family name. Individuals previously estranged from their families may find themselves back in the fold, once again cherished (see, e.g., Eck 2003: 56–58). Should they be sent to prison, they will be treated with respect by the other prisoners. In short, these perpetrators "are not seen as having committed any kind of crime, but are considered "men" who have fulfilled their duty and are thus entitled to admiration" (Ginat 1997: 16). "Honoring the Killers" is the apt title of a human rights report on such killings in Jordan (Peratis 2004.)

Victims of honor killings, by contrast, attract very little sympathy. Even the other members of the family tend to support the harsh action. A Pakistani mother whose daughter and her alleged paramour had been killed told a journalist, "There is no grief in *ghariat* [honor], it was right to kill them." Indeed, the mother was more concerned about her three sons who had been arrested for the homicide. In another case, an eighteen-year-old woman and her alleged paramour were killed by her brothers and brothers-in-law. The woman's mother-in-law stated, "I have been robbed, my honor has been robbed, I have been violated. This was a zulm [injustice] against me. So we axed her." These sentiments are not confined to benighted rural areas. In a case that became widely known, a woman seeking a divorce was killed by her family in April 1999 in the office of her lawyer in the city of Lahore. A witness reported the victim's mother as being "cool and collected during the getaway, walking away from the murder of her daughter as though the woman slumped in her own blood was a stranger" (see Amnesty International 1999b: 6–7).

A case among the Israeli Arabs reveals the contrasting reputation that attaches to those who kill and are killed in the name of honor:

> A father discovered that his unmarried daughter had a sexual relationship with a man, and killed her. The father confessed his crime to the police. Not knowing this, the man's son (the girl's brother) made a false confession to the police, seeking to spare

> his father the ordeal of imprisonment. Both men were convicted and sentenced to life imprisonment. After serving ten years, the father was released on humanitarian grounds. To help get the son released, an anthropologist proposed to make a television program highlighting his innocence. However, the prisoner's brother initially objected to the proposed program. He was about to marry a woman from a higher-status family, and was concerned that after the program aired her family might refuse the marriage—not because they would learn that his father and brother had served time for murder, but because his sister had been a "prostitute." (see Ginat 1997: 86–87)

Remarkably, even the victims themselves sometimes refuse to criticize their killers: "'He shouldn't have let me live,' said Roweida, 17, who was shot three times by her father after she confessed to an adulterous affair, and, along with dozens of girls with similar stories, is being held for her own protection in a Jordanian prison. 'A girl who commits a sin deserves to die'" (Jehl 1999, quoted in Levy 2002: 184).

LAW AND POPULAR JUSTICE

Popular justice plays an important role in homicide cases for a second reason: it helps to explain the severity of legal sanctions. Black (1976: 107) proposes that law varies inversely with other social control. Where popular justice is strong, law ought therefore to be weak. And indeed, self-help tends to be most frequent and severe where law is absent or unavailable (though law's absence does not guarantee self-help) (Black 1983). Conversely, where popular justice is weak, law ought to be strong. This would explain why the role of popular justice has receded as law has expanded its jurisdiction over the centuries. Consequently, popular sanctions today are generally light (shunning, toleration), with most people leaving it to the law to sanction those who perpetrate homicide.

Law tends to respect nonlegal authority. Among groups with internal procedures and penalties for handling wrongdoing—doctors, priests, and police, for example—legal sanctions are less common and less severe than usual. Moreover, killings of those in position of authority, such as heads of families, are often punished with considerable severity. It has always been so. In Sung Dynasty China (960–1279), for instance, killings by subordinates of their superiors attracted more law than killings by superiors of their subordinates (McKnight 1992: 100).

Subordinates who kill persons other than their superior, however, tend to be treated more leniently. Dependents—those subject to the control or authority of others—evoke greater legal protection than independent individuals. Thus, homicides committed by dependents attract less severity, while those committed against them attract more. Consider several applications of this principle.

THE YOUNG AND THE ELDERLY

In many societies, the young and the elderly are dependent on others to one degree or another. The dependency of the young is evident in the authority that parents, schoolteachers, and others exercise over them. The dependency of the elderly is rooted in their reduced ability to provide and care for themselves. Hence, while age, like race and gender, is not in itself a sociological variable, its strong correlation with social conditions, including dependency, ensures that it systematically affects the handling of cases.

Perhaps because it lacks the political resonance of sex or race, age attracts less scholarly attention as a predictor of legal outcomes. Even so, age effects have been reported in a number of modern studies of homicide, and they indicate that very young and elderly victims enjoy high degrees of legal support. In Texas, defendants convicted of murdering victims under the age of twenty-two faced an elevated risk of getting the death penalty in the years 1942–71. Similarly, in the period 1974–88, a Texas defendant convicted of capital murder was more likely to receive a death sentence if the victim was under twenty-one years of age (Marquart, Ekland-Olson, and Sorensen 1994: 87–88, 173). A California study of first-degree murder trials found that people who killed victims under twenty-one or over sixty had an increased risk of being sentenced to death (Judson et al. 1969: 1394–95, 1485–87). Two studies of Georgia capital sentencing found that killing a child under the age of thirteen raised the defendant's odds of a death sentence, other factors held constant, by a factor of 10 and 4.8 respectively (Baldus, Woodworth, and Pulaski 1990: 588, 319).[7]

The law also handles young killers more leniently. In the United States, the 2005 decision of the United States Supreme Court in *Roper v. Simons* prohibited the execution of anybody under eighteen years of age on constitutional grounds. But for many years previously, individuals accused of homicide who were less than fifteen years of age were virtually never sentenced to death (Gross and Mauro 1984: 41, note 10). Older teenagers and young adults enjoyed less, though still some, immunity from the death penalty. In Florida, 1973–77, among persons indicted for first-degree murder, defendants aged eighteen or younger were less likely to be convicted of first-degree murder (and hence less likely to get the death penalty) (Bowers 1983: 1079). In Georgia before, though not after, the Supreme Court decision in *Furman v. Georgia* (1972), the younger the defendant, the less likely he or she was to get the death penalty (Baldus, Woodworth, and Pulaski 1990: 600). In Texas, 1974–88, individuals convicted of capital murder between the ages of seventeen and twenty-four had a lower probability of being sentenced to death than those over twenty-five (Marquart, Ekland-Olson, and Sorensen 1994: 173). In Ohio too, offenders under twenty-five were less likely to be sentenced to death in the period 1981–97 (Holcomb, Williams, and Demuth 2004).

WOMEN

Many cultures concentrate personal and household authority in the hands of adult men. When they do, men are the rulers, and women and children, their subjects: men decide what is right and wrong, give orders, and impose punishments. Like children, dependent women attract less law.

Dependency can be measured by a woman's source of support. Women who rely on their husbands or others for material necessities are more beholden and subservient than women who support themselves financially (Black 1980: 124–28). Courts handle economically dependent women less severely than women who are self-supporting (Krutschnitt 1982). A homicide committed by a dependent woman is therefore less serious than one committed by an independent woman.

In America today, female dependency varies across racial and ethnic groups. Latina and white women, as Black (1980: 124–28) observes, are more often involved in traditional marriages in which the man is the primary and often the sole breadwinner. By contrast, lower-income black women commonly head their own households and are relatively independent of the men in their lives. Whereas white women receive more lenient sentences for the same offense than white men, black women appear to attract the same sentences as white men (Spohn, Welch, and Gruhl 1985). This differential is not likely to disappear any time soon. Census data show that rates of marriage among black women continue to decline: between 1990 and 2005, the percentage of black women aged eighteen and older who had never been married increased from 33 percent to 40 percent. By contrast, in 2005 only 19 percent of white women had never been married (U.S. Census Bureau 2006: 50). Lower rates of marriage imply that black women are more independent than ever.

The killing of a dependent is more serious as well. White female victims attract more protection than other victims. Those accused of killing white women run a somewhat greater risk of being sentenced to death than those accused of killing black women, black men, or white men (Holcomb, Williams, and Demuth 2004; Williams, Demuth, and Holcomb 2007; compare Stauffer et al. 2006).[8]

Good and evil, right and wrong, morality and immorality—these are the stuff of myths, the tales we tell our children, the movies we watch, and the books we read. Even as we have come to accept that right and wrong vary from culture to culture, their eternal struggle continues to fascinate and entertain us.

"Social control" is the term Blackian sociologists give this normative dimension of social space. Two aspects of normative space, Blackian theory proposes, explain the handling of homicide. The research literature confirms both effects. Individuals who are subject to the authority or control of others, such as women and children in many societies, attract less law as offenders and more law as victims. Individuals who have acquired a reputation for deviance—who have been subject to social control—occupy a lower elevation in normative space and the sanctions they attract vary accordingly. In diverse parts of the world, at diverse times, unrespectability operates to confer legal and popular disadvantages on those who kill, and advantages on those who kill victims so tainted. Join the two normative variables, and the effects are all the stronger. The killing of a respectable dependent by an unrespectable independent is among the most heinous of all homicides. Conversely, the killing of an unrespectable independent by a respectable dependent is among the most understandable and forgivable. It may even be commendable. The same can be said of certain killings in the cultural dimension of social space, as the next chapter makes clear.

7 THE CULTURAL DIMENSION

Around the year 1317—the exact date is unknown—the king of the Irish province of Ulster, Donal O'Neill, composed a remonstrance, or formal letter of complaint, to Pope John XXII. Writing on behalf of the chiefs and people of Ireland, O'Neill complained of the cruel and unjust manner in which the English were ruling his land (Duffy 1998: 480). Among his grievances was that no Englishman "is punished for the murder of an Irishman, even the most eminent." "The English of Ireland," the complaint continued, "differ so widely in their principles of morality from those of England and all other nations that they may be called a nation of the most extreme degree of perfidy. Lay and cleric, they assert it is no more sin to kill an Irishman that it is to kill a dog" (quoted in Curtis 1938: 192).

The king's lament is a familiar one in human history—two ways of life, two standards of morality. For dividing the English and the Irish at the time was a litany of civilizational contrasts. Each nation had its own language, music, history, traditions, folklore, etiquette, and entertainments.[1] Sociologists call this dimension of social life culture, and it profoundly affects the morality of killing.

CULTURAL GEOMETRY

Culture "is the symbolic aspect of social life" (Black 1976: 61). A quantitative dimension of social space, culture includes all forms of individual and collective expression, such as language, religion, art, folklore, and science. Culture varies in several ways, including its frequency or conventionality. In America today, English is a more conventional language than Spanish, Christianity a more conventional religion than Buddhism, and a business suit more conventional male attire than a loin cloth.

Conventionality is an elevated location in social space, a form of social status. Hence, Blackian theory holds that the familiar fourfold status effect applies: homicide is more serious in a direction toward more conventionality than toward less conventionality; in a direction toward more conventionality, seriousness increases with cultural distance; in a direction toward less conventionality, seriousness decreases with cultural distance; and seriousness increases with the conventionality of both parties.[2]

Cultures can be more or less distant from one another, quite apart from their conventionality. Even when all religions are numerically equal, Protestantism and Catholicism are less distant than Protestantism and Islam—they have more beliefs and practices in common. Similarly, as languages, French and Italian are less distant than French and Korean—their vocabulary and syntax are more similar. Black (1976: 74) proposes that the relationship between law and cultural distance is curvilinear: little law is found between culturally close disputants and between those who are so distant as to live in different social worlds; between these extremes, greater cultural distance increases law. Within modern societies, the last part of the curve can generally be ignored and the proposition simplified: law increase with cultural distance.

Conventionality and cultural distance, then, overlap to some degree.[3] Nonetheless, the concepts are separate, as cultural distance does not necessarily imply unconventionality. Both help to explain the handling of homicide.

LAW

Conventionality manifests itself in many ways—in how people think, dress, and speak, in what they say, believe, and worship. Blending in with the crowd, however constituted, is generally an advantage in legal disputes. In modern Western nations, such as the United States, it is more serious to kill a house-dweller than a tent-dweller, a beauty queen than a drag queen, a bourgeois than a bohemian. Elsewhere, the killing of members of majority groups likewise triggers greater penalties. For instance, in Islamic countries, such as Saudi Arabia, the killing of a Muslim generates more punishment and compensation than the killing of a non-Muslim (U.S. Department of State 2006).

Racial and ethnic groups commonly have distinctive cultures, and their members may be legally advantaged or disadvantaged, depending in part on the group's frequency in the population. Frontiers provide many examples.

FRONTIERS

Frontiers serve as natural laboratories for the study of the effects of cultural differences and particularly majority-minority relations. The commingling of disparate languages, attire, beliefs, and traditions increases the potential for conflict if only because of the heightened potential for misunderstanding (see, e.g., Reid 1999). Perhaps the most renowned frontier is the nineteenth-century American West (Hines and Faragher 2000). Hundreds of books, articles, and movies have been made about the "Wild West," creating a popular image of a vast, sparsely populated land into which came outlaws, gunslingers, cattle rustlers, and heroic sheriffs often locked in combat with each other and with their common enemy, the Indian. Much in that image is exaggerated and wrong. The West, like all frontiers, was a place where people cooperated and helped one another, displayed remarkable degrees of trust and honesty, and formed rudimentary but strong civic organizations. In many ways, the most striking feature of the West was how so many people coming together so rapidly from so many different backgrounds coexisted so peaceably (Hollon 1974: chap. 10).

Yet there is no denying that there was violence, and that much of it was intercultural. Feuds, lynchings, vigilantism, and gunfights across racial and ethnic lines were part of the social landscape (see, e.g., Gard 1949). Here again, though, the popular image requires modification (see, e.g., Rosa 1969). Indians were involved in violent conflict with white settlers, but they were by no means the only group. Mexicans, Asians, and, to a lesser extent, blacks fought with whites and with each other.

Little law operated on the frontier itself. All justice was popular. But law followed close behind, in the frontier's wake. As camps and towns, farms and businesses, families and schools took root, legal officials increasingly intervened in conflicts. The system of justice they built strongly favored their own kind. Killings of whites by members of other ethnic groups were treated as considerably more serious than killings of members of other ethnic groups by whites.

One group consistently at the receiving end was the Chinese, who were often in competition with whites for scarce jobs. A stark example occurred in 1885 at Rock Springs, Wyoming Territory, when some fifty Chinese miners were killed. Not a single person was indicted. This was not an isolated incident: "A few days after the attack at Rock Springs, a group of white men attacked and killed several Chinese hop pickers asleep in their tents in Washington Territory. Several men were arrested and brought to trial, but nobody was convicted" (Hollon 1974: 95–100, 101–2).

There were comparatively few African Americans in the West, and they were said to have "enjoyed a surprising degree of equality and prestige on the frontier" (Hollon 1974: 209). Even so, when push came to shove, the legal system did not always treat their murder as being of any great moment. For example, "A New Mexican rancher employed three black cowboys after the Civil War. One Christmas Day, after a few drinks, one of the blacks 'got out of line' and was killed by several of the other cowboys. The rancher ordered the victim buried. A few months later, one of the other blacks 'talked back' to a white cow puncher. Both men went for their guns but the black was killed before he could get off a shot. He too was buried on the property. Neither death resulted in an indictment" (Hollon 1974: 184–85).

Despite such instances, it is true that the most extreme examples of the toleration of homicide come from white-Indian conflict. The whites who came and settled in the West were worlds apart from the Indians whose hunting grounds they entered and eventually appropriated. White and Indian cultures were barely intelligible to one another, separated as they were by customs and values, languages and worldviews. While the two groups were often initially friendly, relations deteriorated over time. To many whites, Indians seemed impossibly alien, less like humans than animals—only more dangerous. To many Indians, whites increasingly appeared to be land-hungry predators who could only be trusted to do one thing—break their promises.

In the early days with plenty of land available, the two sides were able stay out of one another's way when disputes arose. If they happened to be thrown together, they could usually negotiate a solution. But as whites continued to encroach, and Indians began to run out of places to go, conflicts grew more violent (Campbell 2008: 22–23).

Some Indians took matters into their own hands, tormenting the white settlers by raiding their horses, destroying their crops, or attacking them in person. Whites began to respond in kind, striking at settlements, sometimes even before they themselves were attacked, and hunting Indians indiscriminately as though they were wildlife. When they did, even mass slaughter had few legal repercussions, as an Arizona incident illustrates:

> In April, 1871, after a group of Pinal Apaches from the mountains had killed a white man and driven off four horses and six head of cattle, Tucson citizens decided to wipe out a camp of peaceful Aravaipa Apaches who had not been involved in the raid. Six white volunteers and forty-eight Mexicans were issued guns and ammunition by the Adjudant General of Arizona and were joined by ninety-two Papago Indians, enemies of the Apaches, armed with clubs. The 146 raiders attacked the Aravaipa village before daybreak and butchered 118 Aravaipas, 110 of them women and children. They carried off as captives 27 children. After President Ulysses S. Grant threatened to place Arizona under martial law, the leaders of the raid were tried but were promptly acquitted by a local jury. (Gard 1949: 13–14)

Entire tribes were eliminated. A particularly well-documented case is the deliberate extermination of the Yahi, a group of California hill foragers, by white settlers. So successful was the campaign to rid the land of these people that in slightly more than twenty years, the Yahi dwindled in number from over two thousand to less than fifty, even though they were in hiding for much of that time (Kroeber 1961: 15, 42–43). Many of the homicides occurred in raids in which the Indians were tracked (sometimes with dogs), ambushed, fired upon, and slaughtered (Kroeber 1961: 79–85). No matter how violent or premeditated these attacks, they attracted little or no law.

Leniency sometimes went beyond toleration to actual praise. Killing Indians could be rewarding. Connecticut and Massachusetts offered bounties for Indian scalps in the early eighteenth century; later, other jurisdictions, such as Pennsylvania, Virginia, and Indiana, did likewise (Gard 1949: 8–9). The practice spread eventually to California (Campbell 2006). In 1859, for example, the California state legislature commissioned Walter E. Jarboe to hunt and kill Yuki Indians who had attacked white livestock and, later, settlers in the Round Valley region where the Yuki had formerly hunted and fished. Five months later, Jarboe reported that he had successfully completed his mission, killing 283 warriors and taking 292 prisoners, whereupon the legislature gratefully awarded him over $9,300 (Madley 2004: 176–81).

When Indians killed whites, the response was conspicuously different. After the bloody Sioux rebellion in Minnesota of 1862, the United States government permanently confiscated the tribe's land. A military court sentenced 307 Indians to death. Many of the trials lasted no more than five minutes. According to one historian, "Many of those judged guilty were convicted on the basis of flimsy or questionable evidence, and most of those sentenced to death were condemned for merely being present at . . . battles" (Shultz 1992: 249). Thirty-eight Sioux were executed in the largest mass execution in the history of the United States. The punishment did not end there. Three years later, the army caught up with two more Indian chiefs who had previously eluded them. The army tried and sentenced the Indians to death for their involvement in the uprising. The day before the men were to be hanged, a local newspaper opined that "no serious injustice will be done by the execution tomorrow, but it would have been more creditable if some tangible evidence of their guilt had been obtained . . . No white man, tried before a jury of his peers, would be executed upon the testimony thus produced" (quoted in Schultz 1992: 276).

THE POST-FRONTIER WEST

The closing of the frontier did not end the legal disparities between whites and Indians. As long as wide expanses of cultural distance separated whites and Indians, legal differentials would continue to flourish. A study of Gila County, Arizona, found that four whites were indicted for killing Apaches in the years 1890–1920. Charges were dropped against three; only the fourth was convicted (McKanna 1997: 146–47). During the same period, ten Apache defendants were indicted for murdering white victims. All ten were convicted. Moreover, the evidence did not have to be clear-cut to convict when an Apache was accused of murdering a white, as in one case in 1890:

> The body of Edwin Baker, a white rancher, was discovered at his home by a neighbor. The body had a bullet wound and the head was partly severed from the trunk. Investigators discovered moccasin tracks near the body. Prosecutors charged four Indians who had been seen in the region on the day of the murder with the crime: Guadalupe, his two sons, Batdish and Nattsin, and Backelcle.
>
> On appeal from the conviction, the defendants' attorneys vigorously attacked the case against their clients. They produced testimony from a respected scout and another rancher that made it difficult to place the defendants at the scene of the crime; the rancher had spent time in the defendants' camp after the killing had occurred and noticed nothing unusual about the defendants; and none of the victim's property had turned up in the defendants' possession. Nonetheless, the conviction was upheld and the defendants were sentenced to life imprisonment. (see McKanna 1997: 140–42; see also 2005: chap. 4)

A study of homicide cases in seven nineteenth-century California counties (1850–1900) revealed similar patterns. While officials displayed considerable clemency toward whites who killed Indians, they were much less forgiving of Indians who killed whites. Of the thirty-five whites accused of killing Indians, only four were indicted and just one convicted. Of the thirty-nine Indians accused of killing whites, eight were sentenced to death and five to life imprisonment (McKanna 2002: 29–31, 93).

The white-Indian disparities were part of a broader set of cultural disparities that resulted in "two standards of justice, one for whites and another for minorities." A Hispanic indicted for killing a white, for example, was twice as likely to be convicted as a white indicted for killing a Hispanic. Sixteen minority defendants were sentenced to death for killing whites; not a single white was sentenced to death for killing a minority, although forty-six whites were sentenced to death for killing other whites (McKanna 2002: 2, 71, 95, 98–99).[4]

These patterns are not peculiar to the American West but are characteristic of frontiers in other eras and locations (McKanna 2005: 1–18). Earlier, in Puritan Massachusetts, "colonial authorities considered killing of whites by Indians or Negroes . . . to be a more serious offense than all other murders" (Kawashima 1986: 151). In colonial Canada, Indians who killed whites were generally punished swiftly and severely, while whites who killed Indians attracted considerably more tolerant treatment (see, e.g., Harring 1998: 112, 197–202, 245–50). And in nineteenth-century Australia, while harsh penalties were the norm for Aborigines arrested for killing white settlers, whites accused of killing Aborigines were rarely punished. Behind these statistics lies a characteristically cavalier approach to questions of guilt or innocence in frontier justice, well illustrated by the Australian case of 1842 in which three white men were tried for the murder of three Aborigine women and one child. As the judge began his summary of the case, he was interrupted by the jury foreman, who announced that the jury had already reached their verdict: not guilty (S. Davies 1990: 112).

Today, many countries have a mix of ethnically diverse tribes and groups, a blend of cultural minorities speaking their own language, worshiping their own gods, and following their own customs. Majority-minority differentials are only one part of a larger series of differentials between minority groups themselves. Cultural distance is therefore likely to play an important role in the handling of cases. Surprisingly, though, few social scientists have systematically investigated who brings and who wins legal conflicts under these conditions.[5] Culture remains the least explored dimension of social space. There is, however, one major exception: race in the United States.

RACE MATTERS

Race as such is not a sociological variable. The term "race" does not refer to social attributes, but physical ones—skin color, hair texture, and the like. However, when those physical differences are systematically correlated with social attributes, race acquires sociological relevance. Such is the case in the United States. The typical black American possesses considerably less economic status than the typical white American. But economic status alone cannot explain the differential treatment of blacks and whites. For instance, the probability of a death sentence in Georgia is influenced by the status of the defendant, the status of the victim, *and* the race of the victim (Baldus, Woodworth, and Pulaksi 1990: 157–60, 588–91). Even wealthy blacks may be somewhat disadvantaged. Pure sociology explains these additional effects with culture.[6]

The cultures of blacks and whites, especially those of low social status, differ in several important ways. Ebonics (sometimes known as African American Vernacular English), soul food, jazz, blues, hip-hop, black churches, and black history month all indicate enduring cultural differences between American blacks and whites (see, e.g., Kochman 1981; see also Lamont 1999). Moreover, since blacks are the minority culture, they are less conventional than whites. Minority status (coupled with low economic status) results in differential treatment of blacks in many walks of life, including law.[7]

Black-white disparities have long been a feature of American justice.[8] In Omaha, Nebraska, for instance, from 1880 to 1920, blacks who killed whites were convicted 90 percent of the time; whites who killed blacks, by contrast, were convicted about 40 percent of the time (McKanna 1997: 68). In Alabama, 1929–85, the severity of sentences handed out to women convicted of homicide varied with their race and that of the victim (Hanke 1995). For example, the percentage of cases receiving the most severe sentence imposed—life imprisonment—was as follows: black-white, 50 percent; white-white, 18 percent; black-black, 7 percent; white-black, 0 percent.[9]

Differentials of this sort extend into more modern times. In Philadelphia during 1970, adult blacks convicted of felony murder were sentenced to one of the two most punitive punishments—life imprisonment or death—in 65 percent of cases with white victims, but in only 25 percent of cases with black victims (Zimring et al. 1976; see also Wilbanks 1984: 99–100). For black youths, the differences were even more marked: when the victim was white, 59 percent of convicted defendants were sentenced to life or death; when the victim was black, a mere 2 percent of defendants received the extreme sentences of life imprisonment or death. Another study of an unnamed northeastern city found that killers of whites were convicted of more serious forms of homicide than killers of blacks, holding constant the sex and occupation of the parties (Farrell and Swigert 1986).

The most extensive study looked at over one thousand first-degree homicide cases adjudicated in 1988 in the nation's largest urban counties. The authors found that, after adjusting for several other factors, including the prior relationship between the parties, white offenders and, in cases that went to trial, killers of black victims were more likely than black offenders and killers of white victims to escape conviction altogether (Beaulieu and Messner 1999; see also Baumer et al. 2000: 298–99). Even after factoring out other effects, then, race continues to influence the handling of American homicide cases, a conclusion buttressed by the large body of research conducted on the death penalty.

RACE AND THE DEATH PENALTY

Systematic evidence of racial differences in the death penalty extends back into the first half of the twentieth century. The first rigorous study drew on data from counties in North Carolina, Virginia, and Georgia in the years 1930–40 to show that a black who killed a white was more likely to be convicted, sentenced to death, and actually executed than a black who killed a black (Johnson 1941). Some years later, another researcher expanded the North Carolina sample from five to ten counties (Garfinkel 1949). He reported that, given an indictment for homicide, black defendant–white victim cases were four times more likely to receive the death penalty than white defendant–white victim cases, and eight times more likely than black defendant–black victim cases. (None of the sixteen whites indicted for killing blacks were sentenced to death [1949: 371, table 3]).[10]

After a lull of some years, research on race and the death penalty picked up momentum in the 1970s and '80s. The spur for the research was the 1972 decision of the United States Supreme Court in *Furman v. Georgia,* 408 U.S. 238, holding that all existing death penalty statutes were unconstitutional. The majority justices gave different reasons for their decision, but a common theme was that because the statutes gave the sentencer (usually the jury) unrestricted discretion, they allowed the death penalty to be imposed in an arbitrary manner. Subsequently, many states drafted new statutes restricting the sentencer's discretion. In *Gregg v. Georgia,* 428 U.S. 153 (1976), and related cases, the Supreme Court upheld the constitutionality of "guided discretion" statutes, which set out explicit aggravating and/or mitigating standards to be followed in imposing the death penalty and provided for automatic review of all death sentences by an appeal court. Common aggravating circumstances, for example, were the killing of a police officer or committing a vile murder. The court reasoned that by directing the decision maker to consider these legislatively determined factors, the statutes eliminated the risk that the death penalty would be imposed on arbitrary grounds, such as race, and that any anomalies would, in any event, be rectified by the automatic appeal process.

Despite the safeguards introduced by the new state laws, extensive research confirms that race continues to influence who attracts and who avoids the death penalty (see, e.g., Paternoster 1991: chap. 4).[11] Consistent with Blackian theory's predictions, the victim's race is a more powerful predictor than the defendant's (see, e.g., Bowers and Pierce 1980). Thus, grand juries in Florida are more likely to bring indictments for first-degree murder in stranger homicides when the case involves a white victim, and because of that, those cases eventually result in a death sentence more often than cases with black victims (Radelet 1981; see also Bowers 1983). Prosecutors in several jurisdictions, including North and South Carolina, Kentucky, New Jersey, and Texas, seek the death penalty more often in white-victim than in black-victim cases (Nakell and Hardy 1984; Paternoster 1984; Keil and Vito 1990; Bienen et al. 1988; Marquart, Ekland-Olson, and Sorensen 1994; Phillips 2008; see also Radelet and Pierce 1985, Sorensen and Wallace 1999). Likewise, juries in Georgia and judges in Florida (acting on jury recommendations) impose the death sentence more often when the victim is white (Baldus, Woodworth, and Pulaksi 1990; Bowers 1983; Foley and Powell 1982). Together, these and other studies in different, albeit mostly southern, states point to a simple conclusion: killers of whites are more likely to be sentenced to death than killers of blacks (Gross and Mauro 1989; see also Zeisel 1981; Murphy 1984; Nakell and Hardy 1987; Smith 1987; Keil and Vito 1989; but see Judson et al. 1969: 1368–76; Arkin 1981).

A strength of these post-*Furman* studies is their methodological rigor. The earlier research, while suggestive, had not taken into consideration other factors that might explain the racial disparities. If, for instance, more black-white murders are committed in the course of a felony, such as a robbery, they would attract the death penalty more often because of their greater legal seriousness, and not because of the race of the parties. The post-*Gregg* studies allow this issue to be resolved because they use large samples and they control or adjust for the nature of the homicide as well as many other variables, such as the number of victims and the age, gender, and criminal record of the parties. The two most elaborate studies conducted to date come from Georgia. Although the studies partly overlap, they are separate—and large: the first analyzes 750 murder convictions from 1969 to 1979 and includes more than 150 variables; the second study examines 1,066 people indicted for murder and convicted of murder or manslaughter, 1973–79, and embraces over 230 variables (Baldus, Woodworth, and Pulaksi 1990: 42–46). The studies reach virtually identical conclusions and confirm what researchers have found in other states: holding constant a large number of factors, killing a white bring an increased risk of the death penalty. Racial disparities are greater at the prosecutorial than the jury stage, but the combined effect of the decisions at both stages is that the defendant's chances of receiving a death sentence are higher when the victim is white, holding constant the nature of the killing and a host of other variables.[12]

The Georgia research was included in a federal constitutional lawsuit brought to invalidate the death penalty. The case—*McCleskey v. Kemp*, 481 U.S. 279 (1987)—went up to the Supreme Court, which held that a statistical study showing racial differentials in death sentencing was, in itself, not sufficient to show that the defendant had been discriminated against on grounds of race, and hence was constitutionally irrelevant.

After *McCleskey*, the pace of research slowed but did not halt. Several later studies confirm and extend the existence of racial differentials (see Pierce and Radelet 2002). Research in Illinois and Maryland, for example, continued to find the familiar racial disparities in death penalty cases (Pierce and Radelet 2002; Paternoster et al. 2003).

THE DEFENDANT'S RACE

Although the impact of the victims' race is generally greater, many studies show a race-of-defendant effect as well. A study of capital murder cases in Philadelphia, 1983–93 found, for example, that "the average black defendant's probability of receiving a death sentence is 14 percentage points higher than a similarly situated nonblack defendant" (Baldus et al. 1998: 1726). A review of twenty-eight studies of racial disparities in the death penalty conducted by the U.S. General Accounting Office (GAO) found that more than half of the studies report a race-of-defendant effect and that more than three-fourths of those found that black defendants were more likely to receive the death penalty (Dodge 1990: 6; see also Baldus and Woodworth 2003). Thus, independent of the race of the victim, black defendants are often, though not invariably, more likely to be sentenced to death than their white counterparts (compare McAdams 1998).

The more subtle nature of race-of-defendant effect is well illustrated by a study conducted in Houston, aptly termed the "capital of capital punishment" because it sends more defendants to their death than any other jurisdiction in America. The study examined all 504 capital murder cases filed against adult defendants in Houston (Harris County), 1992–99. When the author first analyzed the data, he found no correlation between the defendant's race and the death penalty: approximately the same percentage of blacks and whites were sentenced to death. However, once he adjusted for other factors, the author found that black defendants typically commit murders that result less often in a death sentence—for example, they are less likely to kill whites, women, or elderly people. The fact that blacks and whites receive the death sentence at the same rate means in effect that the bar for sentencing a black defendant to death is lower than for a white defendant (Phillips 2008a).

Finally, what about executions? Only 5 percent of persons sentenced to death in America are put to death (Liebman, Fagan, and West 2000). But here again, race matters. In a study of sixteen states over thirty years (1972–2002), blacks who killed whites were significantly more likely, adjusting for several factors, to be executed than other capital defendants (Jacobs et al. 2007).[13]

To summarize: A strong line of research establishes that the death penalty in America is imposed in a racially unequal, though not racially arbitrary, manner. For the same homicide, blacks who kill whites are consistently most likely to receive the death penalty, followed, in order, by whites who kill whites, blacks who kill blacks, and, finally, whites who kill blacks.

THIRD PARTIES

Culture also explains the behavior of third parties. Whether and how partisans and settlement agents intervene in cases is influenced by their cultural geometry. The evidence is particularly strong for settlement. But, first, consider partisanship.

PARTISANS

Conventional parties are more attractive than unconventional parties. Third parties side more often and more strongly with conventional killers and victims. Black's principle of relative status applies: the greater the contrast in conventionality between the two sides, the greater the contrast in the amount of partisanship the more conventional side attracts (1993: 127).

Conventional partisans are more valuable. In North America the testimony of a white is, all else equal, more credible than that of a black (see, e.g., Comack and Balfour 2004: 84). Conventional partisans are harder to attract, however, particularly for unconventional parties.

Conventional killers and victims therefore garner more partisan support than their unconventional counterparts. Indeed, unconventionals may find it hard to get people to represent or testify for them at all. In modern America, homicides involving members of racial minorities often fail to attract witnesses who are prepared to testify, even when the killing occurred in public. In one of my Virginia cases, for example, a young black man was shot and killed in a crowded public park on a Saturday afternoon. Of the approximately one hundred people who witnessed the event, only one was willing to testify.[14]

Unconventional parties are less likely to attract conventional partisans, but when they do, they benefit all the more from the attendant boost in status. In nineteenth-century California, Mexicans and Indians accused of homicide were typically not represented by attorneys (all of whom have some degree of conventionality). Chinese defendants, however, did have lawyers to represent them (usually paid for by a fraternal organization) and were less likely to be convicted than their Mexican and Indian counterparts (McKanna 2002).

Third parties are also drawn to those culturally close to themselves. Here a second principle of social gravitation applies: *Partisanship is a joint function of the third party's social closeness to one side and social distance from the other* (Black 1993: 127). Thus, all else the same, whites side with whites, blacks with blacks, bohemians with bohemians, and fundamentalist Christians with fundamentalist Christians. These tendencies may also affect the settlement of cases.

SETTLEMENT AGENTS

Conventionality

Conventional settlement agents are more severe, decisive, and formalistic (Black 1989: 15–16; 1993: chap. 8). In America, white judges are more likely than black judges to convict defendants of felonies (Uhlman 1979: 65–69). White jurors are similarly more likely than black jurors to find defendants guilty (Bernard 1979). In capital cases, white jurors are more willing to impose a death sentence. Researchers conducting a large multistate study known as the Capital Jury Project interviewed over one thousand people who served on capital juries in fourteen states. They found that in cases where racial differentials tend to be most pronounced—black on white killings—the probability of a death sentence varied significantly with the number of white and black jurors (Bowers, Steiner, and Sandys 2001). As table 1 indicates, in black-white capital cases, the more whites on a capital jury, the greater the chance of a death sentence. Equally, the more blacks on a capital jury, the lower the chance of a death sentence:

When whites and blacks serve on the same jury, whites vote more often for death. Blacks harbor more doubts about the defendant's guilt, regardless of whether the defendant is black or white. And more blacks believe defendants who say they are remorseful: where whites interpret statements of remorse as feigned, blacks more often see them as sincere. Blacks and whites construe the same evidence differently.[15]

Cultural Distance

Settlement agents who are culturally distant from both parties tend to decide cases in a severe, decisive, and formalistic manner (Black 1993: chap. 8). Colonial judges, for example, are more apt to convict and punish than native judges. They are also more likely to render zero-sum (all-or-nothing) decisions and to be sticklers for the rules.

TABLE 1 Percentage of black-white capital murder trials ending in death penalty by number of white and black jurors

No. of white jurors	% of cases with death sentences	No. of black jurors	% of cases with death sentences
0–3	46	0	64
4	35	1	53
5	63	2	48
6+	65	3+	36

Source: Bowers, Steiner, and Sandys (2001: 192, table 1).

Settlement agents are sometimes culturally closer to one side than the other. Modern legal systems bar family members and friends from serving as judges and jurors, but not co-religionists or people of the same race or ethnicity. That is not always so. In thirteenth-century England, disputes between Jews and Christians required a jury composed of equal numbers of members of the two groups. In late-seventeenth-century America, the Plymouth Colony (Massachusetts) frequently added Indians to juries hearing cases between Indians and colonists. Until the nineteenth century, in England and North America, juries composed of six aliens and six citizens judged cases in which aliens were accused of crimes (Van Dyke 1977: 11).[16]

Whether the law acknowledges or ignores cultural partisanship, it is a fact of life: third parties of all types, including settlement agents, tend to side with litigants with whom they share cultural characteristics. A culturally close jury saved Dan White from a capital murder conviction in San Francisco after he killed Mayor George Moscone and City Supervisor Harvey Milk in 1978:

> Milk became the first openly gay politician in a major United States city when he was elected to represent the Castro district, an area increasingly populated by gay men and women. Moscone was a liberal mayor, sympathetic to the cause of gay rights. White represented a traditional, conservative, family-oriented section of San Francisco. White resigned his seat on the city's board of supervisors, but soon changed his mind and wanted his seat back.

At first Moscone agreed, but after being lobbied by Milk and other liberals he decided to deny White's request. White armed himself with a pistol, put extra bullets in his pocket, and entered city hall through a side window, apparently to avoid the metal detectors at the front door. He went to Moscone's office, argued with him, and then shot him four times. After reloading he gun, White walked down the hall, confronted Milk, and shot him five times. As with Moscone, the last shot was through the skull.

White's lawyer asserted that good people like Dan White do not commit murder; something else must have been going on. He argued that White had been provoked by Moscone's change of mind about the reappointment, and that he was clinically depressed. Several psychiatrists testified that White's mental condition drove him to his desperate actions. One argued that White's consumption of junk food, such as Twinkies and Coca-Cola, changed his blood sugar and intensified his depression, leading to the killing. (This became popularly known as the "Twinkie defense.") Another testified that White had entered the building through the window out of consideration of the feelings of others: he did not want to embarrass the police officer staffing the metal detectors by having to confront a gun-carrying politician.

These arguments resonated with the jury, four of whom wept when White's tape-recorded confession was played in court. The jury contained no gays, blacks, or Asians—the principal minorities in the city—but was mainly composed of white ethnic Catholics, like White. Their verdict: voluntary manslaughter. (see Shilts 1982: 254–55, 266–69, 304–23)

Cultural closeness was also very helpful to any whites who happened to be accused of crimes against blacks in the Jim Crow South (see, e.g., Dollard 1957). With whites firmly in control of all legal institutions—police, courts, and prisons—blacks experienced blatantly unequal legal treatment. Whites who lynched a black could expect to escape all punishment. If the lynching did spawn a legal inquiry, it was usually stopped by an all-white grand jury finding that the victim died, in the tried and trusted phrase, "at the hands of persons unknown." In later years some cases began to make it to trial. But since the juries were composed entirely of local whites, convictions were extremely rare, often despite overwhelming evidence of guilt. Consider, for instance, the trial of two white defendants for the murder of a fourteen-year-old black boy, Emmett Till, in the Mississippi Delta town of Sumner in 1955 (Whitfield 1988):

> On a visit from Chicago to his relatives, Till made sexually suggestive comments or advances to a white woman working alone in a store (the precise facts are disputed). The woman reacted by getting a gun, at which point Till departed. When the woman's husband heard about the incident, he and his half-brother and another man went looking for Till after dark. They abducted him from his great-uncle's cabin. The boy disappeared, never to be seen alive again. Three days later, the corpse of a severely beaten male, weighed down by a heavy fan, was fished out of a local river, bearing Till's ring. Till's mother identified the body as that of her son. A grand jury indicted the woman's husband and half-brother for capital murder. The breach of racial solidarity was soon corrected. From that point on, white (and local) partisanship prevailed:
>
> All five lawyers—all of whom were white—practicing in Sumner volunteered to represent the defendants pro bono, an offer the defendants accepted.
>
> The sheriff testified, not for the prosecution, but for the *defense.* He claimed that the body recovered from the river was not that of Till, and speculated that the boy was safely back up north. (At the conclusion of the trial, however, he told a television audience that if any of the people who had been sending him threatening mail came down to Mississippi, "the same thing's gonna happen to them that happened to Emmett Till.")
>
> Unmoved by the boy's great-uncle's in-court identification of one of the defendants as the man who had abducted the boy from his cabin, the all-white jury returned a verdict of not guilty, taking an hour and seven minutes to do so only because the sheriff-elect instructed them to make it "look good."[17]

With the disappearance of legal segregation and the softening of black-white divisions, legal decisions in the South and elsewhere are less overtly unequal than in the past. But racial partisanship continues to rear its head (see, e.g., Ugwuegbu 1979).

Contrasts in the racial composition of the jury largely explain why O. J. Simpson (the famous African American former football player and media personality) was able to win his criminal trial for murder but lost his civil trial arising out of the very same incident. Simpson, recall, was accused of killing two whites in Los Angeles in 1995: his ex-wife and a young man, a waiter, who was returning a pair of spectacles to her left at the restaurant. Although Simpson was acquitted of all criminal charges, he was held liable by a civil jury two years later for the same two killings, and ordered to pay $33,500,000 in damages. Why were the decisions so different?

The answer lies in the race of the jurors. In the criminal case, nine of the twelve jurors were African Americans, two were white, and one was a Latino. By contrast, in the civil trial brought by the families of the victims, eleven of the jurors were white and one was Asian American.

Civil cases, it is true, have a lower standard of proof than criminal cases. In civil cases plaintiffs only have to prove their case on a preponderance of the evidence; in criminal cases the state has to prove its case beyond a reasonable doubt. But neither the amount of evidence nor the standard of proof explains the divergent results. The evidence against Simpson in the criminal trial was itself very considerable. One veteran ex-prosecutor remarked of the criminal charges, "In all my years, other than in cases where the killer has been apprehended during the perpetration of the homicide, I have never seen a more obvious case of guilt" (Bugliosi 1996: 20). Thus, by most standards, the case against Simpson was established well beyond a reasonable doubt. Yet a black jury was not going to convict Simpson. Opinion polls taken at the time revealed a deep racial divide on the question of Simpson's guilt: about 70 percent of whites thought Simpson guilty, while about 90 percent of African Americans said he was not guilty (see Black 2002: 123).

The racial divide carried over to the civil case. All blacks interviewed for the civil jury thought Simpson was not guilty, while all whites thought that he was guilty (Black 2002: 123). When attorneys for the civil plaintiffs conducted a simulated trial a month before the actual trial, a sharp split emerged between the white jurors, who would hold Simpson liable, and the black jurors, who would not. Probing deeper, the lawyers asked the jurors a series of questions designed to discover how much evidence of guilt they would require before ruling against Simpson. The attorneys were dismayed by the answers: "The degree to which the pro-Simpson jurors, especially African-American women, would discount, disregard, or dismiss evidence damning to Simpson was mind-boggling. It was clear that, no matter how strong the evidence, some jurors would simply not convict" (Petrocelli 1998: 335).

The reason for the divergent verdicts in the criminal and civil trials, then, had much less to do with the amount of evidence or legal standard of proof than with who sat on the jury: "The African-Americans were culturally closer to Simpson, while the white Americans were closer to the victims" (Black 2002: 123).[18]

POPULAR JUSTICE

Popular justice responds strongly to the cultural geometry of cases. The application and severity of popular sanctions for homicide varies with the conventionality and cultural distance of the parties and third parties.

CONVENTIONAL AND CULTURALLY DISTANT VICTIMS

Conventional victims attract more popular justice than unconventional victims. To kill a person who conforms to her group's traditions and accustomed way of life elicits both partisanship and severity. But to kill somebody who has unorthodox religious views, unusual dietary habits, or an eccentric manner of dress evokes less support and less severe sanctions.[19]

Conventional killers, on the other hand, benefit from greater forbearance. In the postbellum American South, offenses (such as homicide) by whites against whites led to a lynching much less often than offenses by blacks against whites. Moreover, when lynched, whites were less often tortured or mutilated than blacks (Brundage 1993: 86, 92).

The killing of culturally distant persons similarly attracts greater severity (provided the parties belong to the same social world) (Black 1990: 46). Lynching, for example, is more probable and severe the more culturally distant the parties are (Senechal de la Roche 1997:

58–60). So too is vengeance (see, e.g., Reid 1999). For instance: "A Blackfoot warrior whose father, brother, or best friend had been killed by the tribe he was fighting was not content merely to take the scalp of a fallen enemy. He mutilated the body of his foe—cut off his hands, feet, and head, or even literally hacked him to pieces" (Ewers 1958: 138).

Homicides across the nineteenth-century American cultural divide separating Indians and whites were also apt to trigger vengeance with particularly violent characteristics, such as multiple victims, mutilation, and scalping (Utley and Washburn 1985). In one of the largest incidents, the Minnesota Sioux attacked white settlements in 1862 in response to a mounting series of grievances. They showed no mercy, killing some six hundred whites and raping, torturing, and scalping many of their victims (Gard 1949: 7). In retaliation, United States soldiers killed many and, despite orders to the contrary, scalped several Indians. After the Sioux leader, Little Crow, was eventually killed, "a cavalry detachment sent out from Hutchinson found Little Crow's body, scalped it, and brought it into town, where it became a major attraction that Independence Day of 1863. The corpse was dumped in the middle of the main street. Boys stuffed firecrackers in the ears and nose and set them off. By evening, however, people had lost interest, and the body was tossed in an offal pit on the outskirts of town. Sometime later, a cavalry officer retrieved it and cut off the head with his saber" (Schultz 1992: 273–74).

Although incidents like these were unusual in their scale, the resort to lethal retaliation was not. Neither was the practice of collective liability whereby all members of a group can be held responsible for the actions of one of them. Cultural distance collectivizes liability (Senechal de la Roche 1996: 116). In many parts of the nineteenth-century American frontier, when an Indian killed a white, any available Indian was liable to be killed in revenge (see, e.g., Kroeber 1961: 80–81). For instance, of Oregon at mid-century it has been said that "any white man found dead was assumed to have been murdered by Indians, and often his death was made an excuse for raiding the nearest Indian village and killing all the men, women, and children found there" (Gard 1949: 11). Similar patterns have been reported for many other groups (see, e.g., Mishkin 1940: 2; Harner 1972: 172; Hallpike 1977: 198).

UNCONVENTIONAL AND CULTURALLY CLOSE VICTIMS

Culturally close killings typically evoke milder sanctions. Among certain Plains Indians groups, such as the Cheyenne, homicides committed by members of other tribes were avenged whenever possible (Hoebel 1960: 70–73). But a Cheyenne who killed a fellow tribesman, although he was typically banished from the tribe for about ten years, was spared (Llewellyn and Hoebel 1941: 167).[20]

The killing of an unconventional is less serious as well. The murder of a minority group member is less often avenged, compensated, or results in the killer being shunned. When the victim is both culturally distant and unconventional, the response is all the more lenient. In the American West, private individuals sometimes offered monetary rewards for Indian scalps (Gard 1949: 8–9). On the Australian frontier too, many killings of Aborigines were of little moment. Some whites boasted of how many Aborigines they had eliminated (Reynolds 1987: 50). And others might praise them. A newspaper correspondent wrote in June 1868:

> I much regret to state that the blacks have become very troublesome about here lately. Within ten miles of this place they appeared and cut steaks from the rumps of several horses. As soon as it was known, the native Police, under Sub-Inspector Uhr, went out, and, I am informed, succeeded in shooting upwards of thirty blacks. No sooner was this done than a report came in that Mr. Cameron had been murdered at Liddle and Hetzer's station, near the Norman. Mr. Uhr went off immediately in that direction, and his success I hear was complete. One mob of fourteen he rounded up: another mob of nine, and a last mob of eight. In the latter lot there was one black who would not die after receiving eighteen or twenty bullets, but a trooper speedily put an end to his existence by smashing his skull. . . . Everybody in the district is delighted with the wholesale slaughter dealt out by the native police, and thank Mr. Uhr for his energy in ridding the district of *five-nine* (59) myalls. (quoted in Reynolds 1972: 22)

Morality reflects its cultural environment. Where cultural differences are most pronounced, as on frontiers, moral contrasts are at their strongest and clearest. In 1883 a British colonial official wrote home to his friend, Prime Minister William Gladstone, that during his six years in Australia he had "heard men of culture and refinement, of the greatest humanity and kindness to their fellow whites, and who when you meet them at home you would pronounce them to be incapable of such deeds, talk, not only of the *wholesale* butchery . . . but of the *individual* murder of natives, exactly as they would talk of a day's sport, or of having had to kill some troublesome animal" (quoted in Reynolds 1987: 51–52; emphasis in original).

The sentiments Arthur Gordon expressed to Gladstone are strikingly similar to those of the Irish king Donal O'Neill in his missive to the Pope half a millennium earlier. Despite great disparities in time and place, conduct and context, they exemplify the same underlying principle: two cultures, two moralities.

Even within the melting pots of modern industrialized societies, cultural differences survive and continue to influence the handling of homicide. How people speak and dress, what they think, and which God they worship still affects the severity of penalties for those who kill their fellow humans. Moreover, cultural patterns are stubborn and resistant to change. In the United States, new statutes enacted after *Furman v. Georgia* introduced two major legislative reforms designed to eliminate racial differentials in the death penalty: guided discretion and automatic review by an appeals court. On their face, these are impressive safeguards. They made decision making less discretionary and more formalistic or rule-like. But they did not succeed in eliminating racial disparities. The aggravating-circumstances scheme has proven to be vague enough to permit the same murder to be evaluated differently depending on who commits it (Baldus, Woodworth, and Pulaski 1990: 22–23). And automatic appellate review has similarly failed to eliminate the racial patterns found at the trial level (Baldus, Woodworth, and Pulaksi 1990: 218; Gross and Mauro 1989: 69–77).

Blackian theory explains why: passing laws forbidding disparities or amending procedures will not succeed as long as the cultural geometry or structure of cases remains unchanged (Black 1989). Unequal outcomes are embedded in the very foundation of law and popular justice—in social life itself. Changing the rules and procedures will have little effect as long as the case structures remain unchanged.

The morality of killing, then, is culturally relative. But it is relative not so much to the cultural characteristics of the society as to the cultural characteristics of the case. Societies with widely divergent cultures may utilize similar sanctions, such as imprisonment, vengeance, and compensation. Equally, sanctions within the same society may diverge sharply, depending on the cultural elevation and distance of the parties. In every society it is more serious to kill a conventional person than an unconventional person, especially when the killer is unconventional. Likewise, to kill a person distant in cultural space is more serious than to kill a person proximate in cultural space.

In sum, the handling of homicide varies with its location and direction in cultural, normative, radial, organizational, and vertical space. But there is still one more spatial dimension to be considered, the relational, the subject of the next chapter.

8 THE RELATIONAL DIMENSION

> O, my offense is rank, it smells to heaven,
> It hath the primal eldest curse upon't,
> A brother's murder.

The speaker of these lines is Claudius, brother and murderer of the King of Denmark in Shakespeare's classic play, *Hamlet.* In a moment of clarity, Claudius is struck by the affinities of his act with the biblical slaying of Abel by Cain. Suddenly, he understands the sheer evil of what he has done. He has not just taken a life; he has murdered a kinsman, a family member, a brother. His is not just an offense, but the very worst kind of iniquity, so putrid it stinks to Heaven itself.

Claudius's insight uncovers a common, perhaps even universal, view of homicide: to kill is wrong, but to kill a family member is an even graver violation of the moral order. Medieval England was certainly not the only society in which "all right-thinking men naturally viewed with profound revulsion violence within the kindred" (Hyams 2003: 203). The Bedouin of North Africa liken a man who kills a member of his own family to an animal, "for no human being would do this," and they call him "one who 'defecates in the tent'" (Peters 1967: 264). The Lugbara of Uganda regard the killing of a family member as unthinkable and unnatural, a sin of the gravest magnitude that no decent person would commit (Middleton 1965: 512). In the Albanian highlands, "a son unnatural enough to kill his own father could surely not have been born by that father, but must be a bastard" (Hasluck 1954: 211).

Although people are unusually shocked and horrified by intimate killing, Black makes a bold prediction: they handle it leniently (1976: 41).

LAW

Intimacy or "relational distance," a component of the morphological dimension of social space, is the degree to which people participate in one another's lives. Measures of relational distance include "the scope, frequency, and length of interaction between people, the age of their relationship, and the nature and number of links between them in a social network" (Black 1976: 41). Spouses and siblings occupy the intimate end of the spectrum; strangers, the distant end.

Relational distance predicts the behavior of law and of popular justice (Black 1976; 1993). Black proposes that law and relational distance are related in curvilinear fashion (1976: 41). Thus, little or no law is found between intimates. As relational distance increases, so too does the amount of law. Law therefore becomes more active in conflicts between distant acquaintances and strangers. However, as relational distance increases to the point that people live in wholly different worlds, law tails off. As with cultural distance, the last part of the curve only applies today across societies.[1] Within modern societies, law generally increases with relational distance (Black 1989: 110, note 71).

HOUSTON

The tendency of intimate relationships to repel law was first demonstrated in American homicide cases in a Houston, Texas, study, published at about the same time as *The Behavior of Law* (Lundsgaarde 1977). The demonstration is all the more cogent since the author does not appear to have been aware of Black's theory (1995: 843). Yet the link between intimacy and leniency turned out to be the central finding of the study.

The study analyzed the handling of all homicides coming to the attention of the Houston police in 1969. That year the city had 176 homicides judged to be criminal in which the relationship between killer and victim was known and in which the offender's case had been legally resolved.[2] Of those, only 40 percent (73) resulted in legal punishment; the remainder were dismissed by the grand jury (also known as "no billed"), were dropped by the prosecutor, or resulted in an acquittal or probation. Intimate cases, he found, were particularly likely to escape punishment: the "severity of the penalty for killers correlates inversely with the degree of intimacy between killer and victim. Thus, 61 percent of killers of relatives escaped any form of legal penalty; 53 percent of killers of friends or associates similarly escaped any form of legal penalty, and 36 percent of killers of strangers escaped legal punishment" (Lundsgaarde 1977: 16).

When punishment was imposed, its severity varied inversely with the parties' intimacy. Five cases attracted the most severe penalty—death; all were stranger killings. Seven cases received the second most severe disposition—life imprisonment; five were stranger killings. When terms of imprisonment were meted out, the maximum term for killing an intimate was 19 years and the average was 8 years; for killing an acquaintance the maximum term was 75 years and the average was 10 years; and for killing a stranger the maximum was 99 years and the average 28 years (Lundsgaarde 1977: 16, 232).

Cases between intimate partners were treated with particular indulgence. A fairly typical instance:

> The couple next door were yelling and screaming. Nothing new about that, though: they drank and quarreled often. Sometimes they could be heard threatening to kill one another. This particular time they argued all night long. Their dispute turned violent: she (aged 55) took a knife and cut his finger. He (aged 70) went to the hospital and got stitched up. When he returned home, the dispute flared up again. This time she shattered a mirror in his face. He yelled at her that he would kill her. She left the apartment, shouting that, no, she would kill him. As she was about to reenter the apartment, he took a shotgun and shot her through the screen door. Hearing the shot, a crowd quickly assembled. The man told the crowd, "Call somebody to come and get her or I will shoot her again."
>
> After the woman died the man was arrested and charged with homicide. The case went to a grand jury, which declined to indict him. (see Lundsgaarde 1977: 57)

This defendant was one of thirteen men who killed their intimate female partner in the city that year. Not one received a sentence of life imprisonment or death, and only four were given a prison sentence of any duration. Even more lenient was the disposition of the twenty-four women who killed their husbands or boyfriends: a majority had their charges dismissed prior to trial, and not a single one was punished.

The Houston study has the great advantage of following a sample of cases from start to finish—from arrest through their final legal disposition—thereby allowing the effects of intimacy to be studied much more fully than a more conventional single or two-stage study would allow. A disadvantage is that it does not take into account how and why the killing was committed. But a closer look at the cases suggests that the conduct of the parties, such as the killer's premeditation, does not account for the case dispositions (see also Dawson 2006). Some intimate homicides evinced (by normal legal criteria) a clear intention to kill and still had very lenient outcomes. In one case a woman shot her sleeping husband at close range in the chest after he had previously struck and threatened her. She received three months' probation (Lundsgaarde 1977: 72–73). Other intimates killed not just intentionally but in the presence of witnesses, and their cases too had a lenient denouement. For instance, a woman who became angry with her husband when he would not leave a saloon with her went outside, got a pistol, returned, and shot him. She was acquitted at trial (70–71). Another woman shot her adult son in the back of the head as he left a store because he "had been fooling around with homosexuals and drugs." She was given a mere five years (87–88).

Even the victim's actions were influenced by intimacy. In several cases victims protected the killer by lying to officials about who had attacked them, even as they lay dying of their wounds. One woman, for instance, argued with her husband, complaining that she was tired of his liaisons with "them whores." The couple quarreled and she wound up shooting him. According to the detective who interviewed him before he died, the husband stated that he "was willing to prosecute the person who had shot him but that he didn't know who had done it!" (Lundsgaarde 1977: 65).

At first glance, these victims are behaving peculiarly: after all, they have just been grievously wounded by their assailant. But a corollary of pure sociology's assumption that social life, not individuals, behaves is that all the parties to the case obey the same principles as law itself. From this perspective it is not surprising that the victims are reluctant to turn the full force of the law on their antagonist. Though beaten, bruised, and bloody, their long shared history with the attacker blunts their natural vengefulness. Intimacy repels severity by officials and victims alike.

ELSEWHERE IN AMERICA

Findings from other American studies confirm the intimacy principle and reveal some of its additional implications. Consider, for instance, homicide in romantic triangles, as in the following two cases, from my Virginia study:

> Rasheed dropped by his girlfriend's apartment one night at about 11 PM and discovered her in bed with another man whom he did not know. Enraged, Rasheed attacked the interloper. Using fists and kitchen implements, the two men went to battle with Rasheed, getting the upper hand before walking away. The interloping man died the following day from the wounds he sustained in the fight.

The second case also involved an emotional killing of an unfaithful partner in the heat of the moment:

> The defendant, Ben, discovered that his wife, Hazel, was "running around" with other men in the company of their oldest daughter. That night, Ben confronted Hazel on her return home, but she refused to acknowledge any wrongdoing on her part. Her nonchalance infuriated Ben. The following day Ben spoke to her parents about the situation. Realizing that he was very upset, Hazel phoned the police when she finished work and asked for an officer to accompany her home while she took some clothes and left. Hazel went inside while the officer waited outside. Ben confronted Hazel and they argued. This inflamed Ben, who opened a closet door, reached to the top shelf, took out his gun, and shot his wife several times, including after she had already fallen to the ground.

Which defendant was treated more severely? Neither had a criminal record. Both killed after their partners cheated on them. If anything, Ben's crimes seems more culpable—he had had time to become accustomed to the infidelity and his wife was sufficiently fearful of him to call the police; Rasheed, by contrast stumbled upon Tricia in flagrante delicto. Yet Rasheed was convicted of first-degree murder and sentenced to sixty years' imprisonment, while Ben was convicted of second-degree murder and sentenced to fifteen years in prison. The principal difference between the cases was that Rasheed killed a stranger whereas Ben killed an intimate, his wife.

In the Virginia sample as a whole, intimates were sentenced less severely than intimates. Table 2 cross-classifies three categories of sentence severity with the relational distance between the parties for cases with a single victim. Even though the total number of cases is not large, and the study does not include all the intimate cases screened out at earlier stages, the pattern is very clear: greater relational distance brings greater severity.

The Houston and Virginia studies provide rich evidence of the power of relational distance, but they do not rule out other possible explanations. Strangers, for example, are more likely to kill for gain while intimates are more likely to kill in the course of conflict (see, e.g., Cooney and Phillips 2003: 86). That might explain why intimates are handled more leniently. Or perhaps stranger killings are more likely to have higher-status victims. That too could explain their greater severity.

Larger studies, however, have held constant, to a greater or lesser degree, the nature of the offense and the social characteristics of the parties and yet continue to exhibit an intimacy effect. One is a Miami study of all 569 homicides coming to the attention of the police in 1980. After taking into account the race, gender, and conduct of the parties, the author found that people who killed intimates were less likely to be charged, charged with a legally more serious homicide, and convicted than those who killed nonintimates (Wilbanks 1984: 96–98). Studies of capital murder lead to the same conclusion.

CAPITAL MURDER

Recall that all five death sentences in the Houston study were imposed for the killing of strangers. That is not unusual. Americans who kill their intimates hardly ever receive the death penalty. One writer dubs the immunity of intimates to capital punishment "the domestic discount" (Rappaport 1994).

TABLE 2 Severity of sentence by relational distance of the principals in Virginia homicide cases (in percentages)

Sentence	Relational distance		
	Intimates	Acquaintances	Strangers
5–19	45	29	22
>20	55	45	44
Life/death	0	26	33
%	100	100	99
N	[20]	[31]	[18]

Gamma = .40; P = .007

There are exceptions, cases in which intimate killers are sentenced to be executed. But take a closer look and additional factors usually surface. The Scott Peterson case is a good example. Peterson was accused of murdering his wife and dumping her body in the Pacific Ocean in 2002. The case attracted enormous publicity and was heavily featured on television, radio, newspapers, and magazines. Following a lengthy trial, Peterson was sentenced to death by the state of California. Importantly, though, his wife was eight months pregnant at the time of her death and Peterson was convicted of two counts of murder, that of his wife and his unborn son (see, e.g., Bailey 2008: 237–58). Defendants who kill just their intimate partner when the relationship is still intact virtually never receive the death penalty in modern America.

Statistical studies from a variety of states confirm the close correlation between the death penalty and stranger killings. Kentucky prosecutors are more likely to charge the defendant with a capital crime when the victim is a stranger (after holding constant the legal seriousness of the killing) (Keil and Vito 1990).[3] In Florida the absence of a prior relationship between killer and victim increases the likelihood of a death sentence (Radelet 1981: 922). In Georgia two studies of capital sentencing found that, after adjusting for a series of variables relating to the characteristics of the parties and the crime, killing a stranger increased the defendant's odds of being sentenced to death (Baldus, Woodworth, and Pulaski 1990: 319–20, 588–90; compare Judson et al. 1969: 1346–47).[4] An analysis of all homicides reported to the FBI over a five-year period (1976 through 1980) in eight states—Arkansas, Florida, Georgia, Illinois, Mississippi, North Carolina, Oklahoma, and Virginia (over 14,000 cases in all)—found that, after controlling for the race of the parties, "those who killed strangers were far more likely to be sentenced to death than those who killed family members, friends, or acquaintances" (Gross and Mauro 1989: 47–48). The stranger-nonstranger differential, for instance, ranged from a high of twelve in Arkansas to a low of four in Florida (1989: 46–48, 236, 238, 240, 242, 244). Aggregated over the entire sample, stranger killings were over seven times more likely to attract a death sentence than homicides between those with a prior relationship (calculated from 1989: 46, 236, 238, 240, 242, 244).

Once sentenced to death row, killers of strangers are more likely to remain there and face execution. Over five decades (1925–72), Texas prisoners had a one in three chance of having their death sentence commuted to life imprisonment by the governor if their victim was a family member or acquaintance, but only a one in eight chance if the victim was a stranger (Marquart, Ekland-Olson, and Sorensen 1994: 117).[5]

Revealing as these statistical studies are, they may also conceal some of the power of relational distance. The studies often separate stranger cases from all others. But nonstrangers vary considerably in their intimacy: they can range from spouses of fifty years to people who have recently developed a nodding acquaintanceship. Reducing relational distance to just two categories may therefore mask much of its influence. More fine-grained analysis may reveal an intimacy effect where initially there was none, or a more powerful effect than first appeared.[6]

OTHER TIMES, OTHER PLACES

Evidence for the intimacy principle extends well beyond the modern American legal system. In nineteenth-century Ireland, for example, "there was a strong sense," a historian notes, that family violence "should not be within the purview of the courts." Thus, "even in homicides, family members often tried to keep the authorities out. While John Farrell, a Limerick fisherman, lay dying after being stabbed by his brother, he insisted to police that he had simply fallen over a metal pot while drunk" (Conley 1999: 51, 52).

If the authorities did intervene, juries were slow to convict and judges slow to impose harsh sentences in family homicides. When, for instance, adult children killed a parent (as happened not infrequently due to conflicts over delayed inheritance of family farms), the official response was typically one of considerable leniency. In a twenty-six-year period (1866–92), thirty-seven men were accused of killing their fathers; only twelve (32 percent) were convicted. Of the twelve convicted, only three (i.e., 8 percent of those accused) served more than a year in prison. The lenient outcomes were not for want of evidence of guilt. In one case, for instance:

> A farmer in County Limerick died shortly after eating a breakfast served to him by his thirty-year-old son. The police became suspicious when they learned that the son had recently purchased strychnine. They had the body exhumed and found traces of poisoning. They questioned the son, who stated: "He was a good father but he had one failing, and that was the prevention of my starting in life; his intention being to continue on until his death. I was doing a servant's work for him and he would keep me there all his lifetime. Look at my age now. What less could I do?"
>
> Notwithstanding his self-incriminating statement and the other evidence against him, the son was acquitted by a jury. (see Conley 1999: 55–56)

Men who killed their wives or girlfriends also attracted little law. Irish courts of the time treated all who killed with weapons with additional severity. Hence, husbands who killed their wives with a weapon were not afforded the same leniency as other intimate killers.[7] But men who pushed or struck their wives without weapons usually got off lightly. Some were acquitted. Of those who were convicted, 70 percent served less than twelve months. Similarly, eight of twelve men accused of killing their girlfriends escaped punishment altogether (Conley 1999: 62–64, 112).

Elsewhere in Europe, intimacy also cast its spell over homicide cases. Nineteenth-century French juries were notoriously lenient in killings committed without premeditation and in the heat of the moment (*crimes passionnels,* or crimes of passion). These cases nearly always involved intimates and arose over matters of adultery, betrayal, and jealousy (Donovan 1981: 95). Some displayed considerable evidence of murderous intent. One such case occurred in 1880 when "the actress Marie Br . . . [,] stage name Béraldi, dressed herself in a large hat and lorgnon and stalked her old lover and his new mistress in the streets of Paris. Ultimately, she walked up behind him, shot him in the back and then, satisfied with the deed, voluntarily gave herself up to the police. Despite her obvious premeditation and the open way in which she acted, Br . . . was acquitted by the jury at her trial" (Harris 1989: 208).

Across the English Channel, a close relationship with the victim was likewise an advantage for a defendant. In the English county of Kent during the mid-nineteenth century, "domestic homicides were rarely treated as murders" because "though not formally recognized in law, the relationship between the victim and the accused was crucial both in deciding whether to call a homicide a manslaughter or a murder, and in determining sentences." Thus, while every defendant accused of killing an employer or superior officer was convicted and executed, "only 13 percent of those killing their child or stepchild (excluding infanticide) and only 23 percent of those accused of killing a spouse were executed" (Conley 1991: 59–60).[8]

INFANTICIDE

Infanticide—the killing of young babies—is another species of intimate homicide that rarely attracts law's full fury. In England, for example, infanticide was probably relatively common in medieval and early modern times, yet it garnered virtually no legal attention. Indictments were scarce and convictions even more so. For instance, of the almost three thousand homicide cases that came before the courts of three English counties in the period 1300–1348, only one involved the killing of a newborn (Hanawalt 1979: 154–57). Under Queen Elizabeth I, however, the moral climate changed and officials began to define infanticide as a social problem that needed to be eliminated. This was part of a larger concern with vice of all types—laws were passed against drunkenness, gambling, swearing, fornication, and other moral transgressions. With infanticide, the trend culminated in a law of 1624 which provided that when a young illegitimate child was found dead, the mother was presumed to have killed the child unless at least one witness swore that it had been stillborn. Although the offense under the new statute was not murder but concealment of birth, it carried the same penalty: death (Beattie 1986: 113–24).

The law of 1624 appears to have been strictly enforced for several generations, but by the beginning of the eighteenth century it was being routinely bypassed by legal officials (Hoffer and Hull 1981: 65–91). For example, if a woman could show that she had made clothing for her child (known as "benefit of linen"), she was almost always acquitted. Preparing for a live birth was taken as evidence that the mother had intended to care for the child and therefore had not killed it. The mother's intention to care for or kill the child was not, logically speaking, relevant to the offense stipulated by the statute—concealing the birth—but the courts accepted it as evidence of innocence anyway. Moreover, collecting linen routinely came to overwhelm evidence of guilt, such as medical testimony that the child had been born alive. For instance, in a 1774 case:

> Mary Clifton, a servant, was accused of giving birth to an illegitimate child and burying its corpse in her master's yard. The child had a small mark around its right eye. Although she initially denied having a child, after a doctor testified that she had recently delivered a baby, she confessed the birth. She claimed that she had cried out for help and sent for linen during her pregnancy. A doctor performed the standard test for live birth—submerging the lungs in water to see if they floated—and declared that the baby had not been stillborn. However, the court discounted the medical evidence, her earlier denial, and the apparently clear attempt to conceal the birth and acquitted Mary. (see Hoffer and Hull 1981: 73–74)

Outcomes such as this became common and convictions for infanticide infrequent. Indictments declined as well. After the cycle of concern with sexual immorality had runs its course, the law-repelling nature of intimacy once again reigned supreme. Infanticide came to be handled with renewed leniency, reflecting the sentiment expressed in 1866 by Sir James Fitzjames Stephens, an eminent Victorian judge, that "the crime is less serious than other kinds of murder" (quoted in Conley 1991: 110). Thus, even when prosecutions were brought, defendants tended to get the benefit of the doubt. Any women who were convicted were usually treated mercifully: of the sixty English women convicted of murdering their newborns in the period 1905–21, fifty-nine had their death sentences commuted (Hoffer and Hull 1981: 162–63).

INTIMATE STRATIFICATION

As the case of infanticide shows, intimacy, like all the variables in Black's theoretical system, can only properly be analyzed when all else is held constant. Other aspects of case geometry may qualify, or even override, the intimacy effect. Consider stratification. In many premodern societies, men were the acknowledged rulers of their families. To kill a patriarchal father or husband was an aggravated crime. In imperial China, for example, the law prescribed and imposed more severe penalties when a father or even an elder brother was killed (see, e.g., Alabaster 1899: 146–49; Davis 2000). In medieval England, the killing of a husband amounted to "petty treason," an aggravated form of homicide (see, e.g., Durston 2004: 682–87). If the killing of patriarchs make up a good percentage of all intimate homicides in societies of this kind, then the intimacy effect is likely to be attenuated or even supressed. Conversely, as patriarchy declines, the killing of a female intimate becomes a more serious matter. In Victorian England, for example, a wave of gender equality served to increase the quantity of law for men who killed their wives (Wiener 2004).[9]

The late twentieth century brought another surge of gender equality, at least in the world's wealthier countries. From about 1970 onwards, women, especially married women with children, entered the workforce in greater numbers, made up a greater percentage of the prestigious professions (such as medicine and law), increased their representation at the top of the corporate and political worlds, and began to earn the same money for the same job as men (see, e.g., Hacker 1997; Caplow, Hicks, and Wittenberg 2001). Even as this happened, women continued to shoulder most of the responsibility for the care of dependent children and elderly people, which raised their degree of social participation or radial status (see, e.g., Daly 1987). Violence against women (most of which is perpetrated by male partners) became a more serious matter: academics undertook large-scale research, legislatures passed laws, and police departments adopted new training procedures and policies (see, e.g., Sherman 1992). The changes were reflected in the handling of homicide cases.[10] In Houston, for example, a later study comparing the period 1985–94 with 1969 revealed that men who killed their wives and girlfriends were more likely to be sent to prison (68 percent versus 60 percent) and for longer terms (20 percent received life imprisonment versus 0 percent).[11] Since male-female cases happened to make up a larger proportion of all intimate homicides in the latter period, the overall result was, as expected, to reduce the size of the intimacy effect (Titterington and Abbott 2004; see also Dawson 2004).[12]

DEGREES OF INTIMACY

Intimacy, recall, is a matter of degree. Even among the relationally close, those who are less intimate should attract somewhat more severity. "Today's lovers may draw apart tomorrow and as this happens, law becomes a possibility in their lives," Black states (1976: 43–44). A Toronto study confirmed this prediction. The study analyzed the legal fate of 144 men convicted of intimate partner homicide over a twenty-year period (1974–96). It found that men who killed a woman from whom they were separating or had already separated were more likely to be found guilty of murder, and less likely of manslaughter, than men who killed their current female partner. The effect was even stronger at the sentencing stage: after adjusting for several other factors, such as the race, age, criminal history, and employment status of the killer, the nature of the killing, and the conviction offense, men who killed in intact relationships received sentences that were two years shorter than men who killed in relationships that were unraveling or had already done so (Dawson 2003).

The intimacy principle implies, then, that the most intimate killings of all should attract the most lenient sanctions of all. They do. Maximal intimacy is found not in killings of current spouses but of selves, and suicide elicits few or no penalties. Most modern nations do not even define it as criminal. In the United States, for example, suicide is not punishable and hence not formally a crime (LaFave 2000: 699).

But isn't there a simpler explanation—the killer is dead and cannot be punished? As the renowned English jurist Sir William Blackstone (1796: 495) elegantly put it, "What punishment can human laws inflict on one who has withdrawn himself from their reach?" However, as Blackstone realized, while the offender cannot be imprisoned or executed, he can be shamed and fined to his own detriment and that of his heirs. In the realm of punishment, death truly has no dominion. Rulers have often claimed a property interest in the lives and labor of their subjects. Those subjects have no right to destroy what belongs to their sovereign. Many cultures have therefore punished people who die by their own hand, employing a variety of tactics to do so, including mutilating and publicly exposing their bodies and then denying them normal rights of burial (see, e.g., Spierenburg 1984: 56–57, 79). In eighteenth-century England, some regions had the custom of "burying suicides at crossroads with stakes driven through their bodies" (McLynn 1989: 51). The property of a suicide may also be forfeited to the government and the family members disinherited, a penalty typically known in advance to the potential self-killer (see, e.g., McLynn 1989: 51). When it is penalized, however, the penalties imposed for killing oneself are typically less severe than those for killing others.

Homicides, then, can be located on a continuum defined by intimacy at one end and relational distance at the other. The most intimate are suicides, followed in order by homicides of family members, friends, close acquaintances, more distant acquaintances, and, finally, strangers. As cases move along the continuum, so does the severity of the sanctions with which the law responds to the killing. The more distant the parties (within the same society), the more serious the homicide and the greater the chance of a severe punishment, including the most severe of all, a death sentence. Conversely, the greater the intimacy of killer and victim, the more leniently it is handled. Indeed, for the most intimate homicides of all, the very idea of punishment is often considered inappropriate.

In short, the intimacy principle is a key component of social geometry. It pulses quietly beneath the skin of the legal system, mediating and even undermining the formal law. Despite its importance, it is largely ignored by traditional legal discourse. It is virtually never mentioned in statutes, judicial opinions, or legal scholarship. Most law professors do not teach it and most law students graduate without ever hearing of it. Lawyers representing clients may become aware of it, though even then many mistake it for something else, such as discrimination against women. Yet the evidence shows that the principle affects men and women, old and young, rich and poor alike. Little wonder, then, that Black (2000b: 707) calls it a "sociological law of law."

THIRD PARTIES

The impact of the relational structure of cases extends to third-party behavior: the more distant the parties, the more third parties intervene, as both partisans and settlement agents (Black 1995: 834–36). Cases between intimates tend to have fewer witnesses than cases between strangers. They also have less settlement—fewer authoritative decisions being made by legal officials. Consequently, intimate cases do not go as far as others in the legal process. To a significant extent, then, third-party behavior reinforces the core case geometry and helps to explain case outcomes.

Nonetheless, because third parties bring an added dimension to conflicts, they may "significantly alter the relational structure of cases" (Black 1989: 14). Thus, lawyers and witnesses can narrow or broaden the relational distance of the two sides. The criminal prosecutors and defense attorneys in a city, for example, will often know one another from prior cases. In a stranger homicide, their participation reduces the relational distance between the opposing sides and increases the chance of a negotiated settlement, such as a plea bargain. On the other hand, when the killer and victim are intimate, bringing in lawyers who are strangers from the parties and each other will increase the relational distance between the sides and raise the odds of a conviction and severe sentence.

Whether and how third parties relate to the case in the first place is strongly influenced by another aspect of intimacy—that between the third party and the principals. Partisanship and settlement behavior alike vary with the third party's intimacy with both sides. Consider, first, partisanship, for which the evidence is particularly strong.

PARTISANS

The support of intimates and associates can greatly strengthen a party's case. For example, the strong partisanship police officers elicit from each other augments the advantages they enjoy in virtue of their own organizational status. When police officers kill or are killed, it is their friends and colleagues who handle the case from start to finish. Consequently, no effort is spared in bringing a perpetrator to justice when police are victims, and only legally grievous cases wind up being prosecuted and punished when police are offenders (see, e.g., A. Collins 1998).

There is an exception that proves the rule, a situation in which the police do not enjoy an imbalance of partisanship—and lose more often. Recall that police fare much worse in civil than in criminal cases (see Klockars 1996: 4). In civil actions for wrongful death, it is the victim's representatives—usually the family—who pursue the case against the officer, and not the police department and the prosecutor's office, as in criminal cases. Instead of being opposed by his friends and colleagues, the officer is opposed by a group of close-knit strangers prepared to mount a more aggressive case against him. Lacking the protection of unequal partisanship, the officer is more likely to lose.

Professional ties can even help to avert suspicion that homicide has occurred at all. In 2000 Doctor Harold Shipman was convicted in England of killing 15 patients and suspected of killing between 220 and 240 others. That same year, an American doctor, Michael Swango, pled guilty to four counts of murder and five counts of attempted murder. In 2003 Charles Cullen, a former nurse in New Jersey, pled guilty to killing at least fourteen patients. These men were able to get away with so many murders for so long in considerable part because the close ties between medical personnel and forensic pathologists inhibit the full and open investigation of medical deaths. Had they left it at just one or two patients, they probably would never have been detected at all (Timmermans 2006: 170–81).

Partisanship is not, however, simply a matter of having close ties to one side. Black's second principle of social gravitation states: *Partisanship increases with the third party's social closeness to one side and social distance from the other* (1993: 127). Third parties close to one side and distant from the other ought, therefore, to provide the strongest support; those close to both sides ought to be nonpartisan, seeking to resolve the conflict, while those distant from both sides ought to remain neutral and uninvolved. Witness behavior exemplifies these predictions.

Coming Forward, Staying Back

Just how vital a role witnesses play in homicide cases is not always widely appreciated. In the movies, detectives solve most homicides with fingerprint, ballistic, DNA, or other forensic evidence. Real-life cases are more prosaic: a member of the public usually identifies the suspect (see Jackall 2005: 257). Witnesses continue to be central at later stages as well. Indeed, many cases ultimately succeed or fail on the continued presence and relative credibility of the opposing witnesses.

Not every witness to a murder is prepared to be a witness in the murder case, however. Giving evidence is an act of partisanship that varies, in part, with the witness's relational distance from the principals. Partisanship therefore strongly influences which version of the facts legal officials come to accept; it shapes legal truth.[13]

Intimates will usually come forward to provide testimony for their side, even if nobody else will. In one of the Virginia cases, for instance, out of the one hundred people who, the defendant estimated, witnessed the killing, the only one prepared to testify in court was the victim's girlfriend. To have no intimates is a disadvantage in modern society, therefore, just as it was in earlier times in which people ("compurgators") swore oaths to the truth of their kinfolk's legal claims (e.g., Pollock and Maitland 1898: 600–610, Black 1993: 143, note 21).

Strangers, by contrast, are harder to attract. Among the Tiv of Nigeria, for example, people are slow to intervene in the disputes of unacquainted others with the result that litigants have "trouble in getting witnesses of this sort, even though the number of people who have seen an act is legion" (Bohannan 1957: 39). In modern America, although strangers will sometimes come forward on their own, more commonly somebody has to track them down and persuade them to testify. If they cannot be persuaded, they can be subpoenaed. But that is risky. Witnesses forced to testify by a subpoena sometimes become uncooperative or hostile. Lawyers may therefore wind up not calling them for fear they will do more harm than good to their client's case (see, e.g., P. Chevigny 1969: 105).

When witnesses are close to both sides, their relative distance from both helps to determine which side they will support. In one case from the Virginia study, for example, a witness who was intimate with the victim and merely acquainted with the defendant provided central evidence for the state. Third parties who have ties of approximately equal closeness to both sides often remain neutral. In three of the Virginia cases, witnesses with close ties to both sides refused to get involved. As one of them told a defendant, "It's not my beef."

Intimacy also explains who stays back. People are generally reluctant to testify against their intimates, as an exchange in a Canadian trial illustrates:

> *Witness:* I don't feel right sitting here.
> *Crown:* How come, what doesn't feel right?
> *Witness:* My cousin [the accused] is sitting right behind me. It hurts me to testify against her. (quoted in Comack and Balfour 2004: 85)

Consequently, people often withhold information, documents, or physical objects (such as weapons) likely to incriminate their intimates. In one of the Virginia cases, the defendant's sister overheard the victim's sister say to a friend during a recess that the victim's boyfriend had lied on the stand. But she could not induce the sister to testify on behalf of her brother. This disinclination of witnesses to testify against their intimates can make it difficult for the state to prosecute a homicide case at all (see, e.g., Lewis 1961: 169).

Shading the Story

When witnesses do come forward, what they say—how they shade their story—is also influenced by their closeness to each side. Intimates appearing for the defense tend to emphasize mitigating circumstances and to play down aggravating circumstances. Testifying for a defendant accused of murder, they will make sure that the authorities know that the victim started the fight. They will appear readily as character witnesses, drawing attention to the defendant's good qualities, such as his service to the community or his strong work ethic. If the defendant decides to lie, they are the most likely people to support his efforts.

Victims' witnesses exhibit the same tendencies. The more intimate a witness is with the victim, the more damaging to the defendant's case the testimony tends to be. The victim's intimates typically move aggravating circumstances to center stage and mitigating circumstances to the wings. They will emphasize any predatory elements in the homicide and downplay any involvement the victim had in his or her own demise. But this tendency only holds if the victim's intimate is distant from the defendant. Where the witness is close to both sides the testimony tends to be more guarded, less clear-cut.

The following case (from my Georgia study) illustrates some of these patterns:

> Reginald, on trial for murdering a friend, Lemarcus, maintains that he acted in self-defense. A number of witnesses are called, each of whom has a different relationship to the parties. The most intimate with the victim is his girlfriend, Latoya, who volunteers that the defendant started the fight. The most intimate with the defendant is his brother who, though he did not himself witness the killing, tells the court that Reginald came to him after the event and told him that he shot Lemarcus after Lemarcus had choked him and stomped him in the face. Caught in the middle is Reginald's ex-girlfriend, Shaquita, who is a close friend of Latoya. Shaquita appears to be very uncomfortable on the witness stand, turning her chair to the side where she is able to look away from Reginald. Her responses are brief and lack detail, but she does say that Lemarcus slammed Reginald to the ground in the prior fight.

Police witnesses too follow the same principles. Police operate under a strict "code of silence" (sometimes known as "the blue curtain"), "an unwritten rule and custom that police will not testify against a fellow officer and that police are expected to help in any cover-up of illegal action" (Rudovsky 1992: 481, note 60). So familiar is the code of silence that a new word has been coined to describe it: "testilying" (Koepke 2000: 221).

The same ethic prevails among another group that finds itself opposite the police in many conflicts: gang members. Though frequent adversaries, and often seeing each other as belonging to separate moral universes, gang members and police behave in the aggregate remarkably similarly as witnesses. Inside and outside the courtroom, members of both groups routinely corroborate their ally's testimony, regardless of its veracity.

When both parties are supported by a corps of intimates who are distant from each other the case is likely to be factually complex with an abundance of conflicting evidence. The truth is likely to be hotly disputed, not just at trial but for long afterward as well. These cases exemplify with particular force the observation that "there's three sides to every story: your side, my side, and what really happened" (quoted in Bogira 2005: 259).

Attracting Strangers

For all their reliability, intimate witnesses have one grave disadvantage: they lack credibility (Black 2000c: 349–50). Their audience expects them to shade their testimony, even to lie, on behalf of their intimates (see, e.g., Gluckman 1967: 110; Conley 1999: 149). So while their word can be helpful when coupled with other evidence, a case founded solely on intimate testimony, such as an alibi, can quickly run aground (see, e.g., Feige 2006: 61). However accurate the testimony, the prosecutor will point to the relationship as a reason for discounting it ("What else would his Mom say?"). Strangers are simply more credible (see Simmel 1908: 402–8).

Litigants who can mobilize relationally distant third parties therefore enjoy a competitive edge. Indirect ties through others are particularly valuable. John does not know witness A, but he knows B who knows A, and as a result of B's request, A agrees to testify on John's behalf. The arrangement has the additional advantage that since John has no prior direct relationship with A, A's testimony has the appearance of being that of a total stranger and is all the more effective as a result.

Parties who can access more distant regions of social space, then, can build stronger cases. Sociologists have shown that ties to distant acquaintances, or "weak ties," are the most effective in extending the reach of people's networks (Granoveter 1973). My intimates typically know most of the same people I do (and I know most of the same people they do). But my distant acquaintances—old school friends, former neighbors, co-workers from previous jobs, and the like—are likely to move in circles largely different from mine. As such, they can provide a bridge to distant networks. When litigation arises, these weak ties can be crucial in recruiting strangers—lawyers, witnesses, investigators, or other allies—to the case.

In short, how a homicide occurs is one thing, but how police, prosecutors, judges, and juries later reconstruct it may be quite another. Legal officials rely on evidence to discover the facts, and evidence only enters a case when witnesses are prepared to come forward and present it, and they do so in a credible manner. Third-party relational distance strongly influences witness involvement and credibility alike. The strongest litigants have a combination of extensive close and distant relationships, enabling them to mobilize partisanship and to have their side of their story advanced and accepted.

SETTLEMENT AGENTS

Settlement agents are usually equally relationally distant from both principals (Black and Baumgartner 1983: 113). "The settlement agent and the principals form an isosceles triangle of relational distance with the settlement agent at the apex" (Black 1984: 22). A proposed judge or mediator, say, who has ties to one party will usually be unacceptable to the other party.[14] Any ties are therefore likely to be indirect—through one of the party's lawyer, for example—but they too can be fateful, as the Lizzie Borden case, probably the most celebrated murder trial in nineteenth-century America, illustrates:

> On August 4, 1892, in the small Massachusetts city of Fall River, Andrew Borden, a wealthy businessman, and his wife, Abby, were found murdered in their locked home. Both had been hacked to death with an axe. Since the two deaths appeared to have occurred ninety minutes apart, it was unlikely that an intruder could have hidden in the house for that time without being spotted. Suspicion soon turned to Andrew's thirty-two-year-old unmarried daughter, Lizzie, who lived in the house with her father and stepmother. Lizzie was known not to get along with her stepmother, and admitted as much to the police. The day before the double murder, Lizzie had attempted to buy a lethal poison. She told investigators that at the time the murders occurred she was in the barn loft gathering the necessities for a fishing trip. However, not only had she never gone fishing before but the loft's thick coat of floor dust showed no signs of having been disturbed. In addition, she had changed her dress shortly after the police ar-

rived at the house, and had burned a dress three days later, saying that it was covered in paint.

Lizzie's high-powered legal defense team offered little evidence to rebut the prosecution's case, focusing instead on her involvement in her church, her charitable work, and other aspects of her good character. The strategy worked, the jury acquitting Lizzie.

Several observers later commented on how favorably disposed the trial judge had been toward the defense. He made several important rulings in its favor and his charge to the jury clearly pointed toward acquittal. He was also something of a protégé of the defense team's lead lawyer, George Robinson, having been promoted to the bench by Robinson when he was governor of Massachusetts. (see Scott 2005: 132–45)[15]

Distant Settlement

Black (1993: chap. 8) proposes that relationally distant settlement agents are more severe than relationally close agents. While strangers are harsh and unforgiving toward wrongdoers, those close to the defendant—friends, associates, and acquaintances—are generally slower to convict and punish. Judges who have had substantial personal and professional contact with the poor—from whose ranks most modern homicide defendants and victims come—tend to punish less severely than judges who have lived and worked more exclusively among wealthier people (Levin 1972). And a jury composed of the accused killer's neighbors is, all else the same, more lenient than a jury of strangers.

Black (1993: chap. 8) additionally proposes that relationally distant settlement agents are more decisive and formalistic. Where intimates will search for a compromise based on considerations of equity, strangers are drawn to all-or-nothing decisions grounded firmly in the written rules. Jury nullification—the substitution of jury notions of right and wrong over the strict requirements of formal legal rules—should therefore be practiced more often by socially close juries than socially distant ones.[16]

An episode from the early law of homicide exemplifies these principles. In twelfth-century England, a reforming monarch, King Henry II, sought to reorganize the handling of homicide as part of his larger drive to restructure the criminal justice system and strengthen royal administration. Henry enacted statutes that replaced the old system of kin-based compensation with legal punishment and defined virtually all homicide as felonious and punishable with the death penalty. The only exceptions allowed were justifiable and excusable homicide. (Justifiable homicide included the killing of a thief or outlaw; excusable homicide included accidental killing, killing in self-defense, or killing from insanity.) But it was not the king or his legislators who decided actual homicide trials. That was in the hands of jurors in the villages, towns, and cities of England, many of which were quite remote, socially and geographically, from the king's court in London. Being so much closer to the defendants and victims, jurors tended to be much less severe, decisive, and formalistic than the authorities wished. As one historian notes: "These new rules on homicide must have clashed with community views on homicide. After all, many slayings took place within the small village community and had the formal rules been implemented, many persons would have been hanged who earlier would have paid compensation" (Green 1976: 420).

The exceptions written into the new rules, particularly the excuse of self-defense, gave jurors their way out. A comparison of homicide cases as initially described in the coroner's roll with the final jury verdicts reveals a consistent set of contrasts: what were initially depicted as aggressive lethal attacks were routinely transformed into acts of last-ditch self-protection. Juries, it appears, frequently constructed elaborate tales to bring the facts of the homicide within the narrow definition of self-defense contained in the law (Green 1972, 1976). Royal law was simply too severe for local juries; they responded by bending it.

POPULAR JUSTICE

Law, partisanship, and settlement, then, all respond strongly to relational distance. Popular justice is no exception. Intermediate sanctions, such as compensation, are most often found at intermediate degrees of relational distance. In my thirty-society cross-cultural study, for example, 40 percent of acquaintance killings typically resulted in the payment of compensation compared to 15 percent of intimate and 4 percent of stranger killings. At the extremes of relational distance, sanctions are more severe and more lenient, for stranger and intimate victims.

STRANGER VICTIMS

Offenses committed by and against strangers attract more popular justice (see, e.g., Phillips 2003; Jacobs and Wright 2006: 36–37). In many societies the only proper response to a distant killing is vengeance (provided the killer's group is not so distant as to render it impossible). In my thirty-society cross-cultural study, 83 percent of stranger killings typically resulted in self-help, compared to 40 percent of acquaintance killings and just 13 percent of intimate killings.

Self-help is not just more frequent in the aftermath of stranger homicides, it is more violent or severe as well (Black 1990: 76–77). In the rare instances in which vengeance is exacted for the slaying of an intimate, almost invariably only a single person will be killed. But where the parties are strangers to one another, several lives may be taken (see, e.g., Senechal de la Roche 1996: 116). And the attack may be more indiscriminate, increasing the chance of generalized warfare between the two sides (e.g., Koch 1974). Among the Mae Enga of New Guinea, avengers who launch a raid on members of their own clan generally spare women and children, but regard it as quite proper when exacting vengeance from a distant clan to set fire to women's houses in order to incinerate the women and children inside (Meggitt 1977: 24). Eritrean practice illustrates the general principle: When the two sides are close, self-help is rare; at intermediate degrees of relational distance, rule-governed feuding is likely; between strangers, all-out war is a realistic possibility (Favali and Pateman 2003: 79).[17]

INTIMATE VICTIMS

Self-help of all kinds, then, occurs less often when the parties are intimate. People are rarely lynched, for example, for killing spouses, siblings, parents, or other intimates (Senechal de la Roche 1997: 52–55). Where vengeance is the standard response to a homicide, intimacy typically provides an exception. For example, among the Mataco of the Gran Chaco, a semi-desert region located in central South America, the tendency to seek vengeance or compensation for a homicide is abrogated when the victim is a family member (Alvarsson 1988:

139). On the Micronesian island of Yap, the victim's relatives avenge all homicides except those within the family. In the case of fratricide, it "would compound the evil should the surviving brother punish the offending brother" (Schneider 1957: 794).

Intimates who are sanctioned typically find themselves shunned (see, e.g., Lindholm 1982: 66). A Somali herder who killed his father in a quarrel over bride wealth, for example, did not have to pay the usual compensation but was snubbed by his kinsmen, who "concluded that the murderer was a bastard and he was dubbed 'Parricide'" (Lewis 1961: 257). Intimate killers, then, do not necessarily get off scot-free. But they attract fewer and milder sanctions than those who kill strangers (but see Lindholm 1982: 83–87). Thus, in an incident among the Comanche Indians of the Great Plains, a man killed his father in a bid to acquire the father's new wife. The father's adopted brother came after the son and took the wife and some horses from the son. However, he did not kill the son, as would have been expected had the son not been an intimate of the victim (see Hoebel 1940: 72).

In sum, intimate killers tend to benefit from popular leniency. Seldom are they assaulted or killed by the victim's relatives or lynched by angry neighbors. Seldom too do they have to pay crippling sums of compensation. While they may be criticized or even ostracized, less is exacted from them than from those who take the lives of strangers. The killing of parents, children, siblings, and other intimates may often be regarded as the gravest of all evils in Shakespearean drama and real life alike, but it typically garners little severity.

THIRD PARTIES

Intimate conflicts evoke lenient popular sanctions in part because their third-party structure is typically not conducive to severity: those on whose shoulders the duty to avenge the victim rests are usually not sufficiently distant from the killer to take severe action. Being close to the victim, they abhor the killing; but being close to the killer, they tread lightly. The spirit is willing, but the structure is weak.

Feuding and lynching, on the other hand, flourish with differential intimacy (third parties close to one side and distant from the other) when partisanship is at its strongest and most committed. The difference between them lies in the symmetry of partisanship. Feuds normally exhibit strong partisanship on both sides: two groups of intimates somewhat distant from each other (Black 2004a: 153; see also Otterbein and Otterbein 1965). Lynchings have partisanship on the victim's side, but not the killer's. Thus, lynchings are most likely when community outsiders kill insiders and least likely when insiders kill outsiders.

Third parties who have ties to both sides find themselves caught in the middle and rarely provide strong partisanship to either. The presence of third parties with connections to both sides ("cross-cutting ties") raises the odds that a conflict will be resolved peacefully (see, e.g., Colson 1953; Ross 1986; Cooney 1998: 89–96). In my cross-cultural study, for example, when cross-cutting ties were present, the percentage of cases in which vengeance was the typical outcome declined from 83 percent to 38 percent, while the percentage of cases typically resulting in compensation increased from 4 percent to 38 percent.[18]

Modernity weakens family ties and partisanship. Smaller families, whose members change and move with greater frequency, help to explain why violent self-help in the wake of homicide is less frequent in the world's wealthier nations. Still, modern people continue to support their close relatives. The victim's family members will often cut off contact with the killer and his family. Fairly typical is one of the Virginia cases in which a man who had been on good terms with his in-laws was never spoken to by them again after he killed his wife in a quarrel. Defendants who kill victims with many close ties will therefore experience the greatest amount of shunning.

Defendants are much less likely to be permanently shunned by their own intimates. Spouses, siblings, and other relatives tend to relate to the case therapeutically, attributing blame to external circumstances that caused the defendant to act the way he did. They often view the killing as a misfortune rather than an iniquity, as something that happened to the defendant rather than something the defendant did. They are slow to blame their relative, and quick to mention any mitigating factors. Often, they blame themselves. For example, a journalist who interviewed the parents of one of the two young men who killed twelve fellow students and a teacher before committing suicide at Columbine High School, Colorado, in 1999 reported: "When they talk about the event, they discuss it as a suicide. They acknowledge but do not emphasize the murders their son committed. They also think about the signs they missed. 'He was hopeless. We didn't realize it until after the end,' Tom said. Susan added: 'I think he suffered horribly before he died. For not seeing that, I will never forgive myself'" (Brooks 2004).

Even if intimates do accept the defendant's guilt, they will often insist on the killer's essential humanity, that he is a good person who did something wrong. As the mother of a man on trial for killing four members of a family in rural Kansas said about her son: "There's lots more to Dick than what you hear back there in the courtroom" (Capote 1965: 323).

The inherent tendency of intimates to maintain partisanship and withhold blame is evident in the 1992 case of Jeffrey Dahmer. Dahmer was accused and convicted of killing fifteen young men in particularly gruesome fashion, raping, dismembering, and cannibalizing his victims. After the story broke in the national news media, his father said that he "labored to minimize" the information that was coming out:

> I allowed myself to believe that although Jeff might be implicated in a homicide, he was not the actual murderer. I accepted the fact that perhaps someone had, indeed, been killed in Jeff's apartment, but I insisted on the notion that the murder might not have been committed by Jeff. Perhaps my son had been framed, set up, I thought. Perhaps all the evidence against him was merely circumstantial. Perhaps Jeff had only found the bodies, and because of that accidental discovery, had been hurled into the center of a series of murders he'd had nothing to do with. Desperately, I tried to keep my son in the role of victim, someone who had haplessly gotten ensnared in a net of terrible circumstances. (Dahmer 1994: 164)

As the terrible reality that Jeff was indeed a multiple murderer became clear, his father said that "some part of me shut down." He continued, "I did not probe for more. . . . I did not ask the police to report on what their criminal investigations were uncovering. Some part of me did not want to know: the part that lingered in denial, minimized, and evaded; the part that, against all reason and the enormous weight of the evidence, still cried out, 'Not Jeff'" (Dahmer 1994: 188).

When people learn of the intimacy principle, their first reaction is usually one of considerable interest. How fascinating. Then comes puzzlement—why does intimacy result in leniency? Some are tempted to try to figure out what lies behind the principle, what explains it (Dawson 2006). A common hypothesis is that intimate violence is treated leniently because people perceive it to be less dangerous, less threatening. But intimate violence is not objectively any less dangerous—it has the same consequence as violence committed by strangers: injury and death. Stranger violence may undermine public order, but intimate violence undermines private safety. Indeed, because people spend more time around their intimates, and because conflict increases with contact, they are more likely to be killed by any given intimate than any given stranger. Rather, the reason people fear stranger violence more is that it comes from an unknown source. Relational distance explains the perception.

In Blackian theory, intimates get off lightly because social control obeys a universal principle: intimacy repels severity. In all known societies, from the tropical rainforests of South America to the verdant countryside of nineteenth-century Ireland, from the rugged highlands of New Guinea to the slums and suburbs of America today, intimacy mitigates the heinousness of homicide. No society has ever been observed in which intimates consistently attract greater severity. Intimacy or relational distance itself therefore provides the most scientific—the most powerful, parsimonious, and testable—explanation of the facts. Nothing lies behind it—except the more general concept of social distance. Intimacy therefore illustrates not just the empirical power but the distinctiveness of pure sociology explanations.

To this point, the effect of several dimensions of social space on the handling of homicide have been reviewed. But what does all this mean for the theory as a whole? That is the question addressed in the next and final chapter.

CONCLUSION

Stand back from the details of particular cases, and the most striking feature of conflict management is its sheer variability. Human societies subject offenders, rule-breakers, deviants to a remarkably wide array of sanctions, even for the same act of wrongdoing, such as homicide. The critical scientific question is "Why?" Why do law and popular justice produce such divergent results across cases?

Traditional legal and moral theory holds that case outcomes vary because the parties' state of mind and conduct varies. In homicide cases we therefore need look no further than the degree of intentionality and aggressiveness with which killers acted to predict their legal fate. But if that is all we do, we are bound to be disappointed: evidence of intentional aggression alone does not explain who wins and loses homicide cases. Some defendants, like James Grant in Richmond in 1868, are popularly praised and legally acquitted in the face of substantial evidence that they freely and deliberately attacked somebody who had not nor was about to attack them or anybody else. Others, such as Dan White, the sometime San Francisco city supervisor, are convicted only of manslaughter despite strong evidence of intentional aggression. Within a stateless society, one premeditated and unprovoked killing gives rise to a feud that lasts for decades, while a second evokes neither harsh words nor deeds.

The only theory that promises to provide answers to these puzzles is Blackian theory. No other theory ranges so widely across time and place. No other theory provides such a powerful array of testable propositions. No other theory addresses case-by-case variation in the handling of homicide in human societies. How well does it succeed? In this chapter I summarize the empirical evidence and look at some of its implications. But, first, I review the theory itself.

THE THEORY RESTATED

Pure sociology, as set out in *The Behavior of Law* and subsequent publications, explains the handling of cases spatially, with their social structure or geometry. Each dimension of social space has at least one elevation or status. And every social status has the same impact on law—a fourfold effect that links sanction severity to the social elevation, direction, and distance of the interaction between the principals. The fourfold status pattern operates in the realm of popular justice as well.

Since the theory predicts identical status effects, it can be restated more concisely by collapsing the individual statuses into a single, composite status.[1] Thus, the higher an actor is on each dimension of status—wealth, organization, integration, respectability, and conventionality—the higher his or her overall social status.[2] Likewise, when legal and popular sanctions are combined, they indicate the wrongness or immorality of homicide. The two composite variables yield a revised version of the familiar fourfold status pattern:

1. Upward homicide is more immoral than downward homicide.
2. In an upward direction, homicide is more immoral as vertical distance increases.
3. In a downward direction, homicide is less immoral as vertical distance increases.
4. The higher the social elevation of homicide, the greater its immorality.

Case outcomes likewise vary with the relational and cultural social distance of the principals.[3] Close killers and distant victims enjoy moral advantages over distant killers and close victims. Combining relational and cultural distance into the broader concept of social distance yields a fifth proposition:

5. The immorality of homicide is a curvilinear function of social distance.

The very same act of homicide, then, will attract sanctions of varying severity, depending on the social status of both parties and the distance between them. Neither the offender's nor the victim's characteristics alone will explain how cases come out. Some portion of the leniency enjoyed by police officers accused of killing citizens, for instance, can be traced to their victims typically being low-income individuals engaged in criminal activity (Klinger 2004). Were police to start killing doctors, lawyers, or corporate executives as they go about their legitimate business, they would attract more hostile treatment. Again, intimate homicide—such as between spouses—generally repels severity. But intimacy is not everything. To kill a wealthy white spouse is more serious than to kill a poor minority spouse. To kill a parent-spouse is more serious than to kill a childless spouse. To kill a spouse who holds down a job, is popular, and contributes time, money, and energy to helping the poor and needy is more serious than to kill an unemployed spouse with few friends and social activities. To kill a spouse with no history of committing domestic violence is more serious than to kill a spouse with such a history. Even the degree of intimacy itself varies across intimate relationships. To kill a spouse one met and married recently is more serious than to kill a spouse of many years. It is the location of the case in all dimensions of social space, not just one dimension, that counts.

The handling of cases further varies with their third-party geometry. Third parties consist of partisans who help one side prevail in the conflict and settlement agents who would conclude the conflict. Blackian theory predicts that attraction of partisans increases with the superiority and closeness of one side and the inferiority and distance of the other. The side that has the most partisanship has an advantage:

> Homicide is more immoral as the victim's partisanship increases; homicide is less immoral as the killer's partisanship increases.

Note that since partisanship is itself a form of social status, this proposition is itself implied by the status propositions above. A separate proposition is required, however, for settlement.

Superior and distant settlement agents tend to be severe (as well as more decisive and more formal). Mediators, arbitrators, or judges who are known to the parties and are of about the same status will usually seek to settle through conciliation or compensation; if they must punish, they will do so with a light hand. But put the decision in the hands of a wealthy, formally educated stranger from a different cultural background—a colonial official, an upper-class judge hearing a case between low-income young men—and the chances of conviction and severe sentence increase drastically. Elites are strict on social inferiors, strangers, and aliens. Hence the final proposition:

6. Homicide is more immoral as the social elevation and social distance of settlement increases.

This, then, is the Blackian theory of moral relativity. It isolates the fundamental principles of moral behavior—with a difference. It describes not the behavior of people, but the behavior of morality itself. It eliminates all untestable elements. It predicts countless facts, many previously unknown. It reduces to six simple propositions. And it is universal, applying equally to hunter-gatherers and farmers, to animal herders and factory workers, to slaves and free people, to kings and commoners, to the inhabitants of the smallest villages and the largest cities, to all past, present, and future societies.[4] In sum, the theory is startlingly original, wholly testable, radically simple, and maximally general.

THE THEORY TESTED

Impressive though the theory of moral relativity is, for most scientists the crucial question is simply, Is it true? Fortunately, a voluminous and varied literature on the handling of homicide allows that question to be answered. Largely the work of people unaware of the theory and hence not predisposed either for or against it, the research literature lends itself to a broad meta-test of pure sociology's predictions. The data do not have to support Black's theory. Consider some examples of what the totality of the research literature could reveal, and what it actually does reveal.

WHAT THE LITERATURE COULD REVEAL, WHAT THE LITERATURE ACTUALLY REVEALS

A series of findings not predicted by Black's theory of law is quite conceivable. Among those findings are

- That homicides committed by slave owners, aristocrats, landowners, colonialists, billionaires, and other wealthy people are invariably punished less severely than those committed by less affluent individuals.

In fact, the homicides of the wealthy only attract less severity when the victims are of lower status.

- That detectives devote as much time and energy to finding the killer of a homeless drug addict as that of a suburban mother of four.

  In fact, detectives investigate murders with varying degrees of energy and thoroughness, depending, in part, on the social standing of the victim.
- That the leniency that greeted police killers is a thing of the past.

  In fact, the police continue to enjoy a presumption of legitimacy when they kill citizens.
- That the contrast in severity for citizen-police and police-citizen homicide is fairly constant across societies.

  In fact, the contrast in severity evoked by citizen-police and police-citizen homicide varies directly with the centralization of the state.
- That while a defendant's prior criminal record matters greatly at sentencing the victim's prior record is irrelevant.

  In fact, the prior criminal record of both defendant and victim is fateful not just at sentencing but throughout the criminal process.
- That whether a murder victim is single or married, childless or a parent, employed or unemployed makes little difference to the handling of the case.

  In fact, the victim's marital, parental, and employment status matters and has always mattered to the outcome of homicide cases.
- That black defendants in the United States invariably receive the death penalty more frequently than white defendants for the same murder.

  In fact, American blacks who kill other blacks are less likely to be sentenced to death than whites who kill other whites.
- That the law punishes those who kill someone socially close, such as a member of their own family, more severely than those who kill a stranger.

  In fact, the law discounts intimate homicide and, accordingly, those who kill a member of their own family are handled leniently, not just today but throughout history.

- That whether witnesses come forward or stay back is simply a matter of chance.

  In fact, witnesses are more willing to testify on behalf of some people than others, favoring, in particular, high-status and intimate parties.
- That judges, with their greater legal training and experience with criminals, are more lenient than jurors on the average defendant.

  In fact, most defendants have a better chance of being acquitted by a jury of their peers than by a judge.

Popular justice is similar. Its research literature could equally reveal a series of findings seriously at odds with Blackian theory. Among the patterns it could disclose are

- That homicide is a crime in every human society.

  In fact, only comparatively recently has homicide acquired the case structure to make it a crime; in most societies it is a wrong to be redressed by the victim's family through self-help, compensation, or other sanctions.
- That the greater wealth of high-status families invariably makes compensation the most attractive option for them when one of their members is killed.

  In fact, wealthy families are often reluctant to forgo vengeance and accept compensation.
- That racism explains the lynching of murderers.

  In fact, the racial characteristics of the parties are but one factor that predicts whether a homicide will trigger a lynching.
- That the killer's state of mind is always relevant to determining whether he or his family is liable for a killing.

  In fact, whether the killer intended the killing is often irrelevant in fixing liability for the homicide, particularly when cases are handled by corporate kinship groups.
- That homicide is universally condemned, that killing is invariably wrong, that all human life is sacred.

  In fact, some killers are, and continue to be, honored for their deed and treated as heroes, not wrongdoers.
- That which homicides urban gangs chose to avenge depends solely on situational, opportunistic factors.

  In fact, consistent with organizational life everywhere, murders of urban gang leaders are more likely to be avenged than the murders of rank-and-file members.

- That tribal societies use compensation to redress inequalities and that poorer victims therefore attract more compensation than wealthier victims.

  In fact, it costs more to kill somebody of higher status—greater compensation must be paid for wealthy and other high-status victims.
- That tribal mediators are obsessed with the past, including case precedents.

  In fact, precedent plays little or no part in tribal mediation.
- That tribal settlement is harsh and unforgiving.

  In fact, tribal settlement rarely results in punishment for those who kill, typically involving a compromise between the two sides.
- That popular sanctions for homicide in modern society obey different principles than popular sanction in premodern societies.

  In fact, popular justice appears to obey similar geometrical principles, in all societies, at all times.

Although it could be otherwise, then, the research literature is highly consistent with the theory. Even so, the theory does not explain everything. There are some anomalies.

ANOMALIES

Reality is complex and does not always conform to the predictions of even the most powerful scientific theories. Yet deeper analysis may bring clarity. Sometimes the answer turns out to be simple: the researchers got their facts wrong (Black 1995: 845–46). At other times, omitted variables provide the answer. Thus, apparent exceptions to the Blackian theory of law can sometimes be explained by third-party effects (Baumgartner 1992a: 148–49). While the core case geometry predicts one result, the third-party geometry may predict another. Consider a historical example, the case of Giuseppe Baretti, an Italian visitor to London in 1769:

> Baretti was strolling down a London street one October evening when he was suddenly accosted by a young woman. She struck him in the genitals, hoping, it later transpired, to provoke him

> so that her male accomplices could intervene, beat him, and rob him. Things initially went according to plan in that Baretti struck the woman, whereupon three men came to her rescue. But Baretti departed from his allotted role by fighting back and stabbing one of them, Evan Morgan, who later died.
>
> The case went to trial. The defendant's prospects did not look good, for two reasons. He was a foreigner being tried by a London jury for the killing of one of their own (he waived his right to have a jury composed of an equal number of foreigners). Second, he used a knife, and the "Stabbing Act" appeared to give the jury no choice but to send Baretti to the gallows.
>
> Despite the formidable odds he faced, the jury acquitted Baretti of murder and manslaughter. Crucial to his success was the strong partisanship he attracted. A writer of some renown, Baretti had close ties to the leading literary figures of the age. A parade of high-status figures, including Dr. Samuel Johnson, Edmund Burke, David Garrick, Oliver Goldsmith, and Sir Joshua Reynolds, came to court and testified to the effect that he was "a man of benevolence, sobriety, modesty and learning." (see McLynn 1989: 39–40)[5]

Partisans can explain not just why underdogs sometimes win, but why overdogs sometimes lose—why those with apparently sociologically strong cases fail to repel law. In Brazil, for example, although the vast majority of police officers who kill citizens are never punished, no matter how aggressively they have acted, an incident that garners the attention of high-status, socially distant third parties, such as newspapers, television stations, or human rights organizations, may disturb law's slumbers. The social conditions that elicit these periodic instances of unusual partisanship are not yet clear, but when they occur, the authorities may be shamed into taking action, and investigations, prosecutions, and even convictions may result (see, e.g., Amnesty International 1997b; 2003: 11). For instance, widespread national and international media coverage contributed to the conviction and thirteen-year sentence of a police officer who killed a twelve-year-old boy he found reading a pornographic magazine (Brinks 2003: 12–13). Outcomes such as these illustrate the validity of Black's observation that while high-status and distant partisans are the hardest to attract (only a tiny minority of them get involved), they are especially valuable when they do lend their support (1993: 127).

Partisanship can help explain anomalies in popular justice as well. The assassination of the wealthy Lord Leitrim in Ireland in 1878 by three impoverished farmers, for example, was just the kind of murder that typically generates severe popular sanctions (Thomson 1974: 196). This time, however, the killers were widely praised for their deed. But the killing was no ordinary murder. Leitrim was an Anglo-Irish landlord, part of a social class embroiled in a rancorous and protracted conflict with their native Irish tenants over the issues of rent and tenure. Tensions between the two groups grew over the course of the nineteenth century and the landed aristocracy became increasingly unpopular among the Irish, nobody more so than Leitrim, who was widely known to have evicted many tenants and their families from his lands. Despite Leitrim's lofty social standing, his murder, though strongly condemned by the Anglo-Irish establishment, was warmly welcomed by many among the Irish population who were socially closer to the killer than to the victim (Slevin 2006: 149–56).

Analysis of third-party effects will not dispel all anomalies, however. Some findings will surely emerge that stubbornly resist explanation by any of the theory's variables. A mere thirty years old, the theory remains a work-in-progress, an unfinished masterpiece. Revisions and extensions will therefore be necessary, and may take years to formulate. Some will be theoretical, such as creatively reimagining in Blackian terms promising variables that do not initially appear to be geometrical.[6] But most will be empirical. Since real-world cases are a swirling mass of variables, experimental investigations that can specify the effect of one variable while others are held constant would be especially valuable. Issues that await investigation include delving deeper into the role of witness, lawyer, judges, jurors, and other third parties, describing and explaining the full range of gender effects (when will men be advantaged compared to women and vice versa?), exploring the cultural aspects of law and popular justice (e.g., what legal and moral arguments are likely to be made and to succeed?), and, perhaps most centrally, developing more sophisticated measures of both the independent and dependent variables (putting numerical values on the quantity of law and popular justice as well as conventionality, intimacy, and the like: see Black 1979a).

Even so, the research literature strongly supports Blackian theory. A large body of evidence from widely differing times and places shows that homicide cases do indeed vary geometrically in precisely the way that the theory predicts. Not a single well-designed study strongly contradicts it. Thus, the theory can be fairly said to have survived a stringent empirical test, its validity validated.

THE THEORY'S IMPLICATIONS

Powerful scientific theories often go beyond just explaining a set of facts; they change our view of reality. Blackian theory is no exception. The theory has important implications for how we understand law, violence, and morality. Some are uncomfortable, even shocking. Consider three such implications.

THE GEOMETRY OF PROOF

Pure sociology explains the handling of cases with their social geometry; legal theory explains it with the violation of rules, as established by evidence. Pure sociologists do not deny that the evidence matters but hold that, on the same evidence, outcomes vary with the location and direction of cases in social space. But what if the evidence is such a powerful factor that it explains the great majority of legal results, particularly in modern society with its more formalized legal system? Is social geometry a peripheral component of case outcomes?

Not according to the facts. Social geometry probably has the greatest impact in cases that are sociologically either very strong or very weak (pointing to either a decisive victory or a decisive defeat for the complainant) and that are of medium legal strength (the rules and evidence are ambiguous). But even strong legal cases can be derailed when the social geometry lines up the right way (e.g., Bernhard Goetz, Lizzie Borden). Recall, too, that in all cases the evidence is itself strongly influenced by case geometry. What evidence is presented, how strongly it is presented, and how credible it is judged to be are each shaped by the social elevation and distance of the principals and third parties.[7]

Social geometry does more: it helps to predict the quantum of proof—the amount of evidence needed to win a case. In traditional legal thought, the quantum of proof is a constant. The standard of proof may differ from case to case—reasonable cause, a preponderance of the evidence, beyond a reasonable doubt—but the quantum of proof required to attain the legal standard applies to everybody equally, regardless of their wealth, race, gender, age, or other personal characteristics. By contrast, in Blackian theory the quantum of proof is variable (Black 2007). Simply put, some parties need more evidence to win, while others require more to lose. Proof is geometrical.

The general theoretical principle is clear: The quantum of proof is the inverse of the quantity of law. Thus, the more law predicted, the less proof needed. Consequently, downward cases demand less proof than upward cases. Prosecutors require less evidence—fingerprints, DNA evidence, gun powder residue, eyewitnesses, and the like—to convict a homeless man with a criminal record accused of killing a respectable mother of four than when the parties are reversed. However, because the standard of proof is effectively higher in intimate cases, they require more evidence to convict a defendant accused of killing a close relative. Evidence sufficient to convict a stranger of murder may be only enough to convict an intimate of manslaughter, or indeed be insufficient for any conviction at all. A defense attorney, on the other hand, can succeed with less evidence negating or mitigating guilt when representing an intimate: the alibi need not be as airtight, the indicators of self-defense as unambiguous, or the demonstration of provocation as clear-cut. Defending a stranger, on the other hand, requires a more complete refutation of guilt.

In extreme cases—when the social geometry points strongly toward a victory or a defeat—proof may be all but irrelevant. No amount of evidence may be enough to acquit a slave who kills his master; no amount of evidence may be enough to convict a master who kills his slave (even when it is technically illegal to do so). The strongest of prosecutions—backed by considerable evidence of intentional aggression—may fail when the jury is considerably closer to the defendant than the victim (e.g., colonial defendants, the O. J. Simpson criminal case). Equally, the flimsiest of prosecutions may succeed when the jury is socially distant from the defendant and close to the victim (e.g., minorities accused of killing members of the majority in frontier societies). Some parties, then, win not because of the evidence but in spite it.

The point has practical applications. If the quantity of proof varies geometrically, then legal mistakes are more apt to occur in some cases than others. Legal mistakes are of two main types—conviction of the factually innocent, and acquittal of the factually guilty.[8] The former is more likely in downward and distant cases with their lower evidentiary standards; the latter is likely in upward and close cases that have higher standards of proof. Just as some people run a greater risk of being railroaded, others have a better chance of getting away with murder.

HOW TO GET AWAY WITH MURDER

Pure sociology can be used instrumentally, by people trying to win cases (Black 1989: chap. 2). Attorneys can apply the theory to assist them in choosing which cases to take on (e.g., defending intimates), what fee structure to use (e.g., in sociologically strong cases, a percentage of any damage awards won; in sociologically weak cases, an hourly fee), and how to manage the trial (e.g., drawing attention to one's client's sociologically advantageous characteristics and the opponent's sociologically disadvantageous characteristics). The theory can even be worked by criminals (Black 1989: 38–39). It can help people who are planning to kill to avoid punishment. It can be used to get away with murder.

In crime mysteries, getting away with murder usually means that the murderer manages to evade detection. But what is undetected now is always open to being detected in the future. Cold cases can be opened years later. In real life, when a killer gets away with murder, he does not merely escape detection but avoids legal punishment and receives the acclaim of his peers, regardless of how he kills. Sociologically, that is the perfect murder.

The perfect murder remains an artistic puzzle but is no longer a scientific mystery. Its social geometry is implied by Blackian theory: it is committed by a high-status killer against a lower-status victim; the parties are relationally and culturally close; the killer enjoys much partisan support, the victim, little or none; and the settlement agents are socially closer to the killer than to the victim. In short, the slaying is downwardly distant yet horizontally close with a third-party geometry that strongly reinforces the core geometry. Conversely, a person is least likely to get away with murder—most likely to attract maximum penalties—in a distant upward killing committed across a wide expanse of social distance with a third-party geometry strongly tilted in the victim's direction: the homicide of a wealthy, white, married, philanthropist by a poor, single, black, homeless stranger with a criminal record, for example.

A variety of killings fit the model of the perfect murder. The killing of a rebellious slave by a master is perhaps the closest fit of all (see, e.g., Schwarz 1982). Other homicides that display much of the requisite geometry include the slaying of "uppity" blacks in the Jim Crow South, "honor killings" such as the killing of a daughter by her father in honor cultures, and the elimination of notorious thieves or bullies among the urban poor of the world: these too are likely to go legally unpunished and be popularly praised (see, e.g., Brundage 1993; Peratis 2004; Jackall 1997: 110). Although police killings typically lack the close social proximity of killer and victim, many of their other characteristics are favorable. To ensure perfection, however, several additional ingredients are required: the killing should take place in an oligarchy or, better still, an autocracy, the officer should be socially integrated (married, a parent, and someone who participates in the community), have a good reputation, and enjoy the support of his fellow officers; the victim, by contrast, should be poor, unemployed, and unmarried, have a criminal record, and have no effective allies to protest his death; the killing ought to be investigated and prosecuted by the professional and personal colleagues of the killer who are strangers to the victim; and the case should be adjudicated by high-status officials.

In sum, to get away with murder, the killer should

- Be of as high a status as possible.
- Select a low-status, socially close victim.
- Have extensive strong partisanship, and the victim none at all.
- Ensure that those making the crucial case decisions are significantly closer, socially, to him than to his victim.

THE PERSISTENCE OF MORAL INEQUALITY

The ideal of moral equality requires that for the same conduct, people ought to receive the same deserts. Punishment and praise should therefore depend on what people do, not who they are. However phrased, the ideal is central to modern conceptions of justice and, more generally, morality. Of no conduct is this more true than homicide. It is one thing for parking offenses or jaywalking citations to display social variation; it is quite another for homicide, the acme of wrongdoing, to do so.

Reality is recalcitrant, however. In no known society are homicide cases handled purely on the basis of the conduct of the parties. Legal and popular sanctions always and everywhere depend on the location and direction of the case in social space. Formal legal rules do not alter this fundamental fact. We have more police, prosecutors, and judges applying more written rules today than ever before, but the outcome of homicide cases continues to vary with their social geometry.[9] Higher-status parties still find ways to prevail in downward cases; lower-status parties still run into legal obstacles, procedural and substantive, in upward cases. Changing the legal rules without changing the case geometry does not equalize case outcomes, as the recent history of American capital punishment racial reform shows. Only when case geometries are identical are results equal. Since cases are rarely geometrically identical among large populations, moral equality is almost never encountered in the real world. Popular justice invariably discriminates; equality before the law is a mirage.

This is not a welcome message. Most people today disapprove of moral inequality, at least in principle. But what, if anything, can they do about it? Pure sociology is of limited help here. As a science, pure sociology cannot determine what is good or bad, just or unjust, what we should or should not do. Even so, its startling implications will have to be confronted at some point.

One tack is to embrace reality. Perhaps, like ancient societies, we might build inequality into the law, calibrating outcomes with the social status and distance of the parties (see Black 1989: 98–99). We could acknowledge, for example, that a woman who kills her abusive husband deserves leniency, that the killing of an active, community-involved altruist is more serious than the killing of a social isolate, that the slaying of an unemployed drug dealer is less important than that of a hard-working, single mother of four. But which social attributes warrant special treatment? Should it be more serious to kill a wealthy person, for instance? If not, why should a victim's record of community service matter, but not her economic standing? Where does rightful consideration of people's social characteristics end and wrongful discrimination begin?

Another approach is to continue pursuing the modern ideal of equality. The challenge is that such inequalities are deeply embedded in social life. Recall, for instance, how black and white jurors respond to apologies by defendants in capital cases. Blacks tend to see them as genuine, whites as feigned. Each group draws a starkly different conclusion from the same set of facts. Divergences of this kind are unlikely to be eliminated by exhorting people to treat everybody equally, or enacting new legal procedures in the hope that they will do so. They are too firmly rooted in the soil of social existence. Something more is needed.

Blind review of cases by legal officials is one possibility. Black describes such a strategy, one he calls "desocialization," arguing that stripping cases of their "social information"—information about the parties' social characteristics—will equalize case outcomes (1989: chap. 4; see also Phillips 2008c). The law of evidence could be amended, for example, to prohibit the introduction of certain kinds of testimony about people, such as their marital, parental, or employment status. But since information can be inferred from the dress, demeanor, and speech of the parties, cases would still be rife with social information. The ultimate in blind review would be trial by computer: electronic justice. An idea that is in line with the trend toward ever-greater use of computers in all areas of life, electronic justice could be readily applied to legal cases, including homicide, eliminating the social disparities now so pervasive. However, because it would liquidate the advantages enjoyed by social elites, it would likely face redoubtable opposition. And it would do nothing to remove inequality from the popular response to cases.

Equalizing the parties to cases represents another way of equalizing the outcomes. Black sketches such a system, based on giving everybody the advantages of organization (1989: chap. 3). A system of legal cooperatives (co-ops) would provide members with the protection of a corporate body. When a conflict arises, the co-op would step in and handle it. Members who called upon their co-ops too often would be penalized by higher dues and, ultimately, by expulsion. Since organizations attract the compensatory rather than the penal style, incorporating conflict in this manner would presumably deemphasize the criminal nature of homicide and eventually make it, once again, a matter to be settled through payment to the victim's group. Like corporate groups in some earlier societies, the benefits and burdens of compensation would likely be born disproportionately by the family of the killer and victim. Tapping into the larger evolutionary trend toward greater organization throughout society, incorporating conflict in this manner would greatly increase equality in the legal and popular handling of cases. But is the populace willing to accept a shift away from crime to compensation, from punishment to restitution? When interviewed, the relatives of murder victims express a strong distaste for compensatory remedies, even when coupled with life imprisonment for the defendant (Kay 2006).[10]

Pure sociology cannot advocate any of these strategies of sociological justice. Desocialization and legal co-ops are simply ways of bringing legal and moral ideals into line with legal and moral reality. Whether the social conditions are ripe for their adoption is unclear. Without them, however, the gap between the real and the ideal is likely to widen. As the demand for equality in all walks of life, including law, seems to be growing, increased global migration is making modern societies more diverse (see, e.g., International Organization for Migration 2005). More diverse populations are almost certain to bring with them more diversity across cases—more people of different races, ethnicities, and cultures appearing as defendants and victims, as police officers and prosecutors, as judges and jurors. And with greater diversity in case geometry will come greater inequality in case outcomes—greater disparities in who gets charged with murder and who with manslaughter, who is convicted and who walks free, who receives life imprisonment and who gets a death sentence, who is reprieved and who is executed.

Consider, in closing, the theory's implications for how we understand an issue of great scientific and human importance: the nature of good and evil. "Thou shalt not kill," the Bible exhorts, an admonition repeated in all of the world's major religions and philosophies. Every society prohibits killing in the abstract, at least within its own boundaries.[11] But rules are not necessarily the same as behavior, philosophy is not identical to sociology. The philosophy of morality addresses what we ought to do, where our obligations lie in difficult cases, and the nature of morality itself. The sociology of morality focuses on what we actually do, on what predicts behavior in complex situations, and what theory best explains moral reality. Of the two, moral philosophy receives far more attention: to it, priests and politicians devote homilies, scholars careers, and public interest groups money, time, and energy. The analysis of moral behavior is newer and more haphazard, dispersed in the findings of social scientists working on diverse topics, scarcely even enjoying its own recognized domain of scholarly inquiry.

The most advanced perspective on moral behavior is that of pure sociology. It holds that moral principles, as known by the severity of sanctions, vary within each society. Yet they do so in the same way across every society. Whatever part of the scale of severity a society uses, the relative placement of acts of deviance on that scale is consistent across societies, despite enormous diversity in how they are organized. The sanctions themselves change, but the homicides that evoke the greatest severity in the mountains of New Guinea are the same as those that do so in the Kalahari desert, the Amazon jungle, and the streets of Tokyo, São Paolo, and New York.[12]

Morality is thus neither universal nor relative, but something else entirely: it is geometrical (Black 2000a). Right and wrong are not constants but variables. The critical axis of explanation is not from culture to culture or from person to person, but from case to case. Good and evil are not absolute, they are contextual, properties of a realm of reality at once ancient and new, familiar and strange, hidden and in plain sight: social space.

Contrast this with the conventional view of morality as dependent on conduct: Do good—help others, be kind and generous—and you shall be praised; act badly—lie, steal, or kill—and you shall be condemned. The study of homicide lays bare the limitations of that moral common sense. Conduct, or at least conduct alone, does not explain how killers are handled. The same act of lethal violence may result in starkly divergent legal and popular outcomes. Even leaving aside the relatively clear case of warfare, the response to the taking of human life varies widely. This homicide is defined as murder, that one as justifiable. One person who kills is hailed as a hero, a second is forever shunned, while a third suffers torture and lynching. Some victims are precious, their slaying widely lamented and severely punished. Others may as well be vermin, their extermination welcomed, a cause for collective celebration. A homeless man is murdered and forgotten instantly, his death not even entered into the official ledger as a crime. The assassination of a president is investigated for decades, spawning theories and countertheories, inspiring commissions of inquiry, books, articles, films, and abiding public fascination.

Is killing wrong, then? Sociologically, the wrongness of homicide depends on who kills whom, and on who handles the case.

NOTES

1 THE MORALITY OF HOMICIDE

1. I define homicide as the lethal assault of a human being. This definition includes killing by beating, shooting, choking, stabbing, suffocating, poisoning, drowning, hanging, burying, and dismembering. It excludes killing through supernatural means, such as witchcraft, or as a by-product of another activity, such as manufacturing. The restriction to intrasocietal homicide confines the analysis to cases with a high expectation of equal treatment. It does not mean, however, that killings between members of different societies are forever beyond the scope of the theory discussed in this book.

2. Throughout this book, I use the "ethnographic present tense" to refer to societies studied by anthropologists. This usage has the drawback of perhaps giving the impression that even at the time they were studied these societies were eternal and unchanging, that they had no history (Rosaldo 1980; Ferguson 1995). It has the virtue, however, of strongly conveying to the reader the immediacy and reality of how people in these societies lived and acted, at least at one time. It should be noted that virtually all these societies have since changed greatly, some beyond recognition (see, e.g., Hutchinson 1996; Knauft 2002).

3. See, for example, http://www.finnvalley.ie/history/lordlifford/index.html. Retrieved August 24, 2008.

4. There is no universally agreed-upon term for communal or nongovernmental social control: "informal social control," "other social control," "law-like processes," and even "law" are among the designations that have been used.

5. Measurement of popular severity is still in its infancy, and the ranking of severity used here may require revision in the future. For example, in at least some cases, shunning may be more severe than compensation: a victim's group might opt to pay mild compensation over being permanently exiled from its home. On average, though, compensation is more severe: compensation payments in preindustrial societies are typically too onerous to be made by a single individual but require contributions from an entire group, and often do not entirely negate the risk of vengeance, while shunning is more typically temporary than permanent, and visited on an individual or the immediate nuclear family than the group as a whole. Hence, until a more fine-grained measure of severity is developed that can rank particular cases of compensation and particular acts of shunning, the more global strategy of ranking all compensation ahead of all shunning will be used here.

6. Modes of popular justice that have died out may sometimes make a comeback. In Albania, for example, feuding had become rare under the Communist regime (1944–91) but resurfaced following its demise (see, e.g., Blumenfeld 2003: 75–86; Waters 2007: 59–61).

7. Severity is an intuitive concept, but it can be measured more precisely by the degree to which social actors avoid the outcome: the more severe the sanction, the more people and groups shy away from it (see Black 1979a). In law, the death penalty is more severe than life imprisonment—people fight lengthy legal battles to turn death sentences into sentences of life behind bars (see, e.g., McFeely 2000). Likewise, a long prison sentence is more severe than a short one, a conviction is more severe than an acquittal, and an arrest is more severe than no arrest. Indeed, as will be seen in chapter 2, each stage of the criminal justice system can be seen as an incremental increase in severity (Black 1976).

Popular justice does not typically have a system of well-defined stages, but its sanctions too can be ranked in terms of their repulsivity. Self-help is more severe than shunning—people take greater steps to avoid it. Praise is the least severe sanction because it attracts rather than repels individuals and groups.

8. For a thorough discussion of the legal process involved in a fairly typical homicide case, see Pohlman (1999).

9. In the United States, about half of the population is served by a coroner, the other half by a medical examiner. A coroner is an elected or appointed public official, who may or may not have medical training, empowered to hold inquests before juries to determine the manner and cause of death. A medical examiner is a physician who makes a determination based on death-scene investigation, medical files, autopsies, and laboratory tests (Timmermans 2006: 4–6).

10. In Philadelphia, 1948–52, 2 percent of those convicted of homicide were sentenced to death; 18 percent to life imprisonment; 7 percent to 10 years or more; 56 percent to less than 10 years; 17 percent to indefinite sentences; and 4 percent to probation (Wolfgang 1958: 304–6). In Miami, 1980, of the 149 offenders convicted of homicide, 3 percent received the death penalty, 31 percent life imprisonment, 24 percent 11 years or more, 37 percent 10 years or less, and 4 percent probation (Wilbanks 1984: 185). In Houston, 1969, 6 percent of the 91 offenders convicted received the death penalty; 4 percent life imprisonment; 70 percent terms of imprisonment ranging from 2 months to 90 years; and 20 percent probation (Lundsgaarde 1977: 224–32).

11. In addition to the state and the society, there are at least two other sources of sanctions: the supernatural and the self. A killer might be criminally prosecuted, be avoided by his neighbors, attempt suicide, and be a supplicant for divine forgiveness. Of the four sources, the state and society generate the most prominent and onerous sanctions, and the present book accordingly focuses on them alone.

12. As it turned out, Durkheim was wrong about societies. Subsequent discoveries by anthropologists revealed that the simplest societies almost never impose communal punishment, and compensatory sanctions typically develop before, not after, penal sanctions (Black 2000a: 109–12).

13. For a discussion of societal-level theories of punishment, see Garland (1990).

2 PURE SOCIOLOGY

1. Submitted as an SJD dissertation at Harvard Law School (for details, see Cooney 1988; 1998: 162–64).

2. Submitted as a PhD dissertation, University of Virginia (for details, see Cooney 1991; 1998: 158–60).

3. Over the course of a year, I spent several weeks observing prosecutors in a district attorney's office in a small southern city, conducting, all told, about 120 hours of observation. Approximately two-thirds of my time was spent in court, mainly observing trials. I was present for three homicide trials from the questioning of the jury pool (*voir dire*) through to sentencing by the judge. I also observed firsthand several others trials. Outside of court I spent my time engaged in a variety of activities, including informal discussions with the prosecutors about their current, past, and upcoming cases.

4. Studies based on victimization surveys, such as the National Crime Victimization Survey and the National Violence against Women Survey, are particularly prone to failure to control for conduct. Blackian theory predicts that survey respondents are less likely to define acts committed against them by an intimate as a crime (Black 1979c). The intimate victimizations that respondents do record in a survey are therefore likely to have other law-attracting properties, such as a different geometry (e.g., more likely to be downward) or greater legal seriousness (Black 1979c). The law-repelling effects of intimacy should therefore be reduced or eliminated in analyses of the subsequent legal fate of the cases (e.g., reporting to police, prosecution): like is not being compared with like. Including probes in the questionnaire to remind respondents that intimate victimizations are often overlooked likely reduce, but do not eliminate, the problem, since intimacy effects are deeply embedded in social life: people are slow to admit to those close to them, or even to themselves, that they have been victimized by an intimate (see, e.g., Ferraro and Johnson 1983; Moran 2003).

5. My thanks to Scott Phillips for suggesting the meta-analysis analogy.

3 THE VERTICAL DIMENSION

1. Black's formulations are "downward law is greater than upward law"; "downward law varies directly with vertical distance"; "upward law varies inversely with vertical distance"; and "law varies directly with rank" (1976: 21, 24, 25, 17).

2. Disparities in the punishments to be inflicted for master-slave and slave-master killings were written into the penal code of Imperial China under the Manchu Dynasty (1644–1911). When a slave intentionally killed his or her master, the penalty was death by dismemberment. The same offense committed by the master carried a penalty of a year's imprisonment, sixty strokes, and freedom for the murdered man's family. If a slave accidentally killed his or her master, the slave was detained in prison for strangulation; when the master was the offender, no punishment was imposed (Ch'u 1961: 191–95).

3. The privileges of the Brahmans appear to be part of a broader set of differential sanctions that reflect the hierarchies of the caste system. Writing about Tanjore in South India, Gough states: "Any murderer of a man lower in caste than himself wa[s] exempt from the death penalty, but that other grave offences, in addition to murder, [of] a man against a person of higher caste were punishable by death" (1962: 48).

4. Similar medical evidence was common grounds for the acquittal of colonists in British India as well (Bailkin 2006; Farmer 2007: 285–86).

5. Only the high-status defendant/low-status victim combination failed to find its predicted ranking, coming in second instead of last in conviction severity. As the authors note, however, this "may be attributable to the small number of cases involving high status defendants alleged to have murdered low status victims" (Farrell and Swigert 1978: 573).

6. This result was significant at the .06 level (thus making the overall status pattern curvilinear). Researchers in Texas discovered that high-status defendants were similarly more likely to get the death penalty at two separate time periods, 1942–71 and 1974–88, although their study did not control for the status of the victim (Marquart, Ekland-Olson, and Sorensen 1994: 87, 173).

7. In 2004, median family income for blacks was $35,158; for whites it was $56,700 (U.S. Bureau of the Census 2006: 449).

8. Occasionally, a study will find that neither race nor status is statistically significant: see, for example, Baldus et al.'s (2002) analysis of noncapital Nebraska homicide cases, 1973–99.

9. A third category of third party need not concern us here: those who remain neutral.

10. The "Matthew effect" is named after a passage in the gospel of Saint Matthew: "For unto every one that hath shall be given, and he shall have abundance: but from he that hath not shall be taken away even that which he hath." Originally employed in the sociology of science, the term is now used to refer to the tendency of high-status people to receive more favorable treatment in diverse areas of life (see Podolny 2005: chap. 2).

11. On the day he was due to turn himself into the police, Simpson fled in a car driven by a friend. After they were caught, Simpson was found to have a gun, a passport, and a false goatee and mustache. Simpson's friend and driver had over $8,000 in cash in his pocket. The prosecution did not use this evidence in the criminal trial, however (Bugliosi 1996: 97–98).

12. For the entire range of criminal cases sampled, the judge and jury agreed in 72 percent, the judge would have been more lenient in 4 percent, and the jury was more lenient in 24 percent (Kalven and Zeisel 1966: 68).

13. Meggitt (1977: 140–41) notes that when the Australian government succeeded in repressing clan fighting among the Mae Enga of New Guinea and compensation was eventually paid for the deaths of three women, those compensation payments were, on average, higher than those paid for men. But he notes that by the time negotiations were conducted for the deaths of the women, there had been considerable inflation in the amount of compensation payable for homicide, and that the size of these payments is probably best explained by the overall inflation in compensation payments that occurred during this period.

4 THE ORGANIZATIONAL DIMENSION

1. Here I address the handling of lethal assaults inflicted by agents of organizations. The related question of the differential legal response to deaths arising as a by-product of other activities of individuals and organizations (e.g., manufacturing) must [illegible]it another occasion.

2. Galanter (1974) argues that those who litigate often ("repeat players") are more likely to win cases. Blackian theory predicts litigiousness itself, proposing that high-status actors such as the state are, all else constant, more likely to bring cases in the first place.

3. Of course, centralization is not the only variable that affects severity across nations. The United States is the least centralized modern democracy, yet has the most punishment (see, e.g., Savelsberg 1996; Sutton 2004; Western 2006). But the United States also has the greatest wealth inequality among modern democracies (see, e.g., Wolff 2006: 13–16). Wealth disparities may result in greater vertical distance, on average, in upward crimes, a factor that would help increase overall punitiveness. Other relevant factors include the greater social diversity of America and hence the likely greater cultural distance of many of its crimes.

4. For those who attend to such matters, it might be noted that citizens and lawyers alike do not always regard the killings as legitimate. Police use of force, lethal and nonlethal, not infrequently results in complaints by citizens, some of which result in civil damage awards. Additionally, some legal scholars have asserted that while many police killings are legally justified, by no means all are (see, e.g., Knoohuizen, Fahey, and Palmer 1972; Uelmen 1973). Others, however, suggest that the great majority of homicides committed by the police are legitimate (see, e.g., Klinger 2004).

5. In some jurisdictions police officers have additional procedural rights denied to other defendants. In Georgia, for instance, police officers are exempt from some of the rules that apply to normal grand jury investigations. Unlike other defendants, police officers are permitted to remain in the room while others give testimony, to appear with a lawyer, and to make a concluding statement (A. Collins 1998: 86–87).

6. In the United States the tolerance of state criminal law can, in principle, be overcome by federal law. However, only rarely do the federal authorities bring cases against police officers who have violated individuals' civil rights. In 1996, for instance, the Department of Justice filed a prosecution in a little more than 0.2 percent of the official misconduct (including police abuse) complaints that they reviewed (A. Collins 1998: 93).

7. Although human rights research is conducted primarily for political reasons, the social structure of the research suggests that it yields valid empirical data. Human rights reports are typically critical of high-status individuals (e.g., politicians) and institutions (e.g., the police) that are usually well positioned to defend themselves; the researchers are therefore under considerable pressure to get their facts right or otherwise they will find themselves publicly discredited and perhaps banned. The reports also evince a high degree of reliability. Investigations conducted by, for example, Amnesty International, Human Rights Watch, and the United Nations Commission on Human Rights paint a remarkably consistent portrait of the circumstances and outcomes of Brazilian police homicides.

8. Amnesty International (2004b) reports that from 2000 to 2004 Jamaican police killed 650 civilians. Not a single officer was convicted.

9. See *Encyclopaedia Britannica*, 15th ed. (2002), vol. 3: s.v. "Damiens, Robert-François."

10. One exception to the advantages of organizations may occur at the final stage compensatory law, with organizations having to pay more compensation for the s injury. In studies of actual and simulated cases alike, organizational defendant

more in civil damages than individual defendants, holding constant the injury and the wealth of the defendant (Chin and Peterson 1985; Hans 1996; McCoun 1996).

11. Baldus, Woodworth, and Pulaksi (1990: 625) report that, after controlling for some 230 variables, a significant factor in predicting the imposition of the death penalty in Georgia homicide cases is whether the prosecution's principal witness is a police officer or a citizen with no credibility problems.

12. Until January 1999 he benefited from parliamentary immunity, but in June the courts decided that he should face a jury trial. He was convicted in 2001 and sentenced to 632 years in prison, though released from custody pending his appeal (Amnesty International 2001).

5 THE RADIAL DIMENSION

1. The effects of marginality on homicide cases in the middle stages of the criminal justice system (e.g., pressing charges, conviction) await investigation.

2. Why social integration should have greater explanatory power in criminal cases, and wealth greater in criminal cases, (see chapter 3) is one of several gender puzzles that await theoretical exploration. Another is the conditions under which women will enjoy advantages in criminal law, a pattern apparently not found in earlier societies (see, e.g., Given 1977: 137; Beattie 1986: 142–43; Conley 1991: chap. 3). Even today, the phenomenon may be confined to wealthy Western countries. For instance, in certain Middle Eastern societies, such as Saudi Arabia where women cannot vote, drive, or divorce, hold a passport, appear unveiled in public, or talk to an unrelated male, it seems unlikely that women are privileged over men in the criminal justice system (see, e.g., Al-Munajjed 1997; Tétreault 2000).

3. They also tend to side with parties closer to themselves, such as police officers (Black 1993: 139–40).

4. A doctor who witnessed the killing was also killed.

6 THE NORMATIVE DIMENSION

1. Murder, armed robbery, rape, or kidnapping with bodily injury.

2. Baumer, Messner, and Felson's analysis is based on an analysis of some two thousand cases from thirty-three counties representing the seventy-five largest urban counties in the United States. But the authors also found that no leniency was accorded to defendants whose victims had previously been convicted of some crime.

3. A South Carolina study revealed no significant association between how capital jurors retrospectively rated their own and their community's admiration of the victim and their initial vote to impose or withhold the death penalty (Eisenberg, Garvey, and Wells 2003). However, the study failed to control for the defendant's conduct, using instead a measure of how "vicious" the jurors rated the killing. That rating predicted death penalty votes, but was also correlated with the rating of victim admirability. Moreover, the study did not measure the impact of the victim's objective normative status (e.g., alcoholism, criminal record) on juror voting.

4. Quoted by Baumgartner (1992a: 139). My discussion in this chapter draws heavily on Baumgartner's treatment of victim unrespectability (1992a: 138–41).

5. Even today, Iran's penal code allows murder charges to be dropped if the ac-[illegible]d can prove that the killing was committed because the victim was morally cor-[illegible]Fathi 2007).

6. See, e.g., *Encyclopaedia Britannica*, 15th ed. (2002), vol. 2: s.v. "Boycott, Charles Cunningham."

7. Note, however, that killing a child was not a statistically significant factor in either study when all the variables in each were included in a multiple regression analysis (Baldus, Woodworth, and Pulaski 1990: 621, 666).

8. Economic dependency may be important in wrongful death actions as well. Goodman et al. (1991: 274–76) found that when mock jurors were given no information about the wife's employment status, they awarded substantially more compensation to female than to male spousal plaintiffs, a difference that shrank considerably when they were informed that the surviving spouse had a job.

7 THE CULTURAL DIMENSION

1. These stark contrasts were to persist for several more centuries. For a vivid description of the cultural distance between the Irish and English in the year 1600, see Foster 1988: 15–35.

2. A second form of cultural status refers to differences in the quantity of culture possessed by social actors (Black 1976: 65–67). Eminent scientists, philosophers, and religious leaders are examples of individuals who possess this status in abundance. The legal advantages it confers are illustrated by the medieval English doctrine of benefit of clergy, which allowed anybody convicted of his first felony who could read a passage from the Bible's Book of Psalms to be spared the death penalty (Durston 2004: 691–703). The doctrine was modified over the centuries and the reading test was finally abolished in 1706. Its repeal ended the exemption from the gallows enjoyed for several centuries by that small segment of English society that could read (see, e.g., Stephen 1883: 459–72; Samaha 1974: 59–62; Beattie 1986: 141–45, 451–52). Even so, Blackian theory predicts a continuing legal advantage for those who have undergone more schooling.

3. Unconventional actors, by definition, have a culture different from the majority; the degree to which it diverges is cultural distance. Hence, minority groups—whether racial/ethnic, religious, linguistic, or something else—are unconventional to the extent that they are minorities, and culturally distant from the majority and from each other to the extent that their culture diverges.

4. Indian-white disparities continue to this day. For example, Native Americans accused of homicide receive shorter sentences than whites, most likely because of the intra-ethnic nature of most homicide (Alvarez and Bachman 1996). Note that Native Americans are, on average, of lower social status than whites on most dimensions of social space, and considerable Indian-white inequalities in the handling of homicide cases are therefore to be expected.

5. In Pakistan the Penal Code incorporates the doctrine of *Diyat* (blood money). According to some observers, a member of the Muslim majority who kills a non-Muslim can escape legal liability by paying compensation to the victim's family. However, a non-Muslim who kills a Muslim does not in practice have that option and must stand criminal trial, where he will face the risk of a term of imprisonment or a death sentence (U.S. Department of State 2000, vol. 2: 2403).

6. Equally, though, race effects are not purely cultural either. If culture alone explained the findings, all whites would be advantaged and all blacks disadvantaged regardless of economic status. In fact, whites are sometimes sentenced to death

murdering blacks and occasionally are even executed. This happens, for instance, when the normal status hierarchy is reversed and poor whites kill wealthy blacks (Radelet 1989; see also G. Johnson 1941: 100, table 2). Race is fateful, then, because it is correlated with systematic social differences that are typically cultural and economic in nature.

7. Sociologists often state that race is a "social construction." But that is a psychological concept that reveals very little about the underlying basis of racial differences. Race might be more fruitfully thought of as a social reflection—wherever sharp social differences separate groups, physical characteristics of group members tend to be singled out and taken as evidence of innate biological differences.

8. There is much less information on civil sanctions. However, a Chicago study sampled over 9,000 civil jury trials decided between 1960 and 1979 and found that after adjusting for the type of case, the plaintiff's economic losses, physical injuries, and other characteristics of litigants, black plaintiffs won fewer cases, and black defendants lost more cases. Moreover, when they were successful, black plaintiffs received smaller damage awards than their white counterparts. For instance, in wrongful death suits arising out of automobile accidents involving a single business defendant, the median damage award was $79,000 for white victims but only $58,000 for black victims, 25 percent less (Chin and Peterson 1985: 36–41). Since one of the avowed purposes of a wrongful death action is to compensate the plaintiff for the income the victim would have earned had he or she not died, and whites generally earn more than blacks, these results are largely to be expected. What remains to be established is to what degree race influences civil cases over and above economic factors.

9. Two qualifications should be noted. First, the number of black-white (12) and white-black (8) cases was small in comparison to the number of intraracial cases (654). Second, the race effects weakened, though they did not disappear, in a multivariate analysis.

10. Much less research has been conducted on the fate of other minorities in death penalty cases, though some is emerging (see, e.g., Kan and Phillips 2003).

11. A study of South African cases (1900–1948) reveal the same pattern (see Turrell 2004).

12. In the second and larger study, the authors summarized their analysis in a statistical model of thirty-nine variables selected for their empirical impact and theoretical importance. In that model, a defendant's odds of receiving a death sentence were 4.3 times greater if the victim were white (Baldus, Woodworth, and Pualski 1990: 314–20, 384; see also 149–57). For their research data, a 4.3 odds multiplier means that the probability of receiving the death sentence is about twice as high for those who kill white rather than black victims (Baldus, Woodworth, and Pulaksi 1990: 384). Thus, if a defendant has a 15 percent probability of receiving a death sentence for killing a black, given the exact same circumstances, the probability jumps to 30 percent if the victim is white.

13. Hispanics who killed whites also faced an elevated risk of execution, though not as great as that of black defendants with white victims.

14. Parties who enjoy cultural status other than conventionality have similar third-party advantages. All else the same, a professor accused of homicide ought, for example, to attract more and stronger partisanship from other educated persons than a high school dropout.

15. Change the percentage of low-status minorities on juries, then, and the percentage of convictions will change as well. In Baltimore an amendment to the procedures for selecting jurors increased minority representation on juries. Instead of juries having at most 30 percent nonwhites, juries began, from September 1969, to have percentages of nonwhite members ranging from 34 percent to 47 percent. Before the change (January 1965–September 1969), the conviction rate of Baltimore juries had averaged 84 percent; after the change (September 1969–June 1974), it dropped to 68 percent (see Van Dyk 1977: 33–34; appendix J). In Los Angeles a temporary change in jury selection procedures between July 1970 and January 1972 increased the number of blacks and Hispanics on juries. Conviction rates dropped from 67 percent in 1969 to 47 percent in 1971. Once the changes to jury selection procedures were removed and minority representation declined, conviction rates rose again—to 67 percent in 1972 and 62 percent in 1973 (Van Dyke 1977: 35: appendix J).

16. Why cultural closeness is sometimes relevant to the eligibility of settlement agents and sometimes not is unclear. Perhaps the principle is nonlinear: only beyond a certain tipping point—rarely found in today's interdependent societies—does cultural closeness preclude eligibility as a settlement agent.

17. The defendants later admitted the killing to a journalist who paid them for their story (see Whitfield 1988: 51–58).

18. Putting together this principle with that considered earlier relating to the greater average leniency of black jurors generates the following pattern: while black jurors are more lenient than white jurors, they are most lenient of all toward black defendants; while white defendants are more severe on all defendants than black jurors, they are most severe of all on black defendants.

19. The killing of persons who enjoyed high cultural status apart from their conventionality is also more serious. The slaying of educated or religiously elevated individuals, for example, attracts more popular justice. For instance, in Buddhist Tibet (before the Chinese takeover), monks occupied a highly honored place in the cultural life of the society. If a monk was killed, three times the normal amount of compensation payable was payable. If a Buddhist leader—a Lama—was killed, the asking price was nine times the normal amount of compensation (Ekvall 1954: 140).

20. Generalizations must be tentative here because the literature on Plains Indians concentrates heavily on inter-tribal killing and has relatively little to say about intratribal homicide. Moreover, vengeance for intratribal homicide has been documented for at least one Plains Indians group, the Comanche (Hoebel 1940: 66).

8 THE RELATIONAL DIMENSION

1. The curvilinear formulation introduces an element of uncertainty into the relational distance proposition. One way of determining where the turning point occurs would be to conceive of strangers in terms of their degree of distance from each other. For instance, one-degree strangers are those separated by one person who knows both; five-degree strangers require five intermediate ties before a link between the strangers is formed. The question then becomes, how many stranger degrees are required before law stops increasing with relational distance?

2. Calculated from Lundsgaarde (1977: 232, table xiii). Excluded are cases in which the offender was deceased, the outcome undetermined, or charges pending.

3. In San Francisco, 1978–88, after controlling for the race and gender of the par-

ties, the number of victims killed, and the defendant's criminal record, the odds that the case would be treated as potentially capital by prosecutors increased by a factor of more than eight when the parties were strangers (Berk, Weiss, and Boger 1993: 101). Curiously, though, a similar study covering the years 1986–93 found that the odds of the prosecutor seeking the death penalty rose more than five times when the victim was an intimate or acquaintance of the defendant (Weiss, Berk, and Lee 1996). Perhaps the latter sample included an unusual number of dependent victims, such as children.

4. Note that in the Georgia studies, killing a stranger was statistically insignificant and marginally significant, respectively, when included in the full models employing 230 and 150 variables.

5. Eighty-two percent of the commuted capital offenders had been convicted of murder, the remainder, rape and robbery (Marquart, Ekland-Olson, and Sorensen 1994: 117).

6. This may explain why an analysis of homicides from thirty-three of the nation's largest urban counties disclosed no evidence of an intimacy effect. Apart from the fact that the study did not control for some other important variables (e.g., wealth, gang membership, whether the homicide arose out of a felony), the parties were simply divided into strangers and nonstrangers (Baumer, Messner, and Felson 2000). Even so, in other analyses, a simple dichotomy between close and nonclose relationship did reduce the likelihood of a conviction for first degree-murder (Beaulieu and Messner 1999).

7. The researcher does not indicate whether intimates who killed with weapons were treated more or less severely than nonintimates who killed with weapons.

8. A study of an earlier period of English history—the thirteenth century—reports that people accused of killing relatives were *more* likely to be convicted (which carried an automatic death sentence) than those who killed nonrelatives (46 percent compared to 19 percent). But there is a red flag: this anomalous result is based on a total of only 46 cases of homicides between relatives compared to 1,205 between nonrelatives (Given 1977: 103). Homicides between relatives were more likely to be screened out prior to trial (75 percent versus 64 percent) (calculated from 1977: 42, 103, 147). The 19 cases in which defendants were sentenced to death for killing relatives are likely, then, to have been exceptionable cases that outraged the community, such as multiple-victim homicides.

9. Wiener argues that Victorian men who killed their wives and girlfriends came to be treated more severely not just than women who killed their husbands and boyfriends but than all killers (2004: 162–67). However, it is unclear what impact the nature of the killing (e.g., the killing of more than one victim) has on his results. In addition, his study does not include cases in which no charges at all were brought against those who killed their spouses or those in which charges were dropped: experience in other jurisdictions reveals that many intimate homicides are screened out prior to a trial.

10. Thus, legal officials now appear to pay more attention to the violence of the killing and the relationship. A study of the conviction offense and sentencing patterns in Philadelphia homicides 1995–2000 found that the leniency afforded defendants who killed their intimate partner was largely confined to cases in which women killed their male partners (Auerhahn 2007). The reason, the author speculated, was that

women who kill their husbands or boyfriends are often defending themselves from a pattern of escalating battering whereas men who kill their intimate female partners often do so as the culmination of such a pattern. Although these differences in the nature of male and female intimate killings have long surfaced in homicide cases, they have acquired greater influence as women have attained greater parity with men. Where male violence was previously defined as social control it is now increasingly defined as deviance. In short, more equality between the genders may render the parties' conduct more fateful and thereby cut across the intimacy effect.

11. Women convicted of killing their intimate male partners were also treated a little more severely in the later period (0 percent imprisoned in 1969, 16 percent in 1985–94), but they were still handled considerably more leniently than were their male counterparts.

12. Whereas 31 percent fewer killers of intimates escaped punishment compared to killers of strangers in 1969, by 1985–94 that gap had fallen to 9 percent. ("Escape punishment" here means that the killers were dismissed, "no billed," or given probation.) In the later period as well, defendants convicted of killing strangers continued to be most likely to receive the most severe punishment the death penalty—9 percent compared to 1 percent for acquaintance killers and 0 percent of intimate killers. Somewhat unexpectedly, for cases between those extremes—those resulting in imprisonment—intimates were not treated more leniently. For example, while 15 percent of defendants convicted of killing intimates received sentences of ten years or less, only a slightly smaller percentage (10 percent) of those who killed strangers received similarly lenient sentences, and a slightly higher percentage (20 percent) of those who killed acquaintances did.

13. This discussion draws heavily upon Cooney (1994b).

14. Too much status superiority and social distance in settlement agents will generally diminish their attractiveness to the principals (Black 1993: 148). Disputants generally prefer their settlement agents to be moderately superior and distant and to avoid high-status strangers, where possible. Only when they can intervene proactively (i.e., on their own initiative) will elite strangers be found consistently settling disputes (see, e.g., Abel 1979). Once involved, however, the settlement agent may find the disputants less than wholly cooperative, making the task of settlement difficult. When the principals and witnesses refuse to testify, or testify falsely, judges will have a hard time getting to the bottom of the conflict, and their view of the facts of the case may be at considerable odds with the reality of what occurred (see, e.g., Cooney 1998: 122–31).

15. Objecting to such a tie is risky, for if the judge decides it does not vitiate his or her impartiality, the side making the objection may have alienated the judge in the process.

16. It is possible that distant settlement agents are less attuned to the nuances of local status and relationships, and may thereby handle cases somewhat more uniformly than their socially close counterparts.

17. Extremely violent self-help, then, is likely to involve relationally distant adversaries. Strangers may sever the heads or cook and eat the bodies of their victims (see, e.g., Middleton 1965: 51–52; Boehm 1984: 91; Barton 1930: 113–16). The Mae Enga of New Guinea, for example, will mutilate their slain enemies when exacting vengeance from relationally distant, but not close, targets (Meggitt 1977: 36). Canni-

balistic vengeance too is nearly always confined to conflicts spanning large expanses of relational distance (Sagan 1974: chap. 1). Thus, the Jalé of New Guinea hold that "people whose face is known should not be eaten" and hence confine anthropophagic vengeance to groups with whom they have few or no ties (Koch 1974: 80).

18. Another implication is that as would-be avengers get to know their intended target personally, they are less likely to exact vengeance (Blumenfeld 2003).

CONCLUSION

1. Composite measures of social status will therefore typically have more predictive power than individual measures. Analyzing prosecutorial and jury decisions in Houston capital cases, Phillips (2008b) found that combining victim economic, radial, cultural, and normative status yielded greater explanatory power than considering them separately. Moreover, the composite measure had just as much predictive power as several central legal variables, such as whether the defendant had prior convictions for violent crime, whether he had killed multiple victims, and whether he committed an especially legally heinous murder (e.g., he had tortured the victim or engaged in overkill).

2. The statuses reviewed in this work do not exhaust all the statuses identified by pure sociology. For instance, should more information come to light in the future, it ought to be possible to analyze the impact on legal and popular sanctions of the contributions of individuals to the performance of the group or their "functional status" (Black 2000c: 349, note 20).

3. A third form of horizontal social distance not addressed in these pages, but predicted to have the same effects as relational and cultural distance, is organizational distance—the distance between organizational actors, such as gangs or states (see Cooney 1998: 71–73).

4. The generality of the theory further implies that the six principles of morality ought to be readily extendable to other forms of deviant behavior, such as robbery or fraud.

5. See further www.exclassics.com/newgate/ng318.htm. Baretti, Johnson, and several other notables appear as characters in Beryl Bainbridge's novel *According to Queeny* (2001).

6. An example is the prevalence of deviance (see Cooney and Burt 2008). Can this variable be conceptualized at some point in geometrical terms?

7. Consequently, it is difficult to isolate a legal component of cases separate from their sociological component. Social geometry penetrates to the very core of the legal case.

8. On conviction of the innocent, see, e.g., Radelet, Bedau, and Putnam (1992) and Dwyer, Neufeld, and Scheck (2003).

9. Whether sociological variables contribute less to modern than premodern outcomes, as Weber argued, simply cannot be answered at this point. Factors point both ways. For instance, legal organization is more consistent today, resulting in a greater percentage of cases entering the legal system and being processed according to standard rules. In addition, the greater interconnectedness of modern societies increases partisanship on behalf of disadvantaged groups. But while premodern legal systems had less formality, they also typically had more homogeneity, on average, across cases,

a factor that predicts more equal outcomes. The answer is not simple, then, and may vary across particular social settings.

10. A third possibility is "delegalization"—the removal of penalties for conduct now prohibited by the law (Black 1989: chap. 5). Abolish the death penalty, for example, and bias in death sentences stops immediately. However, eliminating all criminal punishment for homicide is not likely to happen any time soon. And delegalization would leave intact inequality in popular justice.

11. The greater leniency often found in cross-societal homicides can be readily explained with Blackian principles.

12. Of course, if the same homicide has a different legal and popular geometry, then it will have quite distinct popular and legal outcomes (e.g., an acquittal and a lynching). O. J. Simpson, for example was acquitted by a predominantly black criminal jury but convicted in the court of white public opinion, a conviction that led to his being shunned in a variety of ways (Toobin 1996; Jordan 2001).

REFERENCES

Aase, Tor. 2002. "The Prototypical Blood Feud: Tangir in the Hindu Kush Mountains." In *Tournaments of Power: Honor and Revenge in the Contemporary World*, ed. Tor Aase, 79–100. Aldershot: Ashgate.

Abel, Richard L. 1979. "Western Courts in Non-Western Settings: Patterns of Court Use in Colonial and Neo-colonial Africa." In *The Imposition of Law*, ed. Sandra B. Burman and Barbara E. Harrell-Bond, 167–200. London: Academic Press.

Adler, Freda. 1973. "Socioeconomic Factors Influencing Jury Verdicts." *New York University Review of Law and Social Change* 3: 1–10.

Alabaster, Ernest. 1899. *Notes and Commentaries on Chinese Criminal Law and Cognate Topics: With Special Relations to Ruling Cases together with a Brief Excursus on the Law of Property, Chiefly Founded on the Writings of the Late Sir Chaloner Alabaster*. Taipei: Ch'eng-wen, 1968.

Allen, Frederick. 2004. *A Decent, Orderly Lynching: The Montana Vigilantes*. Norman: University of Oklahoma Press.

Allen, Hilary. 1987a. "Rendering Them Harmless: The Professional Portrayal of Women Charged with Serious Violent Crimes." In *Gender, Crime, and Justice*, ed. Pat Carlen and Anne Worrall, 81–94. Milton Keynes, UK: Open University Press.

———. 1987b. *Justice Unbalanced: Gender, Psychiatry and Judicial Decisions*. Milton Keynes, UK: Open University Press.

Al-Munajjed, Mona. 1997. *Women in Saudi Arabia Today*. New York: St. Martin's Press.

Alvarez, Alexander, and Ronet Bachman. 1996. "American Indians and Sentencing Disparity: An Arizona Test." *Journal of Criminal Justice* 24: 549–61.

Alvarsson, Jan-Åke. 1988. *The Mataco of the Gran Chaco: An Ethnographic Account of Change and Continuity in Mataco Socio-economic Organization*. Uppsala: Almqvist and Wiksell International.

Amnesty International. 1989. *When the State Kills—The Death Penalty, a Human Rights Issue*. New York: Amnesty International USA.

———. 1993. *Pakistan: Torture, Deaths in Custody, and Extrajudicial Executions*. New York: Amnesty International USA.

———. 1994. *France: Shootings, Killings, and Alleged Ill Treatment by Law Enforcement Officers*. New York: Amnesty International USA.

———. 1996a. "Pakistan: The Death Penalty." *Amnesty International Index:* ASA 33/101/1996.

———. 1996b. "The Candelária Trial: A Small Wedge in the Fortress of Impunity." *Amnesty International Index:* AMR 19/020/1996.

———. 1997a. "Against the Tide: The Death Penalty in Southeast Asia." *Amnesty International Index:* ASA 03/001/1/1997.

———. 1997b."Brazil: Candelária and Vigário Geral: Justice at a Snail's Pace." *Amnesty International Index:* AMR 19/011/1997.

———. 1999a. "Brazil: 7th Anniversary of Carandiru Massacre: Contempt and Neglect for 111 lives." *Amnesty International Index:* AMR 19/25/99.

———. 1999b. "Pakistan: Women Killed in the Name of Honor." *Amnesty International Index:* ASA 33/20/99.

———. 2000. "Algeria: Truth and Justice Obscured by the Shadow of Impunity." *Amnesty International Index:* MDE/011/2000.

———. 2001. "A Victory for Brazilian Justice: Carandiru Prison Massacre Police Colonel Convicted." *Amnesty International Index:* NWS 21/007/200.

———. 2003. "Rio de Janeiro 2003: Candelária and Vigário Geral 10 Years On." *Amnesty International Index:* AMR 19/015/2003.

———. 2004a. "Brazil: The World Has Not Forgotten." *Amnesty International Index:* AMR AMR 19/019/2004 (Public).

———. 2004b. "Jamaica: Five Years of Impunity Must Come to an End." *Amnesty International Index:* AMR 38/016/2004 (Public).

———. 2005a. *Report 2005: Brazil.* Retrieved August 24, 2008. http://www.amnestyusa.org/annualreport.php?id=ar&yr=2005&c=BRA.

———. 2005b. "'They Come in Shooting': Policing Socially Excluded Communities." *Amnesty International Index:* AMR 19/025/2005.

———. 2007. "'From Burning Buses to Caveirões': The Search for Human Security." Retrieved August 24, 2008. http://www.amnestyusa.org/document.php?lang=e&id=ENGAMR190102007.

Andrew, Donna T. 1980. "The Code of Honour and Its Critics: The Opposition to Dueling in England, 1700–1850." *Social History* 5: 409–34.

Applebaum, Anne. 2003. *Gulag: A History.* New York: Anchor Books.

Aptheker, Herbert. 1983. *American Slave Revolts.* 5th ed. New York: International Publishers (1st ed., 1943).

Arkin, Stephen. 1981. "Discrimination and Arbitrariness in Capital Punishment: An Analysis of Post-*Furman* Murder Cases in Dade County, Florida, 1973–1976." *Stanford Law Review* 33: 75–101.

Auerhahn, Kathleen. 2007. "Adjudication Outcomes in Intimate and Non-intimate Homicides." *Homicide Studies* 11: 213–30.

Ayers, Edward L. 1984. *Vengeance and Justice: Crime and Punishment in the 19th Century American South.* New York: Oxford University Press.

Bailey, F. Lee. 2008. *When the Husband Is the Suspect.* With Jean Rabe. New York: Tom Doherty Associates.

Bailkin, Jordanna. 2006. "The Boot and the Spleen: When Was Murder Possible in British India?" *Comparative Studies in Society and History* 48: 462–93.

Bainbridge, Beryl. 2001. *According to Queeny.* New York: Carroll and Graf.

Balicki, Asen. 1967. "Female Infanticide on the Arctic Coast." *Man* (n.s.) 2: 615–25.

Baldus, David C., Charles A. Pulaski Jr., George Woodworth, and Frederick P. Kyle. 1980. "Identifying Comparatively Excessive Sentences of Death: A Quantitative Approach." *Stanford Law Review* 33: 1–75.

Baldus, David C., and George Woodworth. 2003. "Race Discrimination in the Administration of the Death Penalty: An Overview of the Empirical Evidence with Special Emphasis on the Post-1990 Research." *Criminal Law Bulletin* 39: 194–226.

Baldus, David C., George Woodworth, and Charles A. Pulaski Jr. 1990. *Equal Justice and the Death Penalty: A Legal and Empirical Analysis.* Boston: Northeastern University Press.

Baldus, David C., George Woodworth, Gary L. Young, and Aaron M. Christ. 2002. "Arbitrariness and Discrimination in the Administration of the Death Penalty: A Legal and Empirical Analysis." *Nebraska Law Review* 81: 486–753.

Baldus, David C., George Woodworth, David Zuckerman, Neil Alan Weiner, and Barbara Broffitt. 1998. "Racial Discrimination and the Death Penalty in the Post-Furman Era: An Empirical and Legal Overview, with Recent Findings from Philadelphia." *Cornell Law Review* 83: 1638–770.

Banivanua-Mar, Tracey. 2007. *Violence and Colonial Dialogue: The Australian-Pacific Indentured Labor Trade.* Honolulu: University of Hawaii Press.

Banner, Stuart. 2002. *The Death Penalty: An American History.* Cambridge: Harvard University Press.

Barth, Fredrik. 1959. *Political Leadership among Swat Pathans.* London: Athlone Press, 1965.

Barton, Roy Franklin. 1919. *Ifugao Law.* Berkeley: University of California Press, 1969.

———. 1930. *The Half-Way Sun: Life among the Headhunters of the Philippines.* New York: Brewer and Warren.

———. 1938. *Autobiographies of Three Pagans in the Philippines.* New Hyde Park: University Books, 1963.

Baumer, Eric P., Steven F. Messner, and Richard B. Felson. 2000. "The Role of Victim Characteristics in the Disposition of Murder Cases." *Justice Quarterly* 17: 281–307.

Baumgartner, M. P. 1978. "Law and Social Status in Colonial New Haven, 1639–1665." In *Research in Law and Sociology: An Annual Compilation of Research,* vol. 1, ed. Rita J. Simon, 153–74. Greenwich: JAI Press.

———. 1985. "Law and the Middle Class: Evidence from a Suburban Town." *Law and Human Behavior* 9: 3–24.

———. 1988. *The Moral Order of a Suburb.* New York: Oxford University Press.

———. 1992a. "The Myth of Discretion." In *The Uses of Discretion,* ed. Keith Hawkins, 129–62. Oxford: Clarendon Press.

———. 1992b. "War and Peace in Early Childhood." In *Virginia Review of Sociology,* vol. 1: *Law and Conflict Management,* ed. James Tucker, 1–38. Greenwich: JAI Press.

———. 1998. "Moral Life on the Cultural Frontier: Evidence from the Experience of Immigrants in Modern America." *Sociological Focus* 31: 155–79.

———. 2002. "*The Behavior of Law* or How to Sociologize with a Hammer." *Contemporary Sociology* 31: 644–49.

Beattie, J. M. 1986. *Crime and the Courts in England, 1660–1800.* Princeton: Princeton University Press.

Beaulieu, Mark, and Steven F. Messner. 1999. "Race, Gender, and Outcomes in First Degree Murder Cases." *Journal of Poverty* 3: 47–68.

Becker, Howard S. 1963. *Outsiders: Studies in the Sociology of Deviance.* New York: Free Press.

Bedau, Hugo Adam. 1982. "The Laws, the Crimes, and the Executions." Chap. 2 in *The Death Penalty in America,* ed. Hugo Adam Bedau, 3rd ed. New York: Oxford University Press (1st ed., 1964).

Berdan, Frances F. 1982. *The Aztecs of Central Mexico: An Imperial Society.* New York: Holt, Rinehart, and Winston.

Berk, Richard A., Robert Weiss, and Jack Boger. 1993. "Chance and the Death Penalty." *Law and Society Review* 27: 89–110.

Bernard, J. L. 1979. "Interaction between Race of Defendant and That of Jurors in Determining Verdicts." *Law and Psychology Review* 5: 103–11.

Bienen, Leigh B., Neil Alan Weiner, Deborah W. Denno, Paul D. Allison, and Douglas Lane Mills. 1988. "The Reimposition of Capital Punishment in New Jersey: The Role of Prosecutorial Discretion." *Rutgers Law Review* 41: 27–372.

Bing, Léon. 1991. *Do or Die.* New York: Harper Collins.

Black, Donald. 1976. *The Behavior of Law.* New York: Academic Press.

———. 1979a. "A Note on the Measurement of Law." *Informationsbrief für Rechtssoziologie, Sonderheft* 2: 92–106 (reprinted as appendix A in Black 1980).

———. 1979b. "A Strategy of Pure Sociology." In *Theoretical Perspectives in Sociology,* ed. Scott G. McNall, 149–68. New York: St. Martin's Press (reprinted as appendix in Black 1993).

———. 1979c. "Common Sense in the Sociology of Law." *American Sociological Review* 44: 18–27.

———. 1980. *The Manners and Customs of the Police.* New York: Academic Press.

———. 1983. "Crime as Social Control." *American Sociological Review* 48: 34–45.

———. 1984. "Social Control as a Dependent Variable." In *Toward A General Theory of Social Control,* vol. 1: *Fundamentals,* ed. Donald Black, 1–36. Orlando: Academic Press (reprinted as chap. 1 in Black 1993).

———. 1987. "Compensation and the Social Structure of Misfortune." *Law and Society Review* 21: 563–84 (reprinted as chap. 3 in Black 1993).

———. 1989. *Sociological Justice.* New York: Oxford University Press.

———. 1990. "The Elementary Forms of Conflict Management." In *New Directions in the Study of Justice, Law, and Social Control,* 43–69. Prepared by the School of Justice Studies, Arizona State University. New York: Plenum Press (reprinted as chap. 5 in Black 1993.)

———. 1993. *The Social Structure of Right and Wrong.* San Diego: Academic Press.

———. 1995. "The Epistemology of Pure Sociology." *Law and Social Inquiry* 20: 829–79.

———. 2000a. "On the Origins of Morality." *Journal of Consciousness Studies* 7: 107–19.

———. 2000b. "The Purification of Sociology." *Contemporary Sociology* 29: 704–9.

———. 2000c. "Dreams of Pure Sociology." *Sociological Theory* 18: 343–67.

———. 2002. "The Geometry of Law: An Interview with Donald Black." *International Journal of the Sociology of Law* 30: 101–29.

———. 2004a. "Violent Structures." In *Violence: From Theory to Research,* ed. Margaret A. Zahn, Henry H. Brownstein, and Shelly L. Jackson, 145–58. Newark: LexisNexis/Anderson Publishing.

———. 2004b. "The Geometry of Terrorism." *Sociological Theory* 22: 14–25.

———. 2007. "Legal Relativity." In *Encyclopedia of Law and Society: American and Global Perspectives,* vol. 3, ed. David S. Clark, 1292–94. Thousand Oaks: Sage Publications.

———. 2008. "How Law Behaves: An Interview with Donald Black." Unpublished paper, Department of Sociology, University of Virginia.

Black, Donald, and M. P. Baumgartner. 1983. "Toward a Theory of the Third Party." In *Empirical Theories about Courts,* ed. Keith O. Boyum and Lynn Mather, 84–114. New York: Longman.

Blackman, Paul H., and Vance McLaughlin. 2003. "Mass Legal Executions of Blacks in the United States, 17th–20th Centuries." *Homicide Studies* 7: 235–62.

Blackstone, William. 1796. *The Commentaries of Sir William Blackstone, Knt. on The Laws and Constitution of England; carefully abridged, in a new manner and continued down to the present time: with notes, corrective and explanatory. By William Curry, of the Inner Temple.* London: W. Clarke and Son (originally published in 4 vols., 1765–69).

Blumberg, Rae Lesser. 1978. *Stratification: Socioeconomic and Sexual Inequality.* Dubuque: Wm. C. Brown Co.

———. 1984. "A General Theory of Gender Stratification." In *Sociological Theory 1984,* ed. Randall Collins, 23–101. San Francisco: Jossey-Bass.

Blumenfeld, Laura. 2003. *Revenge: A Story of Hope.* New York: Simon and Schuster.

Boehm, Christopher. 1984. *Blood Revenge: The Enactment and Management of Conflict in Montenegro and Other Tribal Societies.* Philadelphia: University of Pennsylvania Press.

Bogira, Steve. 2005. *Courtroom 302: A Year behind the Scenes in an American Criminal Courthouse.* New York: Vintage Books.

Bohannan, Paul. 1957. *Justice and Judgment among the Tiv.* London: Oxford University Press.

Bonczar, Thomas P., and Tracy L. Snell. 2004. *Capital Punishment, 2003.* Washington DC: Bureau of Justice Statistics, U.S. Department of Justice (available at www.ojp.usdoj.gov/bjs/pub/pdf/cp03.pdf).

Borg, Marian J. 1992. "Conflict Management in the Modern World System." *Sociological Forum* 7: 261–82.

Boris, Steven Barnet. 1979. "Stereotypes and Dispositions for Criminal Homicide." *Criminology* 17: 139–58.

Bowers, William J. 1983. "The Pervasiveness of Arbitrariness and Discrimination under Post-*Furman* Capital Statutes." *Journal of Criminal Law and Criminology* 74: 1067–1100.

Bowers, William J., and Glenn L. Pierce. 1980. "Arbitrariness and Discrimination under Post-*Furman* Capital Statutes." *Crime and Delinquency* 26: 453–84.

Bowers, William J., Benjamin Steiner, and Maria Sandys. 2001. "Death Sentencing in Black and White: An Empirical Analysis of the Role of Jurors' Race and Jury Racial Composition." *University of Pennsylvania Journal of Constitutional Law* 3: 171–274.

Breman, Jan. 1989. *Taming the Coolie Beast: Plantation Society and the Colonial Order in Southeast Asia.* Delhi: Oxford University Press.

Brinks, Daniel M. 2003. "Informal Institutions and the Rule of Law: The Judicial Response to State Killings in Buenos Aires and São Paolo in the 1990s." *Comparative Politics* 36: 1–19.

Brooks, David. 2004. "Columbine: Parents of a Killer." *New York Times,* May 15, sec. A.

Brown, Donald E. 1991. *Human Universals.* Philadelphia: Temple University Press.

Brown, Jodi M., and Patrick A. Langan. 2001. *Policing and Homicide, 1976–1998: Justifiable Homicide by Police, Police Officers Murdered by Felons.* Washington DC: U.S. Department of Justice, Bureau of Justice Statistics.

Brown, Keith M. 1986. *Bloodfeud in Scotland, 1573–1625: Violence, Justice and Politics in an Early Modern Society.* Edinburgh: J. Donald.

Brown, Richard Maxwell. 1975. *Strain of Violence: Historical Studies of American Violence and Vigilantism.* New York: Oxford University Press.

Brundage, W. Fitzhugh. 1993. *Lynching in the New South: Georgia and Virginia, 1880–1930.* Urbana: University of Illinois Press.

Bugliosi, Vincent. 1996. *Outrage: The Five Reasons Why O. J. Simpson Got Away with Murder.* New York: W. W. Norton.

Bush, M. L. 1983. *Noble Privilege.* New York: Holmes and Meier.

Cain, Maureen, and Alan Hunt, eds. 1979. *Marx and Engels on Law.* London: Academic Press.

Calder, Bobby J., Chester A. Insko, and Ben Yandell. 1974. "The Relation of Cognitive and Memorial Processes to Persuasion in a Simulated Jury Trial." *Journal of Applied Social Psychology* 4: 62–93.

California Department of Justice. 2000. *Homicide in California, 1999.* Sacramento: Criminal Justice Statistics Center.

Callahan, Lisa, Henry J. Steadman, Margaret McGreevey, and Pamela Clark Robbins. 1991. "The Volume and Characteristics of Insanity Defense Pleas: An Eight-State Study." *Bulletin of the American Academy of Psychiatry and Law* 19: 331–38.

Campbell, Bradley. 2006. "The Collectivization of Genocide." Paper presented at the annual meeting of the American Society of Criminology, November 1, Los Angeles.

———. 2009. "Genocide as Social Control." *Sociological Theory* 27: 150–72.

Caplow, Theodore, Louis Hicks, and Ben J. Wattenberg. 2001. *The First Measured Century: An Illustrated Guide to Trends in America, 1900–2000.* Washington DC: AEI Press.

Capote, Truman. 1965. *In Cold Blood: A True Account of a Multiple Murder and Its Consequences.* New York: Signet Books.

Carneiro, Robert L. 1997. "A Theory of the Origin of the State." *Science* 169: 733–38.

Cavallaro, James. 1997. *Police Brutality in Urban Brazil.* New York: Human Rights Watch.

Chafetz, Janet Saltzman. 2004. "Gendered Power and Privilege: Taking Lenski One Step Further." *Sociological Theory* 22: 269–77.

Chagnon, Napoleon. 1977. *Yanomamö: The Fierce People.* 2nd ed. New York: Holt, Rinehart, and Winston (1st ed., 1968).

Chambliss, William J. 1964. "A Sociological Analysis of the Law of Vagrancy." *Social Problems* 12: 67–77.

Cheh, Mary H. 1996. "Are Lawsuits an Answer to Police Brutality?" In *Police Violence: Understanding and Controlling Police Abuse of Force,* ed. William A. Geller and Hans Toch, 247–72. New Haven: Yale University Press.

Chevigny, Bell Gale, and Paul Chevigny. 1991. *Police Violence in Argentina.* New York: Human Rights Watch.

Chevigny, Paul. 1969. *Police Power: Police Abuses in New York City.* New York: Vintage.

———. 1993. *Urban Police Violence in Brazil: Torture and Police Killings in São Paolo and Rio de Janeiro after Five Years.* New York: Human Rights Watch.

———. 1995. *Edge of the Knife: Police Violence in the Americas.* New York: New Press.

Chin, Audrey, and Mark A. Peterson. 1985. *Deep Pockets, Empty Pockets: Who Wins in Cook County Jury Trials.* Santa Monica: Rand Corporation.

Chiricos, Theodore G., and William D. Bales. 1991. "Unemployment and Punishment: An Empirical Assessment." *Criminology* 29: 701–24.

Ch'u, T'ung-tsu. 1961. *Law and Society in Traditional China.* Paris: Mouton.

Coleman, James S. 1982. *The Asymmetric Society.* Syracuse: Syracuse University Press.

———. 1990. *Foundations of Social Theory.* Cambridge: Harvard University Press.

Collins, Allyson. 1998. *Shielded from Justice: Police Brutality and Accountability in the United States.* New York: Human Rights Watch.

Collins, Hugh. 1982. *Marxism and Law.* Oxford: Clarendon Press.

Colson, Elizabeth. 1953. "Social Control and Vengeance in Plateau Tonga Society." *Africa* 23: 199–212.

Comack, Elizabeth, and Gillian Balfour. 2004. *The Power to Criminalize: Violence, Inequality and the Law.* Halifax: Fernwood Publishing.

Conley, Carolyn A. 1991. *The Unwritten Law: Criminal Justice in Victorian Kent.* New York: Oxford University Press.

———. 1999. *Melancholy Accidents: The Meaning of Violence in Post-Famine Ireland.* Lanham: Lexington Books.

Cooney, Mark. 1988. "The Social Control of Homicide." Unpublished SJD dissertation, Harvard Law School.

———. 1991. "Law, Morality, and Conscience: The Social Control of Homicide in Modern America." Unpublished PhD dissertation, Department of Sociology, University of Virginia.

———. 1994a. "The Informal Social Control of Homicide." *Journal of Legal Pluralism* 34: 31–59.

———. 1994b. "Evidence as Partisanship." *Law and Society Review* 28: 833–58.

———. 1997a. "The Decline of Elite Homicide." *Criminology* 35: 381–407.

———. 1997b. "From Warre to Tyranny: Lethal Conflict and the State." *American Sociological Review* 62: 316–38.

———. 1998. *Warriors and Peacemakers: How Third Parties Shape Violence.* New York: New York University Press.

———. 2002. "Still Paying the Price of Heterodoxy: *The Behavior of Law* a Quarter-Century On." *Contemporary Sociology* 31: 658–61.

———. 2003. "The Privatization of Violence." *Criminology* 41: 1377–1406.

———. 2009. "Ethnic Conflict without Ethnic Groups: A Study in Pure Sociology." *British Journal of Sociology,* forthcoming.

Cooney, Mark, and Callie Harbin Burt. 2008. "Less Crime, More Punishment." *American Journal of Sociology,* forthcoming.

Cooney, Mark, and Scott Phillips. 2002. "Typologizing Violence: A Blackian Perspective." *International Journal of Sociology and Social Policy* 22: 75–108.

Corwin, Miles. 2003. *Homicide Special: A Year with the LAPD's Elite Detective Unit.* New York: Owl Books.

Courtois, Stéphane, Nicolas Werth, Jean-Louis Panné, Andrzej Paczkowski, Karel Bartošek, and Jean-Louis Margolin. 1999. *The Black Book of Communism: Crimes, Terror, Repression.* Cambridge: Harvard University Press.

Crone, Patricia. 1989. *Pre-Industrial Societies.* Oxford: Basil Blackwell.

Cullen, Francis T., and Robert Agnew, eds. 2006. *Criminological Theory: Past to Present.* 3rd ed. Los Angeles: Roxbury Publishing (1st ed., 1999).

Curra, John. 2000. *The Relativity of Deviance.* Thousand Oaks: Sage.

Curtis, Edmund. 1938. *A History of Medieval Ireland, from 1086 to 1513.* 2nd ed. New York: Barnes and Noble, 1968 (1st ed., 1923).

Dahmer, Lionel. 1994. *A Father's Story.* New York: William Morrow.

Dale, Elizabeth. 2006. "Getting Away with Murder." *American Historical Review* 111: 95–103.

Daly, Kathleen. 1987. "Structure and Practice of Familial-Based Justice in a Criminal Court." *Law and Society Review* 21: 267–90.

Das, Sukla. 1977. *Crime and Punishment in Ancient India (c. A.D. 300 to A.D. 1100).* New Delhi: Abhinav.

Davies, R. R. 1969. "The Survival of the Bloodfeud in Medieval Wales." *History* 54: 338–57.

Davies, Susanne. 1990. "Aborigines, Murder and the Criminal Law in Early Port Phillip, 1841–1851." In *Through White Eyes,* ed. Susan Jason and Stuart Macintyre, 101–19. Sydney: Allen and Unwin.

Davis, Adrian. 2000. "Fraternity and Fratricide in Late Imperial China." *American Historical Review* 105: 1630–40.

Dawson, Myrna. 2003. "The Cost of 'Lost' Intimacy: The Effect of Relationship State on Criminal Justice Decision Making." *British Journal of Criminology* 43: 689–709.

———. 2004. "Rethinking the Boundaries of Intimacy at the End of the Century: The Role of Victim-Defendant Relationship in Criminal Justice Decisionmaking over Time." *Law and Society Review* 38: 105–38.

———. 2006. "Intimacy and Violence: Exploring the Role of Victim-Defendant Relationship in Criminal Law." *Journal of Criminal Law and Criminology* 96: 1417–49.

Dean, Trevor. 2001. *Crime in Medieval Europe, 1200–1500.* Harlow: Longman.

Dershowitz, Alan. 1996. *Reasonable Doubts: The O. J. Simpson Case and the Criminal Justice System.* New York: Simon and Schuster.

Devine, Philip E. 1978. *The Ethics of Homicide.* Ithaca: Cornell University Press.

Dimenstein, Gilberto. 1991. *Brazil: War on Children.* London: Latin American Bureau.

Dodge, Lowell. 1990. "Death Penalty Sentencing: Research Indicates Pattern of Racial Disparities." Report T-GGD-90–37. Washington DC: U.S. General Accounting Office.

Dollard, John. 1957. *Caste and Class in a Southern Town.* 3rd ed. Garden City: Doubleday Anchor Books (1st ed., 1937).

Donovan, James M. 1981. "Justice Unblind: The Juries and the Criminal Classes in France, 1825–1914." *Journal of Social History* 15: 89–107.

Duffy, Sean. 1998. "Remonstrance of the Irish Princes." In *The Oxford Companion to Irish History*, ed. S. J. Connolly, 480. Oxford: Oxford University Press.

Dunne, Dominick. 2001. *Justice: Crimes, Trials, and Punishments.* New York: Crown Publishers.

Durkheim, Émile. 1893. *The Division of Labor in Society.* New York: Free Press, 1964.

Durston, Gregory. 2004. *Crime and Justice in Early Modern England: 1500–1750.* Chichester: Barry Rose Publishers.

Dwyer, Jim, Peter Neufeld, and Barry Scheck. 2003. *Actual Innocence: When Justice Goes Wrong and How to Make It Right.* Rev. ed. New York: New American Library (1st ed., 2000).

Eck, Clementine van. 2003. *Purified by Blood: Honour Killings among Turks in the Netherlands.* Amsterdam: Amsterdam University Press.

Eckert, Julia. 2005. "Death and the Nation: State Killing in India." In *The Cultural Lives of Capital Punishment: Comparative Perspectives,* ed. Austin Sarat and Christian Boulanger, 194–218. Stanford: Stanford University Press.

Eisenberg, Theodore, Stephen P. Garvey, and Martin T. Wells. 2003. "Victim Characteristics and Victim Impact Evidence in South Carolina Capital Cases." *Cornell Law Review* 88: 306–42.

Ekvall, Robert B. 1954. "Mi Tsong: the Tibetan Custom of Life Indemnity." *Sociologus* 4: 136–45.

———. 1964. "Peace and War among the Tibetan Nomads." *American Anthropologist* 66: 1119–48.

———. 1968. *Fields on the Hoof: Nexus of Tibetan Nomadic Pastoralism.* New York: Holt, Rinehart, and Winston.

Ericson, Richard V, and Patricia M. Baranek. 1982. *The Ordering of Justice: A Study of Accused Persons as Dependants in the Criminal Process.* Toronto: University of Toronto Press.

Ewers, John C. 1958. *Blackfeet: Raiders of the Northwestern Plains.* Norman: University of Oklahoma Press.

Farmer, Lindsay. 2007. "Criminal Responsibility and the Proof of Guilt." In *Modern Histories of Crime and Punishment,* ed. Markus D. Dubber and Lindsay Farmer, 42–65. Stanford: Stanford University Press.

Farr, James. 2005. *A Tale of Two Murders: Passion and Power in Seventeenth-Century France.* Durham: Duke University Press.

Farrell, Ronald A., and Victoria Lynn Swigert. 1978. "Legal Disposition of Inter-Group and Intra-Group Homicides." *Sociological Quarterly* 19: 565–76.

———. 1986. "Adjudication in Homicide: An Interpretive Analysis of the Effect of Defendant and Victim Social Characteristics." *Journal of Research in Crime and Delinquency* 23: 349–69.

Fathi, Nazila. 2007. "Iran Exonerates Six Who Killed in Islam's Name." *New York Times,* April 19. http://www.nytimes.com/2007/04/19/world/middleeast/19iran.html?ex=1334635200&en=b068db1afcbc0c50&ei=5088.

Favali, Lyda, and Roy Pateman. 2003. *Blood, Land, and Sex: Legal and Political Pluralism in Eritrea.* Bloomington: Indiana University Press.

Federal Bureau of Investigation. 2005. *Crime in the United States: Uniform Crime Reports, 2004.* Washington DC: U.S. Department of Justice.

Feige, David. 2006. *Indefensible: One Lawyer's Journey into the Inferno of American Justice.* New York: Little, Brown.

Ferguson, R. Brian. 1995. *Yanomami Warfare: A Political History.* Santa Fe: School of American Research Press.

Ferraro, Kathleen J., and John M. Johnson. 1983. "How Women Experience Battering: The Process of Victimization." *Social Problems* 30: 325–39.

Fletcher, George. 1988. *A Crime of Self-Defense: Bernhard Goetz and the Law on Trial.* New York: Free Press.

———. 1995. *With Justice For Some: Victims' Rights in Criminal Trials.* Reading: Addison-Wesley Publishing .

Fletcher, Richard. 2003. *Bloodfeud: Murder and Revenge in Anglo-Saxon England.* New York: Oxford University Press.

Foley, Linda, and Richard Powell. 1982. "The Discretion of Prosecutors, Judges, and Juries in Capital Cases." *Criminal Justice Review* 7 (2): 16–22.

Foster, R. F. 1988. *Modern Ireland, 1600–1972.* London: Penguin Books, 1989.

Foucault, Michel. 1975. *Discipline and Punish: The Birth of the Prison.* New York: Vintage Books, 1979.

Freeman, Milton M. R. 1971. "A Social and Ecological Analysis of Systematic Female Infanticide among the Netsilik Eskimos." *American Anthropologist* 73: 1011–18.

Galanter, Marc. 1974. "Why the 'Haves' Come Out Ahead: Speculations on the Limits of Legal Change." *Law and Society Review* 9: 95–160.

Gambino, Richard. 1977. *Vendetta: The True Story of the Largest Lynching in U.S. History.* Toronto: Guenica, 1998.

Ganesan, Arvind. 1996. *Police Abuse and Killings of Street Children in India.* New York: Human Rights Watch.

Gard, Wayne. 1949. *Frontier Justice.* Norman: University of Oklahoma Press.

Garfinkel, Harold. 1949. "Research Note on Inter- and Intra-Racial Homicides." *Social Forces* 27: 369–81.

Garland, David. 1990. *Punishment and Modern Society: A Study in Social Theory.* Chicago: University of Chicago Press.

Gaskill, Malcolm. 2000. *Crime and Mentalities in Early Modern England.* Cambridge: Cambridge University Press.

Gellner, Ernest. 1969. *Saints of the Atlas.* Chicago: University of Chicago Press.

Genovese, Eugene D. 1972. *Roll, Jordan, Roll: The World the Slaves Made.* New York: Vintage Books, 1976.

Geremek, Bronislaw. 1971. *The Margins of Society in Late Medieval Paris.* Cambridge: Cambridge University Press, 1987.

Gilbert, Dennis, and Joseph Kahl. 1993. *The American Class Structure: A New Synthesis.* 4th ed. Belmont: Wadsworth (1st ed., 1957).

Gilsenan, Michael. 1976. "Lying, Honor, and Contradiction." In *Transaction and Meaning: Directions in the Anthropology of Exchange and Symbolic Behavior,* ed. Bruce Kapferer, 191–219. Philadelphia: Institute for the Study of Human Issues.

Ginat, Joseph. 1997. *Blood Revenge: Family Honor, Mediation and Outcasting.* 2nd ed. Brighton: Sussex Academic Press (1st ed., 1987).

Given, James Buchanan. 1977. *Society and Homicide in Thirteenth-Century England.* Stanford: Stanford University Press.

Gluckman, Max. 1967. *The Judicial Process among the Barotse of Northern Rhodesia.* Manchester: Manchester University Press.

Goffman, Erving. 1963. *Behavior in Public Places: Notes on the Social Organization of Gatherings.* New York: Free Press.

Goldstein, Donna. 2003. *Laughter out of Place: Race, Class, Violence, and Sexuality in a Rio Shantytown.* Berkeley: University of California Press.

Goodman, Jane, Elizabeth F. Loftus, Marian Miller, and Edith Greene. 1991. "Money, Sex, and Death: Gender Bias in Wrongful Death Damage Awards." *Law and Society Review* 25: 263–85.

Gossman, Patricia. 1992. *Police Killings and Rural Violence in Andhra Pradesh.* New York: Human Rights Watch.

Gough, Kathleen. 1962. "Caste in a Tanjore Village." In *Aspects of Caste in South India, Ceylon, and North-West Pakistan,* ed. E. R. Leach, 11–60. Cambridge: Cambridge University Press.

Gould, Roger V. 2004. *Collision of Wills: How Ambiguity about Social Rank Breeds Conflict.* Chicago: University of Chicago Press.

Grann, David. 2004. "The Brand: How the Aryan Brotherhood Became the Most Murderous Prison Gang in America." *New Yorker,* February 16 and 23: 157–71.

Granovetter, Mark S. 1973. "The Strength of Weak Ties." *American Journal of Sociology* 78: 1360–80.

Green, Thomas A. 1972. "Societal Concepts of Criminal Liability for Homicide in Medieval England." *Speculum* 47: 669–94.

———. 1976. "The Jury and the English Law of Homicide, 1200–1600." *Michigan Law Review* 74: 413–99.

Grönfors, Martti. 1986. "Social Control and Law in the Finnish Gypsy Community: Blood Feuding as a System of Justice." *Journal of Legal Pluralism* 24: 101–25.

Gross, Samuel R., and Robert Mauro. 1989. *Death and Discrimination: Racial Disparities in Capital Sentencing.* Boston: Northeastern University Press.

Hacker, Andrew. 1997. *Money: Who Has How Much and Why.* New York: Scribner.

Hallpike, C. R. 1977. *Bloodshed and Vengeance in the Papuan Mountains: The Generation of Conflict in Tauade Society.* Oxford: Clarendon Press.

Hamm, Richard F. 2003. "A Good and Efficient Remedy for Libel." In *Murder, Honor, and Law: 4 Virginia Homicides from Reconstruction to the Great Depression,* 12–57. Charlottesville: University of Virginia Press.

Hanawalt, Barbara A. 1979. *Crime and Conflict in English Communities, 1300–1348.* Cambridge: Harvard University Press.

Hanke, Penelope J. 1995. "Sentencing Disparities by Race of Offender and Victim: Women Homicide Offenders in Alabama, 1929–1985." *Sociological Spectrum* 15: 277–97.

Hans, Valerie P. 1996. "The Contested Role of the Civil Jury in Business Litigation." *Judicature* 79: 242–48.

Harner, Michael J. 1972. *The Jívaro: People of the Sacred Waterfalls.* Garden City: Anchor Books, 1973.

Harring, Sidney L. 1998. *White Man's Law: Native People in Nineteenth-Century Canadian Jurisprudence.* Toronto: University of Toronto Press.

Harris, Ruth. 1989. *Murders and Madness: Medicine, Law, and Society in the Fin de Siècle.* Oxford: Clarendon Press.

Hasluck, Margaret. 1954. *The Unwritten Law in Albania.* Cambridge: Cambridge University Press.

Hauser, Marc D. 2006. *Moral Minds: How Nature Designed Our Universal Sense of Right and Wrong.* New York: HarperCollins.

Hellie, Richard. 1982. *Slavery in Russia, 1450–1725.* Chicago: University of Chicago Press.

Highland, Gary. 1994. "A Tangle of Paradoxes: Race, Justice and Criminal Law in Queensland, 1882–1894." In *A Nation of Rogues? Crime, Law and Punishment in Colonial Australia,* ed. David Philips and Susanne Davies, 123–40. Melbourne: Melbourne University Press.

Hines, Robert V., and John Mack Faragher. 2000. *The American West: A New Interpretive History.* New Haven: Yale University Press.

Hoebel, E. Adamson. 1940. *The Political Organization and Law-Ways of the Comanche Indians.* Memoirs of the American Anthropological Association, no. 54. Menasha: American Anthropological Association.

———. 1954. *The Law of Primitive Man.* New York: Atheneum, 1979.

———. 1960. *The Cheyennes: Indians of the Great Plains.* New York: Holt, Rinehart, and Winston.

Hoffer, Peter C., and N. E. H. Hull. 1981. *Murdering Mothers: Infanticide in England and New England, 1558–1803.* New York: New York University Press.

Hoffmann, Heath. 2006. "Criticism as Deviance and Social Control in Alcoholics Anonymous." *Journal of Contemporary Ethnography* 35: 669–95.

Holcomb, Jefferson E., Marian Williams, and Stephen Demuth. 2004. "White Female Victims and Death Penalty Disparity Research." *Justice Quarterly* 21: 875–902.

Hollis, Martin, and Steven Lukes, eds. 1982. *Rationality and Relativism.* Cambridge: MIT Press.

Hollon, W. Eugene. 1974. *Frontier Violence: Another Look.* New York: Oxford University Press.

Horowitz, Ruth. 1987. "Community Tolerance of Gang Violence." *Social Problems* 34: 437–50.

Horowitz, Ruth, and Gary Schwartz. 1974. "Honor, Normative Ambiguity, and Gang Violence." *American Sociological Review* 39: 238–51.

Horwitz, Allan V. 1982. *The Social Control of Mental Illness.* New York: Academic Press.

———. 1990. *The Logic of Social Control.* New York: Plenum.

———. 2002. "Toward a New Science of Social Life: A Retrospective Examination of *The Behavior of Law.*" *Contemporary Sociology* 31: 641–44.

Howell, P. P. 1954. *A Manuel of Nuer Law: Being an Account of Customary Law, Its Evolution and Development in the Courts Established by the Sudan Government.* London: Oxford University Press.

Howell, Signe, and Roy Willis. 1989. *Societies at Peace: Anthropological Perspectives.* London: Routledge.

Huggins, Martha. 2000. "Modernity and Devolution: The Making of Police Death Squads in Brazil." In *Death Squads in Global Perspective: Murder with Deniability,* ed. Bruce D. Campbell and Arthur D. Brenner, 203–28. New York: St. Martin's.

Huggins, Martha K., Mika Haritos-Fatouros, and Philip G. Zombardo. 2002. *Violence Workers: Police Torturers and Murderers Reconstruct Brazilian Atrocities.* Berkeley: University of California Press.

Human Rights Watch. 1998–2007. *World Report.* New York: Human Rights Watch (available at www.hrw.org).

Human Rights Watch. 2001. "Colombia" in *World Report, 2000.* New York: Human Rights Watch. Retrieved August 24, 2008. http://www.hrw.org/wr2k1/americas/index.html.

Hutchinson, Sharon E. 1996. *Nuer Dilemmas: Coping with Money, War, and the State.* Berkeley: University of California Press.

Hyams, Paul R. 2003. *Rancor and Reconciliation in Medieval England.* Ithaca: Cornell University Press.

Innes, Martin. 2003. *Investigating Murder: Detective Work and the Police Response to Criminal Homicide.* Oxford: Oxford University Press.

International Organization for Migration. 2005. *World Migration, 2005.* Geneva: International Organization for Migration.

Jackall, Robert. 1997. *Wild Cowboys: Urban Marauders and the Forces of Order.* Cambridge: Harvard University Press.

———. 2005. *Street Stories: The World of Police Detectives.* Cambridge: Harvard University Press.

Jacobs, Bruce A., and Richard Wright. 2006. *Street Justice: Retaliation in the Criminal Underworld.* Cambridge: Cambridge University Press.

Jacobs, David, Zhenchao Qian, Jason T. Carmichael, and Stephanie L. Kent. 2007. "Who Survives on Death Row? An Individual and Contextual Analysis." *American Sociological Review* 72: 610–32.

Jacques, Scott, and Richard Wright. 2008. "The Relevance of Peace to the Study of Drug Market Violence." *Criminology* 46: 221–53.

Jahangir, Asma. 2004. Report of the Special Rapporteur on Extrajudicial, Summary, or Arbitrary Executions, Asma Jahangir, on her mission to Brazil (September 16–October 8, 2003). Retrieved August 24, 2008. http://daccessdds.un.org/doc/UNDOC/GEN/G04/105/98/PDF/G0410598.pdf?OpenElement.

Jehl, Douglas. 1999. "Arab Honor's Price: A Woman's Blood." *New York Times,* 20 June, sec. 1.

Johnson, Guy B. 1941. "The Negro and Crime." *Annals of the American Academy of Political and Social Science* 271: 93–104.

Johnson, Robert. 1998. *Death Work: A Study of the Modern Execution Process.* 2nd ed. Belmont: West/Wadsworth (1st ed., 1990).

Jordan, Pat. 2001. "The Outcast." *New Yorker,* July 9: 42–47.

Judson, Charles J., James J. Pandell, Jack B. Owens, James L. McIntosh, and Dale L. Matschullat. 1969. "A Study of the California Penalty Jury in First-Degree Murder Cases." *Stanford Law Review* 21: 1302–1497.

Kalven, Harry Jr., and Hans Zeisel. 1966. *The American Jury.* Boston: Little, Brown.

Kan, Yee W., and Scott Phillips. 2003. "Race and the Death Penalty: Including Asian Americans and Exploring the Desocialization of Law." *Journal of Ethnicity in Criminal Justice* 1: 63–92.

Karonen, Petri. 2001. "A Life for a Life versus Christina Reconciliation: Violence and the Process of Civilization in the Kingdom of Sweden, 1540–1700." In *Five Centuries of Violence in Finland and the Baltic Area,* by Heikki Ylikangas, Petri Karonen, and Martti Lehti, 85–132. Columbus: Ohio State University Press.

Katz, Jesse. 1991. "Is Training of Deputies for Deadly Clashes Adequate? Despite Extensive Instructions on When to Shoot, Critics Say Officers Are Too Quick on the Trigger." *Los Angeles Times,* September 8, secs. A1, A22, A23.

Kawashima, Yasuhide. 1986. *Puritan Justice and the Indian: White Man's Law in Massachusetts, 1630–1763.* Middeletown: Wesleyan University Press.

Kay, Judith W. 2006. "Is Restitution Possible for Murder? Surviving Family Members Speak." In *Wounds That Do Not Bind: Victim-Based Perspectives on the Death Penalty,* ed. James A. Acker and David R. Karp, 323–47. Durham: Carolina Academic Press.

Keil, Thomas J., and Gennaro F. Vito. 1989. "Race, Homicide Severity, and Application of the Death Penalty: A Consideration of the Barnett Scale." *Criminology* 27: 511–31.

———. 1990. "Race and the Death Penalty in Kentucky Murder Trials: An Analysis of Post-Gregg Outcomes." *Justice Quarterly* 7: 189–207.

Kiefer, Thomas. M. 1972. *The Tausug: Violence and Law in a Philippine Moslem Society.* New York: Holt, Rinehart, and Winston.

Kirk, Robin. 1994. *Generation under Fire: Children and Violence in Colombia.* New York: Human Rights Watch.

Klinger, David. 2004. *Into the Kill Zone: A Cop's Eye View of Deadly Force.* San Francisco: Jossey-Bass.

Klockars, Carl B. 1996. "A Theory of Excessive Force and Its Control." In *Police Violence: Understanding and Controlling Police Abuse of Force,* 1–22. New Haven: Yale University Press.

Knauft, Bruce M. 1985. *Good Company and Violence: Sorcery and Social Action in a Lowland New Guinea Society.* Berkeley: University of California Press.

———. 2002. *Exchanging the Past: A Rainforest World Before and After.* Chicago: University of Chicago Press.

Knoohuizen, Ralph, Richard P. Fahey, and Deborah J. Palmer. 1972. *The Police and Their Use of Deadly Force in Chicago.* Evanston: Chicago Law Enforcement Study Group.

Kobler, Arthur L. 1975. "Police Homicide in a Democracy." *Journal of Social Issues* 31: 163–84.

Koch, Klaus-Friedrich. 1974. *War and Peace in Jálémó: The Management of Conflict in Highland New Guinea.* Cambridge: Harvard University Press.

Kochman, Thomas. 1981. *Black and White Styles in Conflict.* Chicago: University of Chicago Press.

Koepke, Jennifer E. 2000. "The Failure to Breach the Blue Wall of Silence: The Circling of the Wagons to Protect Police Perjury." *Washburn Law Review* 39: 211–42.

Kooistra, Paul. 1989. *Criminals as Heroes: Structure, Power and Identity.* Bowling Green: Bowling Green State University Press.

Kroeber, Theodora. 1961. *Ishi in Two Worlds: A Biography of the Last Wild Indian in North America.* Berkeley: University of California Press, 1976.

Kruttschnitt, Candace. 1982. "Women, Crime, and the Law: An Application of the Theory of Law." *Criminology* 19: 495–513.

Kubrin, Charis E., and Ronald Weitzer. 2003. "Retaliatory Homicide: Concentrated Disadvantage and Neighborhood Culture." *Social Problems* 50: 157–80.

LaFave, Wayne R. 2000. *Criminal Law.* 3rd ed. St. Paul: West Group (1st ed., 1972).

La Fontaine, Jean. 1960. "Homicide and Suicide among the Gisu." In *African Homicide and Suicide*, ed. Paul Bohannan, 94–129. Princeton: Princeton University Press.

Lamont, Michèle, ed. 1999. *The Cultural Territories of Race: Black and White Boundaries.* Chicago: University of Chicago Press.

Landale, James. 2005. *The Last Duel: A True Story of Death and Honor.* Edinburgh: Canongate.

Landy, David, and Elliot Aronson. 1969. "The Influence of the Character of the Criminal and His Victim on the Decisions of Simulated Jurors." *Journal of Experimental Social Psychology* 5: 141–52.

Lane, Roger. 1997. *Murder in America: A History.* Columbus: Ohio State University Press.

Langan, Patrick A., and John M. Dawson. 1995. *Spouse Murder Defendants in Large Urban Counties.* Washington DC: Bureau of Justice Statistics, U.S. Department of Justice.

Lanni, Adriaan. 2006. *Law and Justice in the Courts of Classical Athens.* Cambridge: Cambridge University Press.

Lee, Richard Borshay. 1979. *The !Kung San: Men, Women, and Work in a Foraging Society.* Cambridge: Cambridge University Press.

Lenski, Gerhard E. 1966. *Power and Privilege: A Theory of Social Stratification.* Chapel Hill: University of North Carolina Press, 1984.

Levin, Martin A. 1972. "Urban Politics and Judicial Behavior." *Journal of Legal Studies* 1: 193–221.

Levy, Neil. 2002. *Moral Relativism: A Short Introduction.* Oxford: Oneworld.

Lewis, I. M. 1961. *A Pastoral Democracy: A Study of Pastoralism and Politics among the Northern Somali of the Horn of Africa.* London: Oxford University Press.

Liebman, James S., Jeffrey Fagan, and Valerie West. 2000. "A Broken System: Error Rates in Capital Cases, 1973–1995." Report: Columbia Law School. Retrieved August 24, 2008. http://www2.law.columbia.edu/instructionalservices/liebman/.

Lindholm, Charles. 1982. *Generosity and Jealousy: The Swat Pukhtun of Northern Pakistan.* New York: Columbia University Press.

Linton, Ralph. 1952. "Universal Ethical Principles: An Anthropological View." In *Moral Principles of Action: Man's Ethical Imperatives,* ed. Ruth Nanda Anshen, 645–69. New York: Harper and Brothers.

Litwin, Kenneth J. 2004. "A Multilevel Multivariate Analysis of Factors Affecting Homicide Clearances." *Journal of Research in Crime and Delinquency* 41: 327–51.

Llewellyn, Karl N., and E. Adamson Hoebel. 1941. *The Cheyenne Way: Conflict and Case Law in Primitive Jurisprudence.* Norman: University of Oklahoma Press.

Lundsgaarde, Henry P. 1977. *Murder in Space City: A Cultural Analysis of Houston Homicide Patterns.* New York: Oxford University Press.

Macaulay, Stewart. 1963. "Non-Contractual Relations in Business: A Preliminary Study." *American Sociological Review* 28: 55–67.

MacCoun, Robert J. 1996. "Differential Treatment of Corporate Defendants by Juries: An Examination of the "Deep-Pockets" Hypothesis." *Law and Society Review* 30: 121–61.

Madley, Benjamin. 2004. "Patterns of Frontier Genocide 1803–1910: The Aboriginal Tasmanians, the Yuki of California, and the Herero of Namibia." *Journal of Genocide Research* 6: 167–92.

Malinowski, Bronislaw. 1925. *Crime and Custom in Savage Society.* Patterson: Littlefield, Adams, 1962.

Manuel, Anne. 1991. *Guatemala: Getting Away with Murder.* New York: Human Rights Watch.

Marquart, James W., Sheldon Ekland-Olson, and Jonathan R. Sorensen. 1994. *The Rope, the Chair, and the Needle: Capital Punishment in Texas, 1923–1990.* Austin: University of Texas Press.

Mars, Joan R. 2002. *Deadly Force, Colonialism, and the Rule of Law: Police Violence in Guyana.* Westport: Greenwood Press.

Marx, Karl, and Friedrich Engels. 1848. *The Communist Manifesto.* Oxford: Oxford University Press, 1992.

Maybury-Lewis, David. 1974. *Akwê-Shavante Society.* New York: Oxford University Press.

McAdams, John C. 1998. "Racial Disparity and the Death Penalty." *Law and Contemporary Problems* 61: 153–70.

McAlary, Mike. 1990. *Cop Shot: The True Story of a Murder That Shocked the Nation.* New York: Jove Books, 1992.

McFeely, William S. 2000. *Proximity to Death.* New York: W. W. Norton.

McGrath, Roger D. 1984. *Gunfighters, Highwaymen, and Vigilantes: Violence on the Frontier.* Berkeley: University of California Press.

McKanna, Clare V., Jr. 1997. *Homicide, Race, and Justice in the American West, 1880–1920.* Tucson: University of Arizona Press.

———. 2002. *Race and Homicide in Nineteenth-Century California.* Reno: University of Nevada Press.

———. 2005. *White Justice in Arizona: Apache Murder Trials in the Nineteenth Century.* Lubbock: Texas Tech Press.

McKnight, Brian E. 1992. *Law and Order in Sung China.* Cambridge: Cambridge University Press.

McLynn, Frank. 1989. *Crime and Punishment in Eighteenth-Century England.* Oxford: Oxford University Press.

McMahan, Jeff. 2002. *The Ethics of Killings: Problems at the Margins of Life.* New York: Oxford University Press.

McMahon, Vanessa. 2004. *Murder in Shakespeare's England.* London: Hambledon and London.

Meggitt, Mervyn. 1977. *Blood Is Their Argument: Warfare among the Mae Enga Tribesmen of New Guinea.* Palo Alto: Mayfield.

Méndez, Juan E. 1992. *Political Murder and Reform in Colombia.* New York: Human Rights Watch.

Merton, Robert K. 1968. "The Matthew Effect in Science." *Science* 159: 55–63.

Michalski, Joseph H. 2004. "Making Sociological Sense out of Trends in Intimate Partner Violence." *Violence against Women* 10: 652–75.

Middleton, John. 1965. *The Lugbara of Uganda.* New York: Holt, Rinehart, and Winston.

Miller, William Ian. 1990. *Bloodtaking and Peacemaking: Feud, Law, and Society in Saga Iceland.* Chicago: University of Chicago Press.

Mills, D. E. 1976. "*Kataki-Uchi:* The Practice of Blood Revenge in Pre-Modern Japan." *Modern Asian Studies* 10: 525–42.

Milton, Catherine, James Wahl Halleck, James Lardner, and Gary L. Abrecht. 1977. *Police Use of Deadly Force.* Washington DC: Police Foundation.

Mishkin, Bernard. 1940. *Rank and Warfare among the Plains Indians.* Seattle: University of Washington Press, 1966.

Moran, Molly Hurley. 2003. *Finding Susan.* Carbondale: Southern Illinois University Press.

Morrill, Calvin. 1995. *The Executive Way: Conflict Management in Corporations.* Chicago: University of Chicago Press.

Morris, Thomas D. 1996. *Southern Slavery and the Law, 1619–1860.* Chapel Hill: University of North Carolina Press.

Moser, Paul K., and Thomas L. Carson, eds. 2001. *Moral Relativism: A Reader.* New York: Oxford University Press.

Murphy, Elizabeth. 1984. "The Application of the Death Penalty in Cook County." *Illinois Bar Journal* 93: 90–95.

Nakell, Barry, and Kenneth A. Hardy. 1987. *The Arbitrariness of the Death Penalty.* Philadelphia: Temple University Press.

Narula, Smita. 1999. *Broken People: Caste Violence against India's "Untouchables."* New York: Human Rights Watch.

Nash, June. 1967. "Death as a Way of Life: The Increasing Resort to Homicide in a Maya Indian Community." *American Anthropologist* 69: 445–70.

Neal, Bill. 2006. *Getting Away with Murder on the Texas Frontier: Notorious Killings and Celebrated Trials.* Lubbock: Texas Tech University Press.

Nicholls, Kenneth. 1972. *Gaelic and Gaelicised Ireland in the Middle Ages.* Dublin: Gill and Macmillan.

Nisbett, Robert E., and Dov Cohen. 1996. *Culture of Honor: The Psychology of Violence in the South.* Boulder: Westview Press.

Nolan, Patrick, and Gerhard Lenski. 2004. *Human Societies: An Introduction to Macrosociology.* 9th ed. Boulder: Paradigm Publishers (1st ed., 1970).

Nye, Robert A. 1993. *Masculinity and Male Codes of Honor in Modern France.* New York: Oxford University Press.

Oberg, Kalervo. 1934. "Crime and Punishment in Tlingit Society." *American Anthropologist* 36: 145–56.

Oliver, Melvin, and Thomas M. Shapiro. 1995. *Black Wealth/White Wealth: A New Perspective on Racial Inequality.* New York: Routledge.

Otterbein, Keith F., and Charlotte Swanson Otterbein. 1965. "An Eye for an Eye, a Tooth for a Tooth: A Cross-Cultural Study of Feuding." *American Anthropologist* 67: 1470–82.

Parsons, Talcott. 1951. *The Social System.* New York: Free Press.

Pate, Antony M., and Lorie A. Fridell. 1993. *Police Use of Force: Official Reports, Citizen Complaints, and Legal Consequences.* Washington DC: Police Foundation.

Paternoster, Raymond. 1984. "Prosecutorial Discretion in Requesting the Death Penalty: A Case of Victim-Based Racial Discrimination." *Law and Society Review* 18: 437–78.

———. 1991. *Capital Punishment in America.* Lexington: Lexington Books.

Paternoster, Raymond, Robert Brame, Sarah Bacon, Andrew Ditchfield, David Biere, Karen Beckman, Deanna Perez, Michael Strauch, Nadine Frederique, Kristin Gawkoki, Daniel Zeigler, and Kathryn Murphy. 2003. "An Empirical Analysis of

Maryland's Death Sentencing System with Respect to the Influence of Race and Legal Jurisdiction." Retrieved August 24, 2008. http://www.newsdesk.umd.edu/pdf/finalrep.pdf.

Patterson, Orlando. 1982. *Slavery and Social Death: A Comparative Study.* Cambridge: Harvard University Press.

Penglase, Ben. 1994. *Final Justice: Police and Death Squad Homicides of Adolescents in Brazil.* New York: Human Rights Watch.

Peratis, Kathleen. 2004. *Honoring the Killers: Justice Denied for "Honor" Crimes in Jordan.* New York: Human Rights Watch.

Peristiany, J. G. 1939. *The Social Institutions of the Kipsigis.* London: Routledge and Kegan Paul.

Peters, E. L. 1967. "Some Structural Aspects of the Feud among the Camel-Herding Bedouin of Cyrenaica." *Africa* 37: 261–82.

Peterson, Elicka S. L. 1999. "Murder as Self-Help: Women and Intimate Partner Homicide." *Homicide Studies* 3: 30–46.

Petrillo, Lisa. 1990. "When a Cop Shoots, Who Takes a Closer Look? Here, Unlike Most Cities, an Outside Probe Rarely Results When Officers Fire." *San Diego Union-Tribune,* December 21, secs. A1, A10.

Petrocelli, Daniel. 1998. *Triumph of Justice: The Final Judgment on the Simpson Saga.* With Peter Knobler. New York: Crown Publishers.

Phillips, Scott. 2003. "The Social Structure of Vengeance: A Test of Black's Model." *Criminology* 41: 673–708.

———. 2008a. " Racial Disparities in the Capital of Capital Punishment." *Houston Law Review* 45: 807–40.

———. 2008b. "Victim Social Status and Capital Punishment." Unpublished paper, Department of Sociology, University of Denver.

———. 2008c. "Racial Disparities in Capital Punishment: Blind Justice Requires a Blindfold." American Constitution Society for Law and Policy. Retrieved November 19, 2008. http://www.acslaw.org/IssueBrief.

Pierce, Glenn L., and Michael L. Radelet. 2002. "Race, Region, and Death Sentencing in Illinois, 1988–1997." *Oregon Law Review* 81: 39–96.

Podolny, Joel M. 2005. *Status Signals: A Sociological Study of Market Competition.* Princeton: Princeton University Press.

Pohlman, H. L. 1999. *The Whole Truth? A Case of Murder on the Appalachian Trail.* Amherst: University of Massachusetts Press.

Pollock, Frederick, and Frederic William Maitland. 1898. *The History of English Law: Before the Time of Edward 1.* Vol. 2. Cambridge: Cambridge University Press, 1968.

Popper, Karl R. 1934. *The Logic of Scientific Discovery.* New York: Harper and Row, 1965.

Powell, Edward. 1989. *Kingship, Law and Society.* Oxford: Clarendon Press.

Public Nuisance Considered Under Such Heads of Complaint As Are Most Notorious within the City and Suburbs of London: With Useful Hints for a Speedy Remedy, and a Plain Scheme for Paving the Streets without Making it a Jobb: To Which is Added Some Thoughts on the Great Grievance of Vagrants and Desperate Poor, With a Proposal to Preserve Us from Robbery and Murder. 1754. London: E. Withers.

Quinney, Richard. 1970. *The Social Reality of Crime.* Boston: Little, Brown.

Radelet, Michael L. 1981. "Racial Characteristics and the Imposition of the Death Penalty." *American Sociological Review* 46: 918–27.

———. 1989. "Executions of Whites for Crimes against Blacks: Exceptions to the Rule?" *Sociological Quarterly* 30: 529–44.

Radelet, Michael L., Hugo Adam Bedau, and Constance E. Putnam. 1992. *In Spite of Innocence: Erroneous Convictions in Capital Cases.* Boston: Northeastern University Press.

Radelet, Michael L., and Glenn L. Pierce. 1985. "Race and Prosecutorial Discretion in Homicide Cases." *Law and Society Review* 19: 587–621.

Rantala, M. L. 1996. *O. J. Unmasked: The Trial, the Truth, and the Media.* Chicago: Catfeet Press.

Rappaport, Elizabeth. 1994. "The Death Penalty and the Domestic Discount." In *The Public Nature of Private Violence: The Discovery of Domestic Abuse,* ed. Martha Albertson Fineman and Roxanne Mykitiuk, 235–43. New York: Routledge.

Reid, John Phillip. 1999. *Patterns of Vengeance: Crosscultural Homicide in the North American Fur Trade.* Pasadena: Ninth Judicial Circuit Historical Society.

Reynolds, Henry. 1972. *Aborigines and Settlers: The Australian Experience, 1788–1939.* Melbourne: Cassell Australia.

———. 1987. *Frontier: Aborigines, Settlers and Land.* Sydney: Allen and Unwin.

Richardson, Jane. 1940. *Law and Status among the Kiowa Indians.* Seattle: University of Washington Press.

Riches, David. 1974. "The Netsilik Eskimos: A Special Case of Selective Female Infanticide." *Ethnology* 13: 351–61.

Rosa, Joseph G. 1969. *The Gunfighter: Man or Myth?* Norman: University of Oklahoma Press.

Rosaldo, Renato. 1980. *Ilongot Headhunting, 1883–1974: A Study in Society and History.* Stanford: Stanford University Press.

Rosoff, Stephen M. 1984. "Physicians as Criminal Defendants: Dr. Williams, Mr. Williams, and the Ambivalence Hypothesis." Unpublished master's thesis, University of California, Irvine.

———. 1989. "Physicians as Criminal Defendants: Specialty, Sanctions, and Status Liability." *Law and Human Behavior* 13: 231–36.

Ross, Marc Howard. 1986. "A Cross-Cultural Theory of Political Conflict and Violence." *Political Psychology* 7: 427–69.

Rubin, Lillian B. 1986. *Quiet Rage: Bernie Goetz in a Time of Madness.* New York: Farrar, Straus, and Giroux.

Rubinstein, Jonathan. 1991. *City Police.* New York: Ballantine.

Rudovsky, David. 1992. "Police Abuse: Can the Violence be Contained?" *Harvard Civil Rights-Civil Liberties Law Review* 27: 465–501.

Rummel, R. J. 1994. *Death by Government.* New Brunswick: Transaction Publishers.

Sagan, Eli. 1974. *Cannibalism: Human Aggression and Cultural Form.* New York: Harper and Row.

Samaha, Joel. 1974. *Law and Order in Historical Perspective: The Case of Elizabethan England.* New York: Academic Press.

Savelsberg, Joachim. 1994. "Knowledge, Domination, and Criminal Punishment." *American Journal of Sociology* 99: 911–43.

Scheper-Hughes, Nancy. 2006. "Death Squads and Democracy in Northeast Brazil." In *Law and Disorder in the Postcolony,* ed. Jean Comaroff and John L. Comaroff, 150–87. Chicago: University of Chicago Press.

Schiller, Lawrence. 1996. *American Tragedy: The Uncensored Story of the Simpson Defense.* New York: Random House.

Schneider, David M. 1957. "Political Organization, Supernatural Sanctions, and the Punishment for Incest on Yap." *American Anthropologist* 59: 791–800.

Schwarz, Philip J. 1988. *Twice Condemned: Slaves and the Criminal Laws of Virginia, 1705–1865.* Baton Rouge: Louisiana State University Press.

Scott, Gini Graham. 2005. *Homicide by the Rich and Famous: A Century of Prominent Killers.* Westport: Praeger.

Senechal de la Roche, Roberta. 1996. "Collective Violence as Social Control." *Sociological Forum* 11: 97–128.

———. 1997. "The Sociogenesis of Lynching." In *Under Sentence of Death: Lynching in the New South,* ed. W. Fitzhugh Brundage, 48–76. Chapel Hill: University of North Carolina Press.

———. 2001. "Why is Collective Violence Collective?" *Sociological Theory* 19: 126–44.

Service, Elman R. 1975. *Origins of the State and Civilization: The Process of Cultural Evolution.* New York: W. W. Norton.

Shakur, Sanyika. 1993. *Monster: The Autobiography of an L.A. Gang Member.* New York: Penguin.

Sherman, Lawrence W. 1992. *Policing Domestic Violence: Experiments and Dilemmas.* New York: Free Press.

Shilts, Randy. 1982. *The Mayor of Castro Street: The Life and Times of Harvey Milk.* New York: St. Martin's.

Shirer, William L. 1959. *The Rise and Fall of the Third Reich: A History of Nazi Germany.* New York: Touchstone Books, 1960.

Shultz, Duane. 1992. *Over the Earth I Come: The Great Sioux Uprising of 1862.* New York: St. Martin's.

Simmel, Georg. 1908. *The Sociology of Georg Simmel,* ed. Kurt H. Wolff. New York: Free Press, 1960.

Simon, David. 1991. *Homicide: A Year on the Killing Streets.* New York: Fawcett Columbine.

Simpson, Antony E. 1988. "Dandelions On the Field of Honor: Dueling, the Middle Classes, and the Law in Nineteenth-Century England." *Criminal Justice History* 9: 99–155.

Slevin, Fiona. 2006. *By Hereditary Virtues: A History of Lough Lynn.* Dublin: Coolabawn Publishing.

Smith, M. Dwayne. 1987. "Patterns of Discrimination in Assessments of the Death Penalty: The Case of Louisiana." *Journal of Criminal Justice* 15: 279–86.

Solomon, Joel. 1999. *Systemic Injustice: Torture, "Disappearance," and Extrajudicial Execution in Mexico.* New York: Human Rights Watch.

Sorensen, Jon, and Donald H. Wallace. 1999. "Prosecutorial Discretion in Seeking Death: An Analysis of Racial Disparities in the Pretrial stages of Case Processing in a Midwestern County." *Justice Quarterly* 16: 559–78.

Sorokin, Pitirim A. 1937. *Social and Cultural Dynamics.* New York: American Book.

Spierenburg, Pieter. 1984. *Spectacle of Suffering: Executions and the Evolution of Repression: From a Pre-Industrial Metropolis to the European Experience.* Cambridge: Cambridge University Press.

Spohn, Cassia, Susan Welch, and John Gruhl. 1985. "Women Defendants in Court: The Interaction between Sex and Race in Convicting and Sentencing." *Social Science Quarterly* 66: 178–85.

Stauder, Jack. 1972. "Anarchy and Ecology: Political Society among the Majangir." *Southwestern Journal of Anthropology* 28: 153–68.

Stauffer, Amy R., M. Dwayne Smith, John K. Cochran, Sondra J. Fogel, and Beth Bjerregaard. 2006. "The Interaction between Victim Race and Gender on Sentencing Outcomes in Capital Murder Trials." *Homicide Studies* 10: 98–116.

Stephen, James Fitzjames. 1883. *A History of the Criminal Law of England.* Vol. 1. London: Macmillan and Co.

Stewart, Frank. 1994. *Honor.* Chicago: University of Chicago Press.

Sumner, William Graham. 1906. *Folkways: A Study of the Sociological Importance of Usages, Manners, Customs, Mores, and Morals.* Boston: Ginn and Co., 1913.

Sundby, Scott E. 2003. "The Capital Jury and Empathy: The Problem of Worthy and Unworthy Victims." *Cornell Law Review* 88: 343–81.

Sutton, John. 2004. "The Political Economy of Imprisonment in Affluent Western Democracies. 1960–1990." *American Sociological Review* 69: 170–89.

Swanson, Guy. 1971. "An Organizational Analysis of Collectivities." *American Sociological Review* 36: 607–24.

Swigert, Victoria Lynn, and Ronald A. Farrell. 1976. *Murder, Inequality, and the Law: Differential Treatment in the Legal Process.* Lexington: Lexington Books.

Swindle, Howard. 1993. *Deliberate Indifference: A Story of Murder and Racial Injustice.* New York: Viking.

Taub, Stuart H. 1988. "Rewards, Bounty Hunting, and Criminal Justice in the West, 1865–1900." *Western Historical Quarterly* 19: 287–301.

Tétreault, May Ann. 2000. "Gender, Citizenship, and State in the Middle East." In *Citizenship and State in the Middle East: Approaches and Applications,* ed. Nils A. Butcheson, Uri Davis, and Manuel Hassassian, 70–87. Syracuse: Syracuse University Press.

Thomson, David. 1974. *Woodbrook.* London: Vintage, 1991.

Timmermans, Stefan. 2006. *Postmortem: How Medical Examiners Explain Suspicious Death.* Chicago: University of Chicago Press.

Titterington, Victoria B., and Barry P. Abbott. 2004. "Space City Revisited: Patterns of Legal Outcomes in Houston Homicide." *Violence and Victims* 19: 83–95.

Tolnay, Stewart E., and E. M. Beck. 1995. *Festival of Violence: An Analysis of Southern Lynchings, 1882–1930.* Urbana: University of Illinois Press.

Toobin, Jeffrey. 1996. *The Run of His Life: The People v. O. J. Simpson.* New York: Random House.

Trotman, David Vincent. 1986. *Crime in Trinidad: Conflict and Control in a Plantation Society, 1838–1900.* Knoxville: University of Tennessee Press.

Tucker, James. 1999. *The Therapeutic Corporation.* New York: Oxford University Press.

Tucker, Lee. 1997. *Guatemala's Forgotten Children: Police Violence and Abuses in Detention.* New York: Human Rights Watch.

Turk, Austin T. 1969. *Criminality and Legal Order.* Chicago: Rand McNally.

Turrell, Robert. 2004. *White Mercy: A Study of the Death Penalty in South Africa.* Westport: Praeger.

Uelmen, Gerald F. 1973. "Varieties of Police Policy: A Study of Police Policy Regarding the Use of Deadly Force in Los Angeles County." *Loyola of Los Angeles Law Review* 6: 1–65.

Ugwuegbu, Denis Chimaeze E. 1979. "Racial and Evidential Factors in Juror Attribution of Legal Responsibility." *Journal of Experimental Social Psychology* 15: 133–46.

Uhlman, Thomas M. 1979. *Racial Justice: Black Judges and Defendants in an Urban Trial Court.* Lexington: Lexington Books.

U.S. Bureau of the Census. 2006. *Statistical Abstract of the United States 2007.* Washington DC: U.S. Bureau of the Census.

U.S. Department of State. 1998–2007. *Country Reports on Human Rights Practices.* Washington DC: U.S. Government Printing Office.

———. 2006. *Country Reports on Human Rights Practices, Saudi Arabia.* Washington DC: U.S. Government Printing Office.

"Use of Capital Punishment by Nation." 2007. Retrieved August 24, 2008. http://en.wikipedia.org/wiki/Use_of_capital_punishment_by_nation.

Utley, Robert M., and Wilcomb E. Washburn. 1985. *Indian Wars.* New York: American Heritage.

van der Sprenkel, Sybille. 1962. *Legal Institutions in Manchu China: A Sociological Analysis.* London: Athlone Press.

Van Dyke, Jon M. 1977. *Jury Selection Procedures: Our Uncertain Commitment to Representative Panels.* Cambridge: Ballinger.

van Onselen, Charles. 1976. *Chibaro: African Mine Labor in Southern Rhodesia, 1900–1933.* London: Pluto Press.

Walker, Samuel. 1998. *Popular Justice: A History of American Criminal Justice.* 2nd ed. New York: Oxford University Press (1st ed., 1980).

Wallace-Hadrill, J. M. 1959. "The Bloodfeud of the Franks." *Journal of the John Rylands Library* 41: 459–87.

Walter, Eugene Victor. 1969. *Terror and Resistance: A Study of Political Violence.* New York: Oxford University Press.

Warner, W. Lloyd. 1958. *A Black Civilization: A Social Study of an Australian Tribe.* New York: Harper (1st ed., 1937).

Waters, Tony. 2007. *When Killing Is a Crime.* Boulder: Lynne Rienner.

Weber, Max. 1922. "Bureaucracy." In *From Max Weber: Essays in Sociology,* ed. Hans Gerth and C. Wright Mills, 196–244. New York: Oxford University Press, 1958.

———. 1925. *Max Weber on Law in Economy and Society.* Ed. Max Rheinstein. 2nd ed. Cambridge: Harvard University Press, 1954 (1st ed., 1922).

Weiss, Robert E., Richard A. Berk, and Catherine Y. Lee. 1996. "Assessing the Capriciousness of Death Penalty Charging." *Law and Society Review* 30: 607–26.

Weitzer, Ronald, and Cheryl Beattie. 1994. "Police Killings in South Africa: Criminal Trials 1986–1992." *Policing and Society* 4: 99–117.

Wells, L. Edward, and Joseph H. Rankin. 1991. "Families and Delinquency: A Meta-Analysis of the Impact of Broken Homes." *Social Problems* 38: 71–93.

Westermeyer, Joseph A. 1971. "Traditional and Constitutional Law: A Study of Change in Laos." *Asian Survey* 11: 562–69.

———. 1973. "Assassination and Conflict Resolution in Laos." *American Anthropologist* 75: 123–31.

Western, Bruce. 2006. *Punishment and Inequality in America.* New York: Russell Sage Foundation.

White, Stephen D. 1986. "Feud and Peace-Making in the Touraine around the Year 1100." *Traditio* 42: 195–263.

Whitfield, Stephen J. 1988. *A Death in the Delta: The Story of Emmett Till.* New York: Free Press.

Wiener, Martin. 1999. "Judges v. Jurors: Courtroom Tensions in Murder Trials and the Law of Criminal Responsibility in Nineteenth-Century England." *Law and History Review* 17: 467–506.

———. 2004. *Men of Blood: Violence, Manliness and Criminal Justice in Victorian England.* Cambridge: Cambridge University Press.

———. 2007. "Criminal Law as a Fault Line of Imperial Authority: Interracial Homicide Trials in British India." In *Modern Histories of Crime and Punishment,* ed. Markus D. Dubber and Lindsay Farmer, 252–71. Stanford: Stanford University Press.

Wilbanks, William. 1984. *Murder in Miami: An Analysis of Homicide Patterns and Trends in Dade County (Miami), 1917–1983.* Lanham: University Press of America.

Williams, David R., and Chiquita Collins. 1995. "U.S. Socioeconomic and Racial Differences in Health: Patterns and Explanations." *Annual Review of Sociology* 21: 349–86.

Williams, Marian R., Stephen Demuth, and Jefferson E. Holcomb. 2007. "Understanding the Influence of Victim Gender in Death Penalty Cases: The Importance of Victim Race, Sex-Related Victimization, and Jury Decision Making." *Criminology* 45: 865–91.

Wilson, Wayne. 1996. *Good Murders and Bad Murders: A Consumer's Guide in the Age of Information.* Lanham: University Press of America. Rev. ed. (1st ed., 1991).

Wolf, Sharon, and Albert M. Bugaj. 1990. "The Social Organization of Courtroom Witnesses." *Social Behavior* 5: 1–13.

Wolff, Edward N. 2006. "International Comparisons of Wealth: Methodological Issues and a Summary of Findings." In *International Perspectives on Household Wealth,* ed. Edward N. Wolff, 1–16. Cheltenham: Edward Elgar.

Wolfgang, Marvin E. 1958. *Patterns in Criminal Homicide.* Philadelphia: University of Pennsylvania Press.

Wormald, Jenny. 1980. "The Blood Feud in Early Modern Scotland." *Past and Present* 87: 54–97.

Ylikangas, Heikki. 2001. "What Happened to Violence? An Analysis of the Development of Violence from Medieval Times to the Early Modern Era based on Finnish Source Materials." In *Five Centuries of Violence in Finland and the Baltic Area,* by Heikki Ylikangas, Petri Karonen, and Martti Lehti, 1–83. Columbus: Ohio State University Press.

Zeisel, Hans. 1981. "Race Bias in the Administration of the Death Penalty: The Florida Experience." *Harvard Law Review* 95: 456–68.

Zimring, Franklin E., Joel Eigen, and Sheila O'Malley. 1976. "Punishing Homicide in Philadelphia: Perspectives on the Death Penalty." *University of Chicago Law Review* 43: 227–52.

INDEX

Page numbers followed by a "t" indicate references to tables.

Aborigines, 95, 123, 153, 154
acquaintances, 157; and law, 158, 162t, 163, 169, 212n3, 213n12; and partisanship, 172–73, 175; and popular justice, 178; and settlement, 177–78. *See also* relational distance
acquittals. *See* courts, dispositions of
Africa, 96, 156. *See also under individual countries and societies*
African Americans, 50–51, 134, 139–40, 206n7, 209–10n6, 215n12; and law, 129–30, 135, 140–41, 148–50, 197, 210n8; —, and death penalty, 141–44, 189; and partisanship, 145, 146; and popular justice, 57, 106, 148, 151; and settlement, 146; —, as jurors, 146, 147t, 150–51, 199, 211n15, 211n18. *See also* race
age, 168, 195; of killers, 129; of victims, 97–99, 128
agrarian societies, 42–45, 62
Alabama, 140
Albania, 58, 123, 204n6
Algeria, 74
Allen, Frederick, 4
America. *See* United States
Amnesty International, 48, 64, 67, 71, 72, 73, 74, 87, 97, 98, 119, 120, 126, 192, 207n7
Apaches, 136, 137–38
Arabs, 83, 85, 126–27
arbitration, 60, 81–83, 187
Argentina, 71, 74
Aristocrats, 42–45, 118–19, 188
Arizona, 105, 136, 137–38
Arkansas, 163
Asia, 96. *See also under individual countries and societies*
Asian Americans, 148, 150. *See also* Chinese Americans
Athens, ancient, 122
attorneys. *See* lawyers
Australia, 95, 123, 139, 153, 154
autocracies, 65, 76–78, 79, 90, 197
autopsy, 9, 204n9
Aztecs, 76

Baldus, David C., 50, 66, 100, 101, 112, 128, 129, 139, 142, 143, 144, 154, 162, 206n8, 208n11, 209n7, 210n12
Baltimore, 69, 113, 211n15
Barreti, Giuseppe, 191–92
Barton, Roy Franklin, 58, 59, 83, 213–14n17
Baumer, Eric P., 12, 81, 113–14, 208n2, 212n6
Baumgartner, M. P., 16, 20, 22, 27, 28, 32, 51, 54, 111, 176, 191, 208n4
Beattie, J. M., 8–9, 44, 95, 119, 166, 208n2, 209n2
Bedouin, 14, 59, 156
Behavior of Law, The. See Blackian theory
benefit of clergy, 209n2
benefit of linen, 166

Berbers, 123
Black, Donald, 5, 6, 7, 16, 18–28, 29–30, 37, 49, 51, 52, 54, 58, 59, 60, 61, 64, 65, 79–80, 81, 88, 89, 92, 93, 102, 110, 111, 118, 121, 122, 127, 129, 132, 145, 146, 150, 151, 154, 156, 157, 170, 171, 175, 176, 179, 191, 193, 194, 198, 199, 200, 204n7, 204n12, 205n4, 205n1, 209n2, 213n14, 214n3, 215n10. *See also* Blackian theory
Blackfeet, 152
Blackian theory, 19–28, 30, 61, 62, 79, 88, 90, 107, 130, 133, 154, 167, 183, 186–88, 193, 195, 196, 209n2, 215n11; of law, 19, 25, 28, 34, 37–39, 64, 92, 111, 133, 156–57, 168, 188, 191; of moralism, 27, 28, 35; of moral relativity, 29–30, 35, 188; of partisanship, 27, 28, 51–52, 80, 90, 101, 102, 145–46, 170, 171, 192–93; of popular justice, 27, 34, 35, 57, 83, 157, 180–81, 190, 207n2; of settlement, 27, 35, 54, 81, 101, 102, 122, 146, 170, 176, 177; testing, 30–34, 35, 188, 205n4; validity of, 30, 35, 188–91, 194. *See also* pure sociology
Blackstone, Sir William, 168–69
blind review of cases, 199
Boehm, Christopher, 61, 81–82
Borden, Lizzie, 176–77, 194
Bowers, William J., 50, 129, 142, 147
boyfriends. *See* intimate partners
Brazil, 10–11, 71, 72, 74, 75, 79, 87, 91, 96–97, 97–98, 103–4, 123, 125, 192, 207n4, 208n12
Britain, 8, 9. *See also under individual countries*
Brundage, W. Fitzhugh, 84, 104, 151
Buenos Aires, 71
Burke, Edmund, 192
Bushmen of the Kalahari, 17, 123

California: nineteenth-century, 53, 70, 73, 79, 86, 112, 136, 137, 138, 145, 147–48, 150, 185, 211n15, 213n3; modern, 12, 70, 85, 100, 114, 128, 162
Cambodia, 77
Campbell, Bradley, 28, 52, 136–37
Canada, 139, 168, 173
capital murder and punishment. *See* death sentence
case, social geometry of the, 23, 34, 39, 92, 111, 151, 154, 167, 186, 198, 215n12; definition of, 21; civil vs. criminal law, 80; core, 61, 62, 102, 170, 191, 197; elements of, 27, 32; and parties' conduct, 32–33; and proof, 194–96; third-party, 62, 187, 191, 197
Cavallaro, James, 10, 72, 74
centralization. *See under* state, the
centrifugal cases/homicide/law/partisanship/settlement. *See under* homicide, direction of; law
centripetal cases/homicide/law/partisanship/settlement. *See under* homicide, direction of; law
Cheh, Mary H., 70
Chevigny, Paul, 71, 72–73, 74, 172
Cheyenne, 6, 153
Chicago, 124–25
children. *See* young people
China: communist, 77, 79; imperial, 10, 43, 76–77, 128, 167, 205n2
Chinese Americans, 135, 145
Christians, 146, 147
citizens, 64, 65; as killers of state officials, 65–67, 71, 77–78, 84, 90; as victims of state officials, 67–77, 79–80, 90, 186–87, 189, 192, 197
collective liability, 6–7, 41, 88, 152
Collins, Allyson, 69, 70, 79, 171
Colombia, 72, 96, 97
colonial societies, 45–47, 95, 146, 147, 187–88
Columbine High School, Littleton, Colorado, 181–82
Comanche, 180, 211n20
compensation, 7, 62, 103, 155, 200, 207–8n10; definition of, 6; and collective liability, 88; for homicides by police, 79–80; for honor killings, 119; and relational distance, 178, 179, 180; replacement by punishment, 8, 15, 89, 177–78, 204n12; severity of, 203n5;

and third parties, 181, 187; and tribal societies, 81–83, 191. *See also* compensation and social status
compensation and social status: of killer, 47–48, 59, 122; of victim, 41, 51, 58, 59, 60, 85, 86, 95–96, 122, 123, 133, 153, 190, 209n5, 211n19
compensatory sanctions. *See* compensation
conciliation, 187
conflict management, 27, 185. *See also* social control
Conley, Carolyn A., 45, 117–18, 163–64, 165, 166, 175
conventionality, 132, 155, 186, 194, 197; and law, 133–40; and partisanship, 145; and popular justice, 151, 153; and settlement, 146, 147t
conviction. *See* courts, dispositions of
conviction of the factually innocent, 196
Cooney, Mark, 9, 27, 28, 32, 33, 49, 76, 83–84, 118, 161, 181, 205nn1–2, 213nn13–14, 214n3, 214n6
coroners, 9, 11, 68–69, 178, 204n9
courts, 117, 137, 163, 165; appellate, 129, 141–42, 143, 154; civil, 54; and evidence, 166, 172, 174; and the evolution of social control, 8–9, 56, 178; of Good Men, 81–83; predicting decisions of, 16, 19, 22, 25, 39, 66, 111. *See also* courts, dispositions of; trials
courts, dispositions of, 11–12, 39–40, 42, 45, 46, 54–56, 66, 67, 96, 116, 120, 137, 139, 140–44, 157–59, 160–62, 164–65, 166–67, 168, 204n10, 206n12, 212n9, 212–13n10, 213nn11–12, 214n1; and acquittals, 3, 45, 46–47, 52–54, 69–70, 116–17, 118, 119, 135, 136, 148–49, 176–77, 191–92; and civil verdicts, 51, 52, 95–96, 150–51, 210n8; and convictions, 49–50, 111–12, 113–14, 145, 147–48, 211n15, 212n8; and punishments, 13–14, 43–44, 50, 68, 78, 110, 112, 146, 162–63, 192, 208nn11–12, 208n3, 209n7, 209n2, 209n4, 210n13, 212nn3–4
criminal record, 22, 33, 55, 111, 160, 168, 214n1; and law, 110, 115, 124, 189, 195; and partisanship, 121; and settlement, 122. *See also* normative status
criminals, 196; as killers, 110, 111–12, 189, 197; as partisans, 121; as settlement agents, 122; as victims, 10, 73–74, 112–13, 186–87, 189, 197. *See also* normative status
cross-cutting ties, 181
culpability. *See* homicide, aggressiveness of; homicide, intentionality of
cultural dimension, the, 21, 131–55
cultural direction, 133
cultural distance, 22, 157, 196, 209n1, 209n3; and law, 133, 137, 139; and the morality of homicide, 155, 186–88; and partisanship, 145–46, 187; and the perfect murder, 196, 197; and popular justice, 151–53; and proof, 194–96; and settlement, 146–51, 187–88, 211n16
cultural geometry, 145, 151, 154
cultural status, 133, 155, 209n2, 210n14, 211n19, 214n1. *See also* conventionality

Dahmer, Jeffrey, 182–83
Dallas, 70
damage awards. *See* compensation
Dawson, Myrna, 159, 168, 183
Dean, Trevor, 8, 41, 43, 84, 116
death sentence, 11, 12, 25, 63, 198, 200–201, 204n1, 208n11, 215n10; and conventionality, 137, 138, 146–47, 209n5; and cultural status, 209n2; and dependency, 128–30; and normative status, 112, 114, 120, 122; and organizational status, 64, 66–67, 78, 83; and race, 139, 140, 141–44, 154, 189, 199, 210n1, 210nn12–13; and radial status, 94, 100; and relational distance, 158, 161–63, 167, 169, 178, 212n3, 212n4, 212n8, 213n12; and vertical status, 41, 42, 42–43, 45, 48, 50, 205n2, 205n3, 209–210n6
death squads, 96–98, 103–4

defendants, 18, 113, 199, 200, 212n3, 214n1; age of, 129, 195; civil cases, 79; and family members, 172–75; gender of, 129–30, 195; organizational status of, 66, 67, 68, 69–70, 72, 75, 78, 171, 207–8n9; race of, 136, 137–39, 140–41, 142, 143–44, 189, 195, 210n8; radial status of, 95, 98, 100, 102, 106–7; relational distance from victim, 157–59, 160–63, 164–65, 166–67, 168, 212n8, 212–213n10, 213n12; respectability of, 111–12, 115–16, 189; and societal inequality, 39; and testing Blackian theory, 32; variable dispositions of, 14–15, 19, 55–56, 114, 146–51, 176–78, 190, 195–96; wealth of, 36–37, 38, 40, 48, 49–50, 54, 61–62, 139, 195; and witnesses, 172–75, 191–92. *See also* killers
delegalization, 215n10
democracies, 65–70, 90
dependent people, 128–130, 131, 209n7, 209n8, 212n3
desocialization of cases, 199, 200
detectives, 9, 121, 159; and defendant social status, 69, 111; and victim social status, 49, 65, 112–13, 189
Detroit, 79
dictators. *See* leaders
dimensions of social space. *See* cultural dimension, the; normative dimension, the; organizational dimension, the; radial dimension, the; relational dimension, the; vertical dimension, the
Dimenstein, Gilberto, 91, 98, 103–4
discretion, 20
doctors: as killers, 36–37, 38, 171; as victims, 187. *See* also medical evidence
downward cases/homicide/law/partisanship/settlement. *See under* homicide, direction of; law
dueling, 118–19
Durkheim, Émile, 15, 18, 21
Durston, Gregory, 42, 93, 117, 167, 209n2

economic status. *See* vertical status
educated people, 187–88, 209n2, 210n14
Egypt, 64, 120
Ekvall, Robert B., 6, 58, 83, 211n19
elderly people, 128–29, 170
electronic justice, 199
employment, 92, 95, 168, 187, 189, 199, 209n8
Engels, Friedrich, 15, 21
England, 42, 147; medieval, 8, 11, 43–44, 60, 147, 156, 165, 167, 177–78, 209n2, 212n8; seventeenth-century, 94–95, 165; eighteenth-century, 44, 117, 166, 169, 191–92; nineteenth-century, 44–45, 117, 118–19, 165, 166, 167; twentieth-century, 167, 171
equality: legal, 23, 36, 154; moral, 1, 198–201
Eritrea, 179
Eskimos, 29
ethnicity, 134, 209n3; and law, 139, 200; and settlement, 147
"ethnographic present tense," 203n2
execution. *See* death sentence
experimental evidence, 52–53, 56, 61–62, 64, 196, 326
extrajudicial executions, 97

family members, 2, 3, 50, 92, 169, 181, 205n4; and the evolution of justice, 8, 88–89, 190, 200; as partisans, 170–71, 180–83; as settlement agents, 146. *See also* family members as victims; family members of killer; family members of victim
family members as victims, 156, 198–99; and law, 36–37, 38, 55–56, 119–20, 158–169, 187, 195, 212nn8–9, 212–13n10, 213nn11–12; and popular justice, 124–25, 126–27, 178–80, 189, 212; as witnesses, 172–75
family members of killer: and compensation, 6, 8, 48, 81–83; and law, 41, 114; and praise, 126; and shunning, 6, 105–7; and vengeance, 9, 58, 85, 88, 179–80
family members of victim, 98, 106; and compensation, 8, 48, 81–83, 200; and law, 8, 75, 80, 171; and shunning, 106;

and toleration, 5, 126; and vengeance, 6–7, 14, 57–58, 85, 123, 179–80, 190
Farrell, Ronald A., 49–50, 100–101, 112, 140
females, 92, 152, 170, 179, 193, 208n2, 209n8; as killers, 100–101, 129–30, 140, 159, 165–67, 212–13n10, 213n11; as victims, 36–37, 38, 58–59, 100–101, 117, 119–20, 130, 158–59, 160–61, 162, 164, 168, 189, 195, 197, 206n13, 212n8
feuding, 7, 61, 62, 103, 134, 179, 180–81, 185
Finland, 88
Fletcher, G., 13, 124
Florida, 129, 142, 162, 163
forensic pathologists, 171
France, 42; eleventh-century, 60; fourteenth-century, 93; eighteenth-century, 77–78; nineteenth-century, 55, 95, 164–65; twentieth-century, 67
frontiers, 14, 134–37, 138–39, 152, 153–54, 195–96
functional status, 214n2
Furman vs. Georgia, 129, 141, 154

Gambino, Richard, 86–87
gangs, 212n6, 214n3; and law, 113; and partisanship, 121, 174; and popular justice, 84, 85, 103, 190–91
Gard, Wayne, 134, 136, 152, 153
Garrick, David, 192
Gebusi, 5, 29
gender, 32, 92, 161, 193, 212n3; and law, 100–101, 129–30, 167–68, 208n2, 209n8, 212n9, 212–13n10, 213n11; and popular justice, 58–59, 206n13. *See also* females; males
Genovese, Eugene D., 40
Georgia, 113, 174; death penalty, 50, 66, 129, 141, 142, 143, 162, 163; popular justice in, 104
Germany, Nazi, 77, 78
getting away with murder, 196–97
Ginat, Joseph, 14, 59, 83, 119, 126–27
girlfriends. *See* intimate partners
Given, James Buchanan, 8, 11, 43–44, 208n2, 212n8
Goetz, Bernhard, 124, 194
Goldsmith, Oliver, 324
grand juries, 15, 18, 19, 207n5; and race, 142, 148, 149; indictments of, 11, 70, 117, 157, 158. *See also* juries
Grant, James, 1, 12, 13, 119, 125–26, 185
Gregg vs. Georgia, 141
Gross, Samuel R., 129, 142, 154, 163
Guatemala, 74, 98
guilty pleas, 11–12, 81
Guyana, 73
Gypsies, 88

Hamlet, 157
Hamm, Richard F., 2–3
Harris, Ruth, 55, 95, 165
Hasluck, Margaret, 7, 58, 123
Hellie, Richard, 41
Henry II (king of England), 177
Hispanic Americans, 130, 210n13, 211n5. *See also* Latinas/Latinos
Hoebel, E. Adamson, 1, 6, 14, 153, 180, 211n20
Hoffer, Peter C., 166
homeless people, 93, 96; and sanction severity, 91, 94, 96–97, 189, 195, 197, 202
homicide: defined, 203n1; frequency of, 17, 97; modern patterns of, 33, 47. *See also* homicide, aggressiveness of; homicide, direction of; homicide, intentionality of; homicide, morality of; homicide, response to
homicide, aggressiveness of: and law, 12–14, 39–40, 72–73, 76–77, 99, 120, 136, 178, 185, 192, 195, 212–13n10; and popular justice, 60–61
homicide, direction of:
—centrifugal vs. centripetal: and law, 92–101; and the morality of homicide, 107–8, 186, 187–88; and popular justice, 103–7
—downward vs. upward, 37, 196–97; and law, 37–51, 64–80, 111–20, 133–44, 147–51, 196; and the morality of homicide, 62, 90, 155, 186, 187–88; and popular justice, 57–61, 83–87, 122–27, 151–52

homicide, intentionality of: and law, 12–14, 39–40, 45, 63, 73, 89, 120, 136, 159, 160–61, 165, 185, 195; and popular justice, 60–61, 88–89, 190
homicide, morality of, 1–2, 17, 35, 38–39, 183; and social geometry, 29–30, 65, 90, 107–8, 130, 155, 186–88, 201–2
homicide, response to, 61–62, 90, 107–8, 130–31, 154–55, 156, 183, 196–97; data on, 30–34, 49, 76, 207n4; delimited, 1, 202, 203n1; explanation of, 14–17, 185–88, 191–94; legal, 10–12, 36–51, 52–56, 64–81, 91–103, 109–22, 127–30, 133–51, 157–78, 188–90; and legal proof, 194–96; and moral and legal theory, 12–14, 29–30, 35, 201–2; and moral equality, 1, 198–201; popular, 1–7, 56–61, 81–87, 103–7, 122–27, 151–53, 178–83, 190–91
homosexuality, 197, 251–53
honor killings, 2–3, 118–20, 125–27, 197
Houston, 13, 14, 16, 66, 157–60, 168, 204n10; death penalty, 144, 161, 214n1
Hull, N. E. H., 166
human rights groups, 30, 70, 75, 192, 207n7
Hungary, medieval, 84
hunter-gatherers, 15, 188. *See also under individual societies*
husbands. *See* intimate partners

Iceland, medieval, 58
Ifugao, 58, 83
Illinois, 143, 163
immorality of homicide. *See* homicide, morality of
imprisonment, 10, 62, 83, 96, 106, 155; and the evolution of social control, 7, 56, 200–201; and honor killings, 120, 126–27; percentage of killers receiving, 21; and pure sociology, 16, 24; severity of, and intimacy, 13–14, 120, 158, 160–61, 162; —, and social status, 54, 66, 67, 72, 110, 114, 117, 140
India: pre-colonial, 43, 76; colonial, 46, 206n4; modern, 48–49, 74, 205n3
Indians, American, 134; and law, 135–39, 145, 209n4; and popular justice, 152–53, 211n20
Indonesia, 64
inequality. *See* societal inequality; vertical dimension, the
infanticide, 29, 94–95, 165–67
innocent, conviction of factually, 196
integration. *See* social integration
intent to kill, 45, 95, 166; and Blackian theory, 13, 30, 32–33; irrelevance of, 14, 88–89, 190; and legal and moral theory, 13; leniency despite, 39–40, 60–61, 63, 73, 97, 120, 136, 159, 165, 195
intimacy and intimacy principle. *See* relational distance
intimate partners: and law, 158–61, 162, 164, 165, 167–68, 187; and popular justice, 179, 181
intimate stratification, 167–68
intimidation in legal cases, 74, 98
investigation, 9, 182, 196, 199, 204n9; forensic, 171; and high-status partisans, 192; independent, 72, 73, 74; and social status of principals, 48–49, 65, 69, 91, 97, 98, 99, 112–13. *See also* detectives; police
Iran, 208n5
Ireland: medieval and early modern, 58, 132; nineteenth-century, 4, 117–18, 154, 163–64, 183, 193
Islamic countries, 41, 119–20, 133. *See also* Arabs *and under individual countries*
Israel, 59, 126–27

Jackall, Robert, 65, 112, 113, 121, 124, 125, 172
jail, 110; before trial, 100, 120; seizure from, 105
Jalé, 213–14n17
Jamaica, 71, 73, 207n8

Japan, medieval, 10
Jewish people, 147
Jívaro, 3, 29
Johnson, Dr. Samuel, 324
Jordan, 120, 126, 127
judges, 4, 118, 139, 166, 175, 193, 198; and the behavior of law, 24, 25–26; and capital cases, 141, 142; compared to juries, 18–19, 55–56, 190, 206n12; and the evolution of law, 8; and honor killings, 3, 118–19; social distance of, 146, 176–78, 200, 213n15; and social distance of principals, 164; social status of, 54, 81, 102–3, 122, 146, 213n14; and social status of principals, 32, 39, 47, 102–3, 115, 164; and sociological theory, 15, 16; and the theory of settlement, 27; as third parties, 51; intimidation of, 74, 98. *See also* courts; trials
juries, 18, 20, 54, 87, 116, 175, 193; and the behavior of law, 25–26; capital, 100, 141, 142, 143; coroners', 2, 204n9; and honor killings, 3, 118–19; and Marxist theory, 15; social distance of, 147–48, 177, 178, 195, 200; —, and race, 148–51, 199, 211n18; and social distance of principals, 164, 165; social status of, 39, 54, 81–83, 102–3, 122, 187–88, 211n15; —, and race, 146, 147t; and social status of principals, 39, 45, 81–83, 102–3, 122, 187–88, 211n15; and the theory of settlement, 27; as third parties, 51. *See also* courts; trials
jury nullification, 178

Kalven, Harry, Jr., 18–19, 55–56, 80
Kansas, 182
Kentucky, 142, 162
killers, 29, 62, 156, 185; equal treatment of, 1, 16, 198–201; evolution of legal sanctions for, 7–10, 89; explaining severity of sanctions for, 12–17, 186–94; and legal proof, 194–96; variability of legal sanctions for, 10–12, 17, 30, 55–56, 102–3, 122, 146, 176–78, 196–97, 202; variability of popular sanctions for, 1–7, 17, 81–84, 202. *See also* killers, social distance of; killers, social status of
killers, social distance of: and law, 147–51, 154, 157–170; and partisanship, 145, 147–51, 170–76, 180–82; and popular justice, 151–53, 178–80
killers, social status of: and law, 36–51, 63–64, 65–80, 90–101, 107–8, 109–20, 127–31, 133–44; and partisanship, 51–54, 60–61, 80–81, 101–2, 121, 145; and popular justice, 57, 59–60, 85, 86–87, 103–7, 108, 122, 124–27, 151, 153
Kiowa, 85
Kipsigis, 58
Kirk, Robin, 96–97
Kobler, Artur L., 68

Laos, 3–4, 95–96
Latin America. *See* South America
Latinas/Latinos, 129–30, 150. *See also* Hispanic Americans
law, 2–3, 61–62, 155; Blackian theory of, 18–26, 31–35, 37–39, 186–90, 191–93, 193–97; centrifugal vs. centripetal, 91–101, 107–8; close vs. distant, 156–70; downward vs. upward, 39–51, 63–80, 90, 109–20, 130–31, 132–44; evolution of, 7–10, 87–89; and other social control, 27–28, 127–30; partisans' social distance and, 145–46, 170–76; partisans' social status and, 52–54, 80–81, 101–2, 121, 145, 146; quantity of, 19; settlement agents' social distance and, 145–46, 147–51, 176–78; settlement agents' social status and, 54–56, 102–3, 122, 146; style of, 20; theories of, 12–17; variability of, 10–12, 185, 198–200, 202. *See also* courts; death sentence; imprisonment; murder versus manslaughter; punishment; sanction severity; settlement; trials

lawyers, 39, 50, 80, 138, 148, 193; absence of, 61–62, 82; and amount of evidence needed to win case, 195–96; and case facts, 175; and case geometry, 32, 170, 171, 200; and discretion, 20–21; and homicide by police, 207n4, 207n5; as homicide victims, 187; human rights, 74; and intimacy principle, 169–70; intimidation of, 98; and legal evolution, 8–9; and O. J. Simpson trials, 52–54, 150–51; as partisans, 27, 52, 53, 101, 145, 149, 176–77; and quantity of law, 19; recruitment of, 175; seeking the death penalty, 142, 143, 162, 212n3; and trial strategy, 103, 115–16, 122, 172, 175, 196, 213n15
leaders, killing of, 29, 90, 188, 202; and law, 64, 77–78; and popular justice, 84, 85–86, 190–91
Lebanon, 85, 120
legal cooperatives, 200
legal evidence, 54, 166, 170, 182, 194–96, 199; credibility of, 52, 80, 146, 172, 175–76, 209n11; strength of, 137, 148–49, 150, 151, 164, 185. *See also* proof; witnesses
legal officials, 39, 103, 134, 159; and desocialization of law, 199; intimidation of, 74; and legal truth, 172, 176; and relational distance, 160, 212n10; and slow partisanship, 102; and social status of parties, 92, 111. *See also* judges; lawyers
legal rules, 2, 39, 67–68, 99, 120, 194, 199; and the death penalty, 64, 66, 129, 141, 143; and formal legal rationality, 15; and intimacy principle, 169; and normative status, 111; and settlement agents, 54, 82, 102–3, 122, 177–78; weak predictive power of, 12–14, 20, 40, 43, 70, 77, 118–19, 198. *See also* settlement, formalism of
legal truth, 172, 175, 213n14
Lewis, I. M., 58, 86, 173, 180
liability: collective, 6–7, 41, 88, 90, 152; subjective, 88–89, 90, 190
Lindholm, Charles, 86, 125, 180
Lithuania, 42
Los Angeles: gangs, 85; police, 70, 73, 79; trials, 53, 150, 211n15
low income. *See* wealth
Lugbara, 156
Lundsgaarde, Henry P., 13–15, 64, 66, 115, 157–59
lynching, 6, 73, 134, 148, 215n12; and partisanship, 61, 180–81, 194; and social distance, 151–52, 179, 180; and social status, 57, 59, 84, 86–87, 103, 104–5, 123; —, and race, 57, 104, 148, 190

males, 193; and domestic authority, 129–30, 167, 209n8; and honor killings, 118–20, 125–27; and intimate partner homicide, 158–61, 162, 167–68, 170, 198–99, 212n9, 212–13n10
marginality. *See* social integration
Marquart, James W., 66, 128, 129, 142, 163
married people, 92, 199; and law, 92, 100, 189, 197; and settlement, 102; and written law of infanticide, 94–95
Marx, Karl, 15, 18, 21
Maryland, 143. *See also* Baltimore
Mataco, 179
Mae Enga, 6, 58, 123, 179, 206n13, 213–14n17
manslaughter. *See* murder versus manslaughter
Massachusetts, 138–39, 147, 176–77
mass media, 53, 87, 150, 162, 192
masters and servants, 44, 205n2
Matthew effect, the, 52
McCleskey vs. Kemp, 143
McKanna, Clare V., 67, 105, 137, 138, 140, 145
McLynn, Frank, 44, 118, 169, 191–92
mediators, 81, 176, 187, 191
medical evidence, 47, 68–69, 74–75, 116, 117, 148, 166
medical examiners. *See* coroners
Meggitt, Mervyn, 6, 58, 123, 179, 206n13, 213–14n17
meta-test, 33–34, 188

Mexican Americans, 134, 136, 145
Mexico, 71, 74, 75
men. *See* males
Miami, 161, 204n10
military, the. *See* state officials
Milk, Harvey, 147–48
Mississippi, 149, 163
monarchs. *See* leaders, killing of
Montenegro, 81–83
moral absolutism, 28–29, 201
moralism, the theory of, 27–28
morality, 132, 153–54, 194; as behavior, 28–30; and equality, 198–201; geometrical nature of, 30, 201–2; of homicide, 1, 12–17, 38–39, 90, 107–8, 131, 155, 156, 186–88; homicide as, 118
moral relativism, 28–29, 155, 201
moral relativity, the theory of, 28–30, 186–88
Morocco, 74
Morris, Thomas D., 40–41
Moscone, George, 147–48
murder versus manslaughter, 89, 119, 122, 200; and officials' discretion, 20–21; and social distance, of principals, 165, 195; —, of settlement agents, 147–48; and social status, of principals, 36–37, 38, 68, 112, 113; —, of settlement agents, 56
Murngin, 123
Muscovite law, 41

Neal, Bill, 84, 105, 115
Nebraska, 50, 105, 140, 206n8
New Guinea, 5, 6, 29, 58, 85–86, 123, 206n13, 213n17. *See also under individual societies*
New Haven Colony, 22
New Jersey, 142
New Orleans, 86–87
newspapers. *See* mass media
New York, 65, 70, 71, 73, 79, 121, 124, 125
Nigeria, 172
normative dimension, the, 21, 108–31
normative direction, 22, 120, 122
normative distance, 121, 122
normative elevation, 120, 122, 131
normative geometry, 121
normative status, 110–11; and law, 10, 73–74, 111–20; and the morality of homicide, 130–31, 186–88; and partisanship, 120–21; and the perfect murder, 196, 197; and popular justice, 3–4, 5, 122–27; and proof, 194–96; and settlement, 122
North Carolina, 141, 142, 163

Oberg, Kalervo, 58, 59, 88–89
offenders. *See* defendants; killers
Ohio, 129
Oklahoma, 163
oligarchies, 65, 71–76, 90, 197
Oregon, nineteenth-century, 152
organizational dimension, the, 21, 63–90
organizational direction, 64, 67, 83, 86, 87, 90
organizational distance, 64, 65, 90, 214n3
organizational elevation, 22, 63, 83
organizational geometry, 68, 80, 88–89, 90
organizational location, 83, 90
organizational status: and the evolution of social control, 87–89; and law, 64–80, 170–71; and the morality of homicide, 90, 186–88; and partisanship, 80–81, 187; and the perfect murder, 196, 197; and popular justice, 83–87; and proof, 194–96; and settlement, 81–83, 187–88
organizational superiority, 65, 76, 79, 81

P's, the three (psychology, purposes, people), 38–45
parents, 199. *See also* family members; parents as killers; parents as victims
parents as killers, 29; and law, 13–14, 94–95, 119–20, 159, 162, 165–67, 197; and popular justice, 126–27; as partisans, 81–83, 85, 116, 175, 181–83
parents as victims, 56, 187, 198–99; and law, 164, 167, 176–77, 189; and popular justice, 105, 106, 124–25, 157, 180

partisanship, 27, 28, 35, 191–93, 197, 214–15n9; Black's principles of, 51, 145–46, 187; and social distance, 68–70, 146–51, 170–76, 178, 180–83, 187; and social status, 51–54, 60–61, 62, 80–81, 90, 101–2, 103, 107, 121, 123, 145, 151, 187; slow, 102
Pakistan, 7, 48, 74, 86, 119–20, 126, 209n5
penal sanctions. *See* punishment
penalties. *See* sanctions
Penglase, Ben, 73, 79, 98
people. *See* P's, the three
Peratis, Kathleen, 3, 120, 126
Peters, E. L., 7, 58, 156
Peterson, Scott, 162
petty treason, 44, 167
Philadelphia, 50, 140, 143–44, 204n10, 212–13n10
Philippines, the, 83
Phillips, Scott, 27, 142, 161, 179, 199, 210n10
poisoning, 164, 203n1
Poland, 42
police, 11, 46, 105, 157, 159, 160, 198, 200; and the evolution of law, 9, 56, 134; explaining the behavior of, 15, 19, 20, 25–26; as investigators, 48, 49, 54, 69, 91, 98, 175, 189; as partisans, 102, 125, 148, 170–71; as witnesses, 80, 149, 174, 208n11. *See also* police as killers; police as victims
police as killers, 90, 127, 189, 197; and law, 10, 67–76, 79, 97, 98, 99, 186–87, 192; and popular justice, 153
police as victims, 90; and law, 47–48, 65–67, 141; and popular justice, 84
popular justice, 27, 111, 117–18, 154, 185, 198; and Blackian theory, 33, 34, 38–39, 190–91, 193; and the evolution of social control, 7–10, 17, 87–89, 200; forms of, 2–7; and law, 127–31; severity of, 5, 203n5, 204n7; and social distance, 151–53, 178–83; and social status, 56–61, 62, 81–87, 90, 91, 103–7, 122–27, 151, 153. *See also under individual forms*
Portugal, eighteenth-century, 42,
plea bargains, 11–12, 170
poverty. *See* wealth
praise, 5, 7, 64, 185, 190, 198, 202; and Blackian theory, 57; legal, 10; —, and social status, 71, 136–37; popular, 2–5, 193; —, and social status, 86–87, 103–4, 124–26; and the perfect murder, 196–97
premeditation. *See* intent to kill
presidents. *See* leaders, killing of
prevalence of deviance, 214n6
priests, 218. *See also* religion
principal parties, 35, 37, 51, 101, 186, 194. *See also* case, social geometry of the; killers; victims
principals. *See* principal parties
prison. *See* imprisonment
probation, 12, 157, 159
proof: social geometry of, 194–96; and social status, 55, 70, 137; standard of, 150
prosecutors. *See* lawyers
provocation, 13–14, 39–40, 45, 46, 185, 195
psychology. *See* P's, the three
punishment. *See* sanction severity
pure sociology, 34–35, 111, 159, 186, 188; and morality, 30, 201–2; as a new science of social life, 16–17, 21–26, 183; practical applications of, 196–97, 199–200. *See also* Blackian theory *and under individual dimensions of social space*
purposes. *See* P's, the three

race, 161, 168, 187, 195, 197; on Australian frontier, 95, 153, 153; of judges, 146; of jurors, 146, 147t, 148–51, 199, 211n15, 211n18; and law, 129–30, 134–44, 154, 189, 200, 210n8; and partisanship, 145, 146, 149, 199; and popular justice, 124; —, lynching, 57, 104, 148, 151–52, 190; —, vengeance, 152–53; sociological significance of, 50–51, 128, 139–40, 209–10n6, 210n7

Radelet, Michael, 142, 143, 162, 209–10n6, 214n8
radial dimension, the, 21–22, 91–108
radial direction, 101
radial distance, 92, 104
radial geometry, 90, 103
radial location, 101
radial status: distinguished from vertical status, 23, 92; and law, 92–101, 167, 214n1; and the morality of homicide, 107–8, 186–88; and partisanship, 101–2, 187; and the perfect murder, 196, 197; and popular justice, 103–7; and proof, 194–96; and settlement, 102–3, 187
rape, 22
relational dimension, the, 21–22, 156–83
relational distance, 183; and law, 119–20, 157–70, 187, 189; and the morality of homicide, 183, 186–88; and partisanship, 170–77, 187, 190; and the perfect murder, 196, 197; and popular justice, 178–80, 180–83; and proof, 194–96; and settlement, 176–78, 187–88
relativity: legal, 23; moral, 28, 29–30, 188
religion: of principal parties, 119, 133, 209n2, 209n5, 211n19; of third parties, 146, 147
respectability, 110–11, 130–31, 195, 197; and law, 111–20, 186–87; and partisanship, 120–21; and popular justice, 3–4, 5, 123–25, 126–27; and settlement, 122
Reynolds, Henry, 153, 154
Reynolds, Sir Joshua, 192
robbery homicide, 109–10, 142
Rio de Janeiro, 71, 72, 91, 98
Roman law, 40
romantic triangles, 160–61
Rummell, R. J., 76, 77

sanctions: civil, 79–80, 171; data on, 30–31, 32; evolution of, 7–10, 89; forms of, 5–7; sources of, 204n11; variability of, 1–2, 5, 10–12, 29, 186, 198, 201, 202
sanction severity, 5, 12, 62, 90, 107–8, 130, 154–55, 183, 196–97; Blackian theory of, 16, 17, 19–28, 29–30, 34–35, 38, 63–64, 92, 111, 133, 157, 186–88, 188–94
sanction severity, legal, 10; and cultural distance, 146–51; and conventionality, 132, 133–44, 146, 147; and normative status, 109–10, 111–20, 122; and organizational status, 63, 64–78; and popular justice, 127–30; and radial status, 91, 92–101, 102–3; and relational distance, 157–70, 171, 176–78; and vertical status, 36–37, 38–51, 52–54, 54–56, 61–62
sanction severity, popular, 5; and cultural distance, 151–53; and conventionality, 151, 153; and normative status, 122–27; and organizational status, 81–83, 83–87; and radial status, 103–7; and relational distance, 156, 178–180, 180–83; theories of, 12–16
San Diego, 70
San Francisco, 112, 147–48, 185, 212n3; Vigilance Committee, 86
São Paolo, 71, 72, 73, 96, 103–4
Saudi Arabia, 47–48, 133, 208n2
Schwarz, Philip J., 41, 42, 197
Scotland, medieval, 8, 58
Scott, Gini Graham, 116, 176–77
self defense, 1, 12, 13, 73, 195; and juries, 55–56, 178
self-help (as a response to homicide), 5, 6–7, 27, 190–91; and social distance, 151–53, 179–80, 181, 213–14n17; and social status, 57–58, 59, 61, 62, 83, 84–87, 88, 123, 151
Senechal de la Roche, Roberta, 28, 57, 61, 84, 88, 104, 151–52, 179
sentencing. *See* courts, dispositions of; death sentence; imprisonment; sanction severity
settlement, 51, 80, 101, 120, 145, 170, 191; Blackian theory of, 27, 35, 187–88; decisiveness of, 54, 81, 82–83, 102–3, 122, 146, 177, 187; formalism of, 54, 81, 82, 102–3, 146, 177, 187; severity of, 54–56, 81, 83, 101–3, 122, 146, 147–51, 176–78, 187–88

Shakespearean drama, 156, 180
Shakur, Sanyika, 3, 9, 84
Shavante, 123
Shilts, Randy, 147–48
Shirer, William L., 78
shunning, 6, 7, 57, 127, 180, 203n5, 207n7; in modern societies, 105–7, 181, 215n12
Simon, David, 49, 69, 111, 113
Simpson, O. J., 52–54, 101, 150–51, 195, 215n12
Sioux, 137, 152
slaves: as killers, 41–42, 195; as victims, 39–40, 195, 197
slave societies, 39–42
social class. *See* vertical status
"social cleansing," 96, 97
social control, 19, 21, 27, 90, 130; and Blackian theory, 34, 37–39, 183; evolution of, 7–10, 87–89; homicide as, 118; and severity of law, 127–30; theories of, 14–17. *See also* law; popular justice
social distance, 183; and law, 119–20, 146–51, 157–70; and the morality of homicide, 155, 183, 186–88; and partisanship, 145–46, 171, 191–92, 193; and the perfect murder, 196–97; and popular justice, 151–53, 177–80, 180–83; and proof, 194–96. *See also* cultural distance; relational distance
social geometry, 21, 69; and the explanation of social life, 22, 23, 26; and morality, 30, 201–2. *See also* case, social geometry of the
social information, 199
social integration, 91, 92, 107–8, 186; and law, 92–101; and partisanship, 101–2; and popular justice, 103–7; and settlement, 102–3
social life, the behavior of, 25–26
social space, 21–22, 139, 186, 198. *See also under individual dimensions*
social status, 21–22, 32, 63–64, 91, 110–11, 133, 189, 202; four-fold pattern, 37, 63–64, 92, 111, 133, 186; and law, 21–22, 38–51, 61, 63–64, 92–101, 111–20, 127–30, 133–45, 189, 209n2, 210n14; and the morality of homicide, 62, 90, 107–8, 131, 155, 186, 187–88; and partisanship, 51–54, 80–81, 121, 145, 190, 191–93; and the perfect murder, 196–98; and popular justice, 56–61, 81–87, 103–7, 127, 151, 153, 190, 191, 211n19; and proof, 194–96; and settlement, 54–56, 81–83, 102–3, 122, 146, 147. *See also* conventionality; normative status; organizational status; radial status; vertical status
social structure. *See* social geometry
societal inequality and sanction severity, 39, 207n3
sociological theory, 14–17, 21; classical, 15; cultural, 14–15; of punishment, 204n13; of rational choice, 16
soldiers, 45, 72, 90, 137, 152. *See also* state officials
Solomon, Joel, 70
Somali pastoralists, 58, 180
South Africa, 75, 210n11
South America, 7, 41, 96, 179. *See also under individual cities and countries*
South Carolina, 142; antebellum, 39–40
Southern Rhodesia, 46–47
Soviet Union, 77, 79
Spain, 42
Spanish Inquisition, the, 76
spouses. *See* intimate partners
stateless societies, 56–57, 87–89, 103, 186
state officials, 64, 71, 76, 80. *See also* leaders, killing of; police; soldiers
state, the, 7–9, 64, 70; centralization of, 64–65, 79, 189, 207n3
storekeeper, killing of, 106–7
strangers, 157, 183, 197; as partisans, 170, 175; as settlement agents, 177–78, 187–88; as victims, and law, 158, 162t, 163, 169, 195; —, and popular justice, 178, 179, 181. *See also* relational distance
suicide: "by cop," 69; response to, 168–69
Sumatra (colonial), 46
Sweden, sixteenth-century, 8

Swigert, Victoria Lynn, 49–50, 100–101, 112, 140
Swindle, Howard, 70

Taude, 86–87
teleology, 24, 26. *See also* P's, the three
television. *See* mass media
testability, 25
"testilying," 174
Texas, 157; death penalty in, 66, 128, 129, 142, 163; nineteenth-century, 84, 104–5. *See also* Dallas; Houston
Thailand, 64
theory, 19; criminological, 16; legal and moral, 12–14, 20–21, 185. *See also* Blackian theory; sociological theory
third parties, 27, 39, 62, 91, 196–97; as essential component of case geometry, 32, 35; partisans, 51–54, 60–61, 80–81, 101–2, 107, 120–21, 145–46, 170–78, 180–83, 191–93, 194; settlement agents, 54–56, 81–83, 102–3, 122, 146–51, 176–78. *See also* case, social geometry of the; family members; judges; juries; lawyers
third world, 11, 47–49, 71, 95–99, 125
Tibet, 6, 58, 83, 211n19
ties, social, 68–69, 175, 181
Till, Emmett, 149
Timmermans, Stefan, 69, 171, 204n9
Tiv, 172
Tlingit, 59, 88–89
toleration: legal, 10–11, 90, 118, 197; —, and social distance, 163, 165; —, and social status, 39, 63, 67, 71, 91, 97, 136, 139, 202; popular, 5, 7, 27, 90, 127; —, and social status, 57, 60, 86, 103, 123
Toronto, 168
trials, 18–19, 20, 31, 170, 196; and evolution of social control, 8–9, 89; of honor killings, 2–3, 118–19, 120; and proof, 194–96; and witnesses, 80–81, 121, 145, 172–76, 190. *See also* courts; death sentence; imprisonment; sanction severity; trials, outcome of
trials, outcome of, 12, 13–14, 16, 87, 185, 187–88, 191–92; and conventionality, 136, 137–39, 140–44, 145, 146, 147t, 189; and cultural distance, 147–51; and normative status, 110, 111–12, 113–14, 116–18, 124; and organizational status, 66, 68, 69–70, 74, 75, 78; and popular justice, 127–30; and radial status, 95, 96, 97, 98, 100; and relational distance, 158–59, 160–63, 164–65, 166–67, 168, 176–78
trial tactics. *See* lawyers
Trinidad, nineteenth-century, 45
Turkey, 120

Uganda, 266
unconventionality. *See* conventionality
unemployment, 187, 197, 199; and law, 94, 96, 99–100, 189; and partisanship, 101–2. *See also* radial status
United States, 31, 71, 73, 185, 201; Constitution, 129, 141, 143; seventeenth-century, 22, 138–39, 147; nineteenth-century law, 2–3, 9, 10, 39–40, 41, 119, 134–38, 145, 176–77; nineteenth-century popular justice, 57, 84, 86–87, 104–5, 123, 125–26, 151, 152–53; modern law, 11–12, 13–14, 16, 26, 36–37, 38, 49–51, 52–56, 65–70, 79–80, 81–82, 99–101, 109–10, 111–16, 121, 128–30, 139–44, 145, 146, 147t, 147–51, 157–63, 167–68, 171, 172–76, 189, 197; modern popular justice, 85, 105–7, 124–25, 181–83. *See also under individual cities and states*
United States Department of State, 47–48, 75–76, 120, 133
unrespectability. *See* respectability
upward cases/homicide/law/partisanship/settlement. *See* homicide, direction of; law

Van Onselen, Charles, 46–47
vengeance as a response to homicide, 6–7, 35, 62, 155; and social distance, 152–53, 179–80; and social status, 57–58, 59, 83–84, 85–86, 103, 123, 190–91; and third parties, 61, 88, 180–81

vertical dimension, the, 21, 36–62
vertical direction, 22, 37, 43, 45, 46, 48, 49, 86
vertical distance, 22, 37, 46
vertical status, 32, 36–37; and law, 37–38, 39–51, 61; and the morality of homicide, 61–62, 186–88; and partisanship, 51–54, 60–61, 187; and the perfect murder, 196, 197; and popular justice, 56–60; and proof, 194–96; and settlement, 54–56, 102, 187–88
victimization surveys, 205n4
victims, 11, 19, 32, 55–56, 132, 178; and legal proof, 194–96; and moral equality, 198–200; provocation by, 13; and sanction severity, 61–62, 90, 107–8, 130–31, 146–47, 154–55, 156, 183, 186–91, 196–97, 202. *See also under individual sanctions and social characteristics*
victims, social distance of: and law, 157–69; and partisanship, 147–51, 170–76; and popular justice, 151–53
victims, social status of: and law, 10, 37, 51, 63–80, 91–101, 109–20, 127–30, 133–45; and partisanship, 60–61, 101–2, 122, 145, 180–81; and popular justice, 57–60, 83–87, 103–7, 122–27, 151, 153, 178–80, 193
vigilantism, 86–87, 123, 134
Virginia: nineteenth-century, 2–3, 11, 125–26; modern, 31, 106–7, 141, 145, 160–61, 162t, 163, 172–3, 181

Wales, medieval, 8
wealth, 62, 71, 90, 106, 111, 170, 186; and getting away with murder, 196–97; and homicide, 33, 49; and law, 22, 24, 36–51, 61, 115–16, 188–89, 195–96, 209–10n6; measurement of, 32; and moral equality, 1, 199; and partisanship, 51–54, 60–61, 187; and popular justice, 56–60; and settlement, 54–56, 102, 187–88
weapons, 45, 164
Weber, Max, 15, 18, 21
White, Dan, 147–48, 186
White, Stephen D., 60
Whitfield, Stephen J., 149
Wiener, Martin, 46, 55, 167
Wilbanks, William, 114, 140, 161, 204n10
witnesses, 32, 117, 138, 159, 170; credibility of, 80–81, 100–101, 121, 145, 175, 192; expert, 53–54, 101; intimidation of, 74; and investigation, 49, as partisans, 27, 171–76, 190
wives. *See* intimate partners
women. *See* females
written law, the. *See* legal rules
wrongful conviction. *See* conviction of the factually innocent
wrongful death cases. *See* courts, dispositions of, civil verdicts

Yahi, 136
Yap, 179–80
young people, 170; and collective liability, 152; as killers, 129, 140; as victims, 97–99, 128, 162, 165–67, 180
Yuki, 137

Ziesel, Hans, 18–19, 55–56, 80, 142
Zimbabwe. *See* Southern Rhodesia
Zulus, 77